Free Software
FOR
DUMMIES®

by Mary Leete

WILEY

Wiley Publishing, Inc.

Free Software For Dummies®

Published by
Wiley Publishing, Inc.
111 River Street
Hoboken, NJ 07030-5774

www.wiley.com

Copyright © 2005 by Wiley Publishing, Inc., Indianapolis, Indiana

Published by Wiley Publishing, Inc., Indianapolis, Indiana

Published simultaneously in Canada

For general information on our other products and services, please contact our Customer Care Department within the U.S. at 800-762-2974, outside the U.S. at 317-572-3993, or fax 317-572-4002.

For technical support, please visit www.wiley.com/techsupport.

Wiley also publishes its books in a variety of electronic formats. Some content that appears in print may not be available in electronic books.

Library of Congress Control Number: 2005923788

ISBN-13: 978-0-7645-9579-0

ISBN-10: 0-7645-9579-2

Manufactured in the United States of America

10 9 8 7 6 5 4 3 2 1

1B/SS/QW/QV/IN

About the Author

Mary Leete is a co-author of *OpenOffice.org For Dummies* and a contributing author to *50 Fast Flash Techniques.* She discovered the cool world of free software several years ago when her husband, Gurdy, suddenly went from spending a fortune on software every year, to spending nothing! This caught her attention and she has ever since been an enthusiastic supporter and user of free software. Mary spent many years working as a computer programmer, so she appreciates the "looking under the hood" feature that free software affords (although she has never looked under its hood herself). Mary is currently in awe of free software's recent meteoric rise, with its new polished and stable versions that are now as good as, and often better than, proprietary software, and she hopes that this book will further the cause of the Free Software movement, whose basis lies in the principle of giving.

Dedication

To the heroes of the Free Software movement who dedicate their time and energy to improve the lives of millions of people around the world by providing powerful applications for all to enjoy — worry-free.

Author's Acknowledgments

I'd like to thank Tom Heine at Wiley for his vision and energy in getting this book approved and published. And I'd like to thank Colleen Totz and Paula Lowell, for their endless hours of editing. I apologize for every confusing sentence and problem, and thank them for making everything right.

I would like to thank my husband, Gurdy, for all his help writing this book. He is a Free Software guru. He helped me write the proposal for this book and taught me how to use the free software that I wasn't familiar with. He also spent many hours reading and editing the book for technical errors — even though he had a full-time job to deal with. I want to thank him not just for the hours of dedicated work he put into the book, but for all his emotional support that he gave me during this project and always.

And thanks to all the heroes of the Free Software movement who are supplying the world with fabulous free software, and doing so, often without any personal gain for themselves other than the satisfaction that they made a profound contribution toward the lives of millions of people around the world.

I'd also like to thank the people at Skype and other companies, who are giving their proprietary software at no charge. Using Skype, far-flung families and friends can keep in touch without paying a fortune in phone calls.

Last, but not least, I would like to thank my children, Porter and Jackie, who had to eat lots of frozen pizza for dinner instead of home-cooked meals, and never complained. (Hmmm.) They also patiently let me take their pictures, to use them as examples of image manipulation using the GIMP. And I want to thank Porter for reading the instructions and teaching me how to play many of the games listed in Chapter 22. And thanks to Jackie for those great SuperTux screenshots and others.

Publisher's Acknowledgments

We're proud of this book; please send us your comments through our online registration form located at www.dummies.com/register/.

Some of the people who helped bring this book to market include the following:

Acquisitions, Editorial, and Media Development

Project Editor: Colleen Totz

Acquisitions Editor: Tom Heine

Copy Editor: Paula Lowell

Technical Editor: Gurdy Leete

Editorial Manager: Robyn Siesky

Editorial Assistant: Adrienne Porter

Cartoons: Rich Tennant (www.the5thwave.com)

Composition Services

Project Coordinator: Adrienne Martinez

Layout and Graphics: Carl Byers, Andrea Dahl, Lauren Goddard, Joyce Haughey, Barry Offringa, Lynsey Osborn

Proofreaders: Leeann Harney, Jessica Kramer, Carl William Pierce

Indexer: TECHBOOKS Production Services

Publishing and Editorial for Technology Dummies

> **Barry Pruett,** Vice President and Publisher
>
> **Richard Swadley,** Vice President and Executive Group Publisher
>
> **Andy Cummings,** Vice President and Publisher
>
> **Mary Bednarek,** Executive Acquisitions Director
>
> **Mary C. Corder,** Editorial Director

Publishing for Consumer Dummies

> **Diane Graves Steele,** Vice President and Publisher
>
> **Joyce Pepple,** Acquisitions Director

Composition Services

> **Gerry Fahey,** Vice President of Production Services
>
> **Debbie Stailey,** Director of Composition Services

Contents at a Glance

Table of Contents

Introduction

. . . .

*F*ree software is becoming so increasingly powerful, sophisticated, and economically viable that it is slowly taking over the world of computing. Free software protocols are at the basis of the birth of the Internet. Free software powers 68 percent of all Web servers, and it is the basis of the Mac OS X desktop as well as the entire Linux desktop. Now free software is making its way up the hierarchy of software and establishing itself powerfully in the realm of application software.

What is "free" software? In this book, it pertains to free as in freedom. Free software in this book is published under a license (such as the GNU Project's popular General Public License) that gives users the freedom to copy it, distribute it, study its source code, modify it, and use it however they want to use it. The only thing that users can't do is publish it without providing these freedoms or without making the source code available.

Why does the free software paradigm work? Because it is based on the principal of giving, which is a powerful force in the universe. People use the programs and make modifications — either for their own use or out of the goodness of their heart — and give those modifications to everyone to use. Also, companies who publish free software are hired by other companies as consultants to install and modify the software, which adds an economic incentive to the free software growth as well.

About This Book

This book explores in depth how to use the major free software packages, listed next, as well as offers a directory of other free software packages (see Chapter 24):

- ✔ **Mozilla Firefox and Thunderbird:** These programs are for surfing the Web and e-mailing safely, without your worrying about malicious programs that might infect your computer via your Web browser or e-mail software. Mozilla Firefox is the second most popular Web browser available today.

- ✔ **The GIMP:** This is a digital image manipulation program, similar to Photoshop. Use its powerful tools and tons of effects to enhance images.

✔ **OpenOffice.org:** This free alternative to Microsoft Office comes with the following modules:

- **Writer:** Word processor similar to Word

- **Calc:** Spreadsheet program similar to Excel

- **Impress:** Presentation program similar to PowerPoint

- **Base:** Database program similar to Access

- **HTML Editor:** Web site design software similar to FrontPage

- **Draw program:** Vector drawing program for making your own clip art and more (including 3D)

✔ **Audacity:** This sound recording and editing software comes with multiple tracks and lots of good effects to clarify and enhance sound.

✔ **Blender 3D:** This is a full-featured 3D animation program.

✔ **Skype:** This is a free Internet phone with conferencing and great sound.

✔ **iPodder:** Use the power of RSS to download the podcasts of your choice and play them on your computer's media player or portable media player.

✔ **Dia:** Use this diagram creation program for flowcharts, electrical diagrams, and more.

✔ **SimplyMEPIS:** This is a powerful, free GNU/Linux alternative to Windows XP.

✔ **SuperTux:** This is a fun, challenging Super Mario-type game with a story and a penguin.

✔ **GNU Chess:** Not only can you play against GNU Chess, but you can watch it play over a dozen chess games that Bobby Fisher played.

✔ **Tux Paint:** This is a delightful painting and stamping program for kids.

✔ **Tux Typing:** This software teaches kids to type in a fun way.

✔ **FlightGear:** Fly around the world from the comfort of your home in dozens of real aircraft and different weather conditions and times of day to any of 20,000 airports. A three-DVD set of the world's surface displays the terrain as you go.

✔ **Celestia:** Explore the universe.

✔ **And more!**

How to Use This Book

You can use this book in several ways:

- ✔ **As a manual** for the programs explored in depth (Chapters 3–20).
- ✔ **For an overview** of what free software is available and where to find it (Chapters 1, 2, 21–24).
- ✔ **To learn more about the philosophy of free software** (Chapter 25 covers that in particular detail.)

Needless to say, you don't have to read this book in order to get the most out of it. Feel free to start at Chapter 25, if you want, which is actually a very good place to start because it gives you ten good reasons for using free software. Or start at Chapter 1 and get a good overview before you plunge in. The choice is yours.

Foolish Assumptions

I assume that you have used computers before and used applications for word processing, Web surfing, and e-mailing, so you already have some understanding of the value of these activities.

Conventions Used in This Book

When I say something like, "Choose File ➪ Open," I mean click on the word *File* in the main menu and continue to hold the mouse down. When the drop-down menu appears, move the mouse to select *Open*. Then release the mouse button. (You can see why I would rather say, "choose File ➪ Open.")

Another convention used is when I say "press A," I mean press the letter *A* on the keyboard (not capital A). And when I say click OK, that means click the OK button with the mouse.

Also, some keyboards have the carriage return labeled Return and others label it Enter. Some keyboards have the Backspace key labeled Delete. And to make matters worse, some keyboards have a Backspace and a Delete key. So I did the following:

✔ When I mean press Return, sometimes I say, "press either Return or Enter, depending on your keyboard," but mostly I just say, "press Return." If I ever inconsistently say Enter, I also mean Return — not the Enter key on the number keypad.

✔ When I say to press Delete, I mean to press Backspace, unless I clearly state that it is the other Del or Delete key.

How This Book Is Organized

This book is divided into six parts, each part containing chapters related to that topic. I start with an overview of all the software and end with the Part of Tens, which includes a directory of ten categories of free software and a chapter on ten compelling reasons why you should use free software.

Part I: Plunging Into Free Software

Part I contains a quickstart guide and overview of the software discussed in this book, as well as the best places to find more free software. Chapter 1 describes some top software packages and easy downloading and installation instructions, which get you up and running in no time. Chapter 2 lists the best places on the Internet to find more free software and find out more about the software explored in this book.

Part II: Using Powerful, Free Office Software

Part II goes deeply into free and powerful word processing, spreadsheet, and database software. Chapters 3 and 4 cover OpenOffice.org Writer in depth. Chapters 5 and 6 cover how to create spreadsheets and use the powerful Functions Wizard. Chapters 6 and 7 cover designing and creating a database, plus generating reports and mail merging (all that useful office-type stuff).

Part III: Exploring the Internet — More Easily, More Securely, and More Featurefully

Part III explores the great free software available for cruising the Internet. Chapter 9 describes how to use the hot new Web browser, Mozilla Firefox, which has been pulling market share away from Internet Explorer on a daily rate because of its high security features as well as other improved features. Chapter 10 describes Mozilla Thunderbird, which also has great new security features as well as RSS integration and more. Chapter 11 goes deeply into how to create your own Web pages using OpenOffice.org Writer's HTML editor. Chapter 12 explores the new world of podcasts with iPodder. And Chapter 13 describes how to make free phone calls with crystal clear reception using Skype.

Part IV: Using Powerful, Free Multimedia Software

This part explores free multimedia software. Chapter 14 describes how to use OpenOffice.org Draw, which enables you to create clip art and even does 3D. Chapter 15 explains the steps of creating a presentation, similar to a PowerPoint presentation, using OpenOffice.org Impress. Chapters 16 and 17 cover the GIMP, which is a free Photoshop-like program with amazing capabilities to transform digital images. Chapter 18 is a short chapter covering diagramming with Dia. Chapter 19 ventures into the world of 3D animation with Blender 3D. Chapter 20 covers Audacity, the great sound editing and recording software.

Part V: More Powerful, Free Software

This part explores, you guessed it, more free software. Chapter 21 describes and explains six different software programs: Solfege for ear training; Flight Gear for simulated flying; Gcompris, which is a suite of games for young children; Celestia for astronomy; and Tux Paint and Tux Typing for painting and typing for kids. Chapter 22 covers ten different games, including GNU Chess, SuperTux, and FreeCiv.

Part VI: The Part of Tens

Chapter 24 includes ten lists of more free software as well as other free stuff, such as free photos, free movies, free sounds, and more. Chapter 25 lists ten reasons to use free software.

Appendix A is where you can find and refer to technical instructions from various places in the book. For example, you can find instructions such as how to download and install free programs using Fink Commander, if you're a Mac OS X user, or how to download and install programs using Synaptic, if you're a GNU/Linux user.

Icons Used in This Book

Every so often, you'll find little icons in the margins of the book, pointing out the following:

 Tips are probably the most common icon. Usually they offer important things you should know, so you probably don't want to skip any.

 The information next to the Technical Stuff icon is optional to read, so you can skip it if you want.

 Better watch out for these guys.

 Notes aren't quite tips, but they are still of some importance.

 Something I wrote previously may come in handy again, as the Remember icons point out.

Where to Go from Here

Free software is based on the idea of giving. If you use it, you may want to consider donating to the group that created it and is actively working to make it better. Or you can donate your time by hanging out on the support forums and helping the newbies. If you're a programmer, you can help to make improvements to the code. Or you can just spread the word about how great the software is by telling your friends.

Part I

Plunging Into Free Software

The 5th Wave   By Rich Tennant

©RICHTENNANT

"Okay people, remember – use your project management software. It's customizable, so those of you collecting 'juice' will use a slightly different entry from those of you doing shakedowns or fencing stolen goods."

In this part . . .

This part provides an overview and a quick-start guide to the major free software packages available, plus information to help you find more. Chapter 1 describes the features of the programs that I explore in depth in this book: OpenOffice.org, Mozilla Firefox and Thunderbird, the GIMP, Audacity, and much more. I also provide detailed instructions on how to download and install them to get you up and running right away.

Chapter 2 describes the major Web sites where you can go and find more free software. I divided this chapter into sections for the different operating systems: Windows, Mac OS X, and GNU/Linux. Reading just these two chapters can get you up and running with dozens of powerful free software applications.

Chapter 1

How to Use Tons of Powerful, Free Software — Fast

- -

In This Chapter

▶ Exploring what free software has to offer

▶ Downloading and installing the top free software package

▶ Getting support for your free software

- -

*T*he Internet offers over 10,000 free software packages available for download. Some of these, of course, stand head and shoulders above the rest. Programs such as Mozilla Firefox, Mozilla Thunderbird, the GIMP, OpenOffice.org, and others are fantastic tributes to what free software stands for.

In the opinion of your humble author and many others, free software is best when it is not just free as in zero cost but also free as in freedom. In the case of software released under the terms of popular free software licenses like the GNU General Public license, you are free to use the software in any way you want, including giving it away, improving it, and modifying it however you want or selling it on a street corner. The only thing you are not free to do under free software licenses like the GNU General Public License is restrict someone else's freedom to do the same. Needless to say, many programmers love free software, which is also known as *open source*. It's like buying a car they can tinker with and not having the hood padlocked. And it is the result of modifications made by businesses and individual programmers that this software grows and evolves.

There's considerable controversy in some circles whether "free software" or "open source software" is a better name for the freely distributable and freely modifiable software described in this book. I and many others think that free software is the proper description, because it highlights the philosophical and ethical value of software freedom. Also, what most people call Linux is actually only a software kernel that is a central but small part of an operating system and is usually combined with an array of software from the Free Software Foundation's GNU project and from others to create a complete operating system. So in this book when I refer to the popular operating system that uses the Linux kernel, I use what I consider the more accurate name for it, GNU/Linux.

The free software packages that I describe in this book are generally as good, if not better than available proprietary software, and you can expect this free software soon to outperform any proprietary software competition. This enormous growth is the history of free software. When the free software protocols of TCP/IP, http, ftp, and others appeared, the Internet was born and soon saw the demise of proprietary networks such as Compuserve. Free software powers 68 percent of all Web servers. And currently, free software is gaining a firm foothold in the application software field. Why? Because it grows through the spirit of giving, which may be one of the most powerful forces in the universe.

So, why not explore the world of free software? It's all free, it's powerful, it's secure, and it's available for everyone to enjoy and improve. And if you're concerned about support for your free software, let me assuage your fears: Support is available, and it's free, too.

In this book, I do occasionally include some proprietary software that is free to download, but not to modify. These software applications are mostly listed in Chapter 24. I also include a chapter on Skype, which is proprietary Internet telephone software that is given freely (meaning with no charge) to anyone for non-commercial use.

Exploring the Web with Mozilla Firefox

Why is Mozilla Firefox increasing its market share of Internet browsers practically on a daily basis, since it appeared in the autumn of 2004? Because exploring the Web with Mozilla Firefox, as shown in Figure 1-1, gives you peace of mind, due to its increased security features, and lets you work more efficiently, using the following features:

- ✔ **Greater security:** It disallows viruses, worms, Trojan horses, and other malicious programs from running in Firefox.

- ✔ **Tabbed browsing:** Using tabs makes viewing and managing Web pages much easier than opening and closing windows.

- ✔ **Search engines right on the toolbar:** What do you like to search? Google? Yahoo!? eBay? Amazon? Ask Jeeves? Wikipedia? All these search engines and more can be listed right on the toolbar. Now there's no need to go to Google to do all your searching.

- ✔ **RSS integration:** Bookmarks can come alive with RSS integration. Just like the news headlines at Yahoo!, you can have bookmarks that give you the latest of whatever you want the latest of — latest news, latest bargains, latest whatever. And it's easy to setup and use.

✔ **Easy bookmarking:** Firefox offers easy and powerful bookmark organizing.

✔ **Pop-up-free browsing:** You can disallow pop-ups, and Firefox lets you know when a Web page is trying to open a pop-up. Then you can decide whether you want to see it or ignore it.

✔ **Best Find feature I've ever used:** This feature alerts you right away if what you're looking for in a Web page is not available — even while you are typing.

Figure 1-1:
Use Mozilla
Firefox Web
browser
for secure
browsing,
tabs, easy-
access
search
engines,
RSS, and
more.

Downloading and Installing Mozilla Firefox for Windows, Mac OS X, and GNU/Linux

To download Mozilla Firefox for Windows or Mac OS X, go to www.mozilla.org and click on the Free Download link for Firefox, unless you want to download Firefox in a language other than English, then choose the Other Systems and Languages link and click the link for your system and language. Save the file to your hard drive. After the file finishes downloading, Windows users can follow the instructions in the sidebar, "Installing applications in Windows," for installing the program.

Installing applications in Windows

Here are the detailed steps that you can follow to install Firefox, as well as virtually any application in Windows: The basic idea is first to see if your downloaded file is compressed, and if it is then uncompress it. (Need some free decompressing software? Go to http://www.thefreesite.com/Free_Software/Unzipping_compression_freeware/ and choose your favorite one.) If the file is not compressed, then you can generally just double-click on it to start the Installation wizard.

To install any application in Windows, you can do the following:

1. **After downloading the file that you want to install, if your browser downloads to the desktop, you may want to move the file into a folder.**

   I have a folder in My Documents called Downloaded Applications where I move all of my downloaded programs.

2. **Open the folder where the downloaded file resides, if it is not already open, click the View button, and choose Details. (Don't double-click on the downloaded file! Just open the folder.)**

   The details of the downloaded files in your folder appear: Name, Size, Type, and so on.

3. **If the Type of the downloaded file is Compressed, then right-click on the file and choose Extract Files. Otherwise, go to Step 6.**

   A dialog box appears with the name and location of the new folder that the file will extract into.

4. **Click OK.**

A progress bar appears, showing the progress of the extracting process. When it finishes, a new folder appears in the same folder as the downloaded file, with the same name, except the type is a File Folder and not a Compressed file.

5. **Double-click to open the newly extracted folder.**

   Often you may see one application file in the open folder. In some cases, such as OpenOffice.org, more than one application file appears, in which case I will let you know what file to double-click on in the next step.

6. **Exit all the programs that you have running in Windows.**

7. **Double-click on the application file in the extracted folder, or if the downloaded file was not compressed, then double-click on the downloaded file.**

   The Installation Wizard appears.

8. **Generally, you probably just want to accept all the default values of the Installation Wizard. Sometimes, you may be required to choose a language and location.**

   If you want more details about the Installation Wizard, see the Appendix.

9. **After you complete the Installation Wizard, you can start the program by choosing Start ⇨ All Programs ⇨ (*Program Name*).**

The steps to install any application in Windows are virtually the same. The basic idea is first to see whether the downloaded file is compressed, and if it is, uncompress it. If it's not, you can generally just double-click on it to start the Installation Wizard.

Mac OS X users can install Firefox by doing the following:

1. **Find the downloaded file with the file format .dmg.** (If you can only find the file that ends with .dmg.gz, double-click on it. Stuff It Expander unpacks it and creates a file ending with .dmg.)

2. **Double-click on the downloaded file ending with .dmg.**

3. **Drag the Firefox application (the globe with the fox on it) into the Applications folder.**

4. **Drag the icon onto the dock, if you want it to be there (which is handy).**

GNU/Linux users can download and install Mozilla Firefox using KPackage. For more details, see the Appendix.

Reading Mail with Mozilla Thunderbird

Mozilla Thunderbird offers the same added security as Mozilla Firefox. No programs can enter your computer through e-mail and start to run automatically in Mozilla Thunderbird, as they can in other email programs. This feature provides peace of mind. Mozilla Thunderbird also has other top-notch features as well:

- ✔ **Intelligent Junk Mail filtering:** Mozilla learns from you, and then you let it take over the task of getting rid of unwanted messages for you.

- ✔ **RSS Integration:** Subscribe to an RSS feed of your choice and have the latest information automatically sent to you as e-mails.

- ✔ **Advanced filtering:** Filter e-mail into folders as it arrives, or easily sort your inbox with a single click.

- ✔ **Smart address book:** This feature fills in addresses automatically as you type them.

- ✔ **Saved Search feature:** You can search e-mails and save them into folders, as shown in Figure 1-2.

To download Thunderbird for Windows or Mac OS X, go to www.mozilla.org and click the Download Thunderbird for Windows, English link under the Get Thunderbird heading. If you want to download for Mac OS X or GNU/Linux, go to www.mozilla.org/products/thunderbird/ and click on the Other Systems and Languages link under Download Now.

Save the file to the hard drive. Then after it finishes downloading, Windows users, follow the instructions in the sidebar in the "Exploring the Web with Mozilla Firefox" section of this chapter to install the program.

Mac OS X users can install Thunderbird by doing the following:

1. **Find the downloaded file with the file format .dmg.** (If you can only find the file that ends with .dmg.gz, double-click on it; Stuff It Expander unpacks it and creates a file ending with .dmg.)

2. **Double-click on the downloaded file ending with .dmg.**

3. **Drag the Thunderbird application into the Applications folder.**

4. **Drag the icon onto the dock, if you want it to be there (which is handy).**

GNU/Linux users can download and install Mozilla Thunderbird using KPackage. For more details, see the Appendix.

Figure 1-2:
Mozilla
Thunderbird
is a
security-
minded mail
client full
of great
features.

Manipulating Images Digitally

Anyone who takes digital photos and wants to improve their look will LOVE the GIMP. The GIMP, which stands for GNU Image Manipulation Program, performs basically the same tasks as Adobe Photoshop. It has a wide array of features, including tools by which you can retouch images, and filters that can enhance their colors and look. Using the GIMP, you can do the following:

✔ **Select, cut, copy, layer, crop, and scale images.**

✔ **Add transparency.**

✔ **Use the Clone tool to repair blemishes,** as shown in Figure 1-3.

✔ **Draw and paint with a paintbrush, pencil, airbrush, even an eraser,** using more than fifty different types of brushes.

✔ **Filter an image in a multitude of ways.** Here are just a few:

- **Color filters** to enhance the colors of an image
- **Edge-detect filters** to make an image look like a line drawing
- **Light effect filters** to add spotlights and other lighting effects
- **Cartoon filter** to give an image a cartoon look
- **Artistic filters** to give an image an artistic flair
- **Rendering filters** for interesting artworks, without the need of any digital photo

Figure 1-3: Using the GIMP's Clone tool, I erased the horse's fence.

Downloading and installing the GIMP for Windows

To download and install the GIMP for Windows, go to http://gimp-win. sourceforge.net/stable.html. Click on the word *Download* to download each of the following programs from this page:

- ✔ GTK+ 2 For Windows
- ✔ The Gimp For Windows
- ✔ GIMP Help 2
- ✔ GIMP Animation Package: Optional, for advanced users

Each time you click the Download link, you can choose a mirror site to download the program from. (For more about mirrors, see the Appendix.) Click in the Download column for a site near you. Save the file to the hard drive. Click the Back button to return to the page to start the other files downloading in the same manner.

After the files finish downloading, follow the instructions in the sidebar in the "Exploring the Web with Mozilla Firefox" section of this chapter, to install the programs. Install GTK+ 2 first, then the Gimp For Windows, and then GIMP Help 2.

Downloading and installing the GIMP for Mac OS X or GNU/Linux

On the Macintosh, the GIMP requires X11, a graphics windowing software used by many GNU/Linux applications. Apple provides a version of X11 for Mac OS X, and you may have installed it if you chose a custom install when installing Mac OS X on your computer — but if you don't remember doing this, you probably didn't. To download and install X11 for Mac OS X, go to http://gimp-app.sourceforge.net and click on the link "Get X11 for OS X 10.3" or on the link "Get X11 preview for OS X 10.2," depending on which version of Mac OS X you have, and then follow the directions in the window that appears to save the file to the hard drive. (If you have a version of Mac OS X later than 10.3, choose the version for 10.3.)

To download and install the GIMP for Mac OS X, go to http://gimp-app. sourceforge.net and click on the link Gimp-2.2.3.dmg. Click in the Download column of a site near you to start the download. Save the file to the hard drive.

After the file has downloaded, Mac OS X users can install the GIMP by doing the following:

1. **Find the downloaded file with the file format .dmg.** (If you can only find the file that ends with .dmg.gz, then double-click on it; Stuff It Expander unpacks it and creates a file ending with .dmg.)

2. **Double-click on the downloaded file ending with .dmg.**

3. **Drag the application into the Applications folder.**

4. **Drag the icon onto the dock, if you want it to be there (which is handy).**

Follow the same steps to install the X11 file you downloaded, if it's not already installed on your Macintosh.

GNU/Linux users generally have The GIMP installed already on their desktops. Or they can use KPackage to download and install it or get the latest version. For more information on KPackage, see the Appendix.

Free Internet Telephone and Conference Calls

Skype is the most popular Internet telephone today with more than 29 million registered users. And it is adding an average of 155,000 users per day. It is not open source software, which means programmers around the world cannot tinker with it and improve it, but it works great and it is given freely. You can make calls from computer-to-computer, or you can make regular phone calls from your computer. The computer-to-computer calls are free, but there's a small charge for the computer-to-phone calls. Even so, as of March 11, 2005, over one million people have enrolled in this SkypeOut service. Skype is user-friendly with its easy-to-use interface and its new Getting Started Wizard, as shown in Figure 1-4. It also has better reception than an ordinary phone.

Skype can also be used as an instant messenger, which is handy when you want to spell out things to people you may be talking to.

To run Skype, you need an Internet connection, either a dial-up with a minimum 33.6 Kbps; or cable, DSL, or other broadband connection. Plus, you need a microphone.

To download Skype, go to www.skype.com and click on the "Download Skype Now. It's Free" button at the top of the page. The download may start immediately. If not, click on the Download Skype For (*your operating system here*). Save the file to the hard drive.

To install Skype on Mac OS X 10.3 or higher, double-click on the downloaded .dmg file. Drag the Skype application to the main Applications folder.

To install Skype on Windows, double-click on the downloaded file, SkypeSetup. Follow the instructions of the Installation Wizard.

Chapter 13 gets you up and running with Skype.

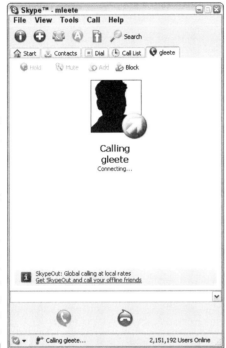

Figure 1-4:
Free telephone calls with great reception and conference calling ability for up to four callers is available with Skype.

Recording and Editing Sound

Audacity is an audio editor and recorder that enables you to basically be your own sound studio. Using Audacity, shown in Figure 1-5, you can record sounds, mix sounds, cut and copy sounds, run filters on sounds, and even change the speed or pitch of the recordings. You can use Audacity to convert tapes or records into digital recordings, or you can use it to convert one type of sound file to another. The filters include Noise Removal, Echo, Tremolo, Equalization, and others.

Downloading Audacity

You can download Audacity from http://audacity.sourceforge.net. Click on the Download tab and click either the Windows or Mac OS 9 Or X link to download the Audacity 1.2.3 installer. Click in the Download column of a site near you. (If you want more information about mirrors, see the Appendix.) Save the file to the hard drive.

You'll also want to download the LAME MP3 encoder. This program allows you to export a sound file into MP3 format. To download the MP3 encoder, Windows users can go to `http://mitiok.free.fr` and click on any lame-3.96.1 link. Mac OS X users can go to `http://spaghetticode.org/lame/` and click on the link for Mac OS X.

Installing Audacity

After the files finish downloading, you may need to extract the zipped files of the LAME MP3 encoder. To do so, Windows users can right-click on the lame-3.96 file and choose Extract files. The unpacking may take place automatically in Mac OS X. If you saw a progress bar for Stuff It Expander when you downloaded Lame, you don't need to unpack it. Otherwise, just double-click on the file.

The first time Audacity needs to use the LAME MP3 encoder, it will ask you where it is. Otherwise, you don't need to do anything else with the LAME MP3 program at present.

To install Audacity, Windows users can follow the instructions in the sidebar in the "Exploring the Web with Mozilla Firefox" section of this chapter.

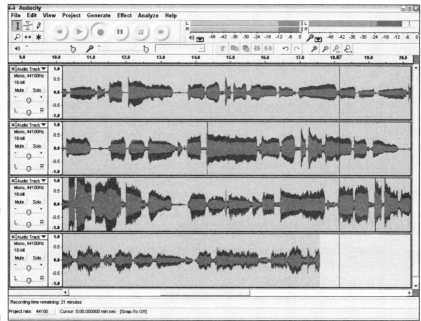

Figure 1-5:
Multi-track your voice and more with Audacity.

GNU/Linux users may already have Audacity installed, but if you don't or if you want to update it to the latest version, you can use KPackage to do so. See the instructions in the Appendix.

Mac OS X users can double-click on the downloaded file and then drag the Audacity application into the Applications folder.

Using Office Software

OpenOffice.org 2.0 rivals, and sometimes surpasses, Microsoft Office in features, reliability, and user-friendliness. OpenOffice.org was designed as a Microsoft Office clone in order to make the migration process easy for people who want to go "free." Sun Microsystems licensed OpenOffice.org under the GNU General Public License, and they also kept a non-free version, called Star Office, which includes a proprietary database, to make available for people or businesses who want the support that Sun offers. OpenOffice.org is a suite of programs that includes a word processor, spreadsheet program, database program, drawing program, HTML editor, and PDF creation software.

 OpenOffice.org 2.0 is available for Windows and GNU/Linux, but the Mac OS X version is only available in an earlier version. You have the choice of using a version that runs on X11, creating the look and feel of the GNU/Linux desktop, or you can use NeoOffice, which runs in the Mac OS X desktop. Currently, NeoOffice is still a beta release candidate, but it may be completely stable by the time you read this. Check out www.openoffice.org for more information about what's available.

Processing words

OpenOffice.org Writer, as shown in Figure 1-6, is a powerful word processor that can handle huge documents and lots of different formats, including Microsoft Word. It can automatically generate indexes, tables of contents, headers and footers, footnotes, and more. You can apply styles and add graphics, as well as scale, position, and improve their color. You can also add columns, generate templates, and much more.

Making calculations

OpenOffice.org Calc is a spreadsheet program for 2D tables and 3D matrices. It can import and export many spreadsheet formats, including Microsoft Excel. It has a capacity for over 65,000 lines and has hundreds of ready-made functions in categories such as Financial, Statistics, Mathematics, Database, and more. Its Function Wizard is shown in Figure 1-7.

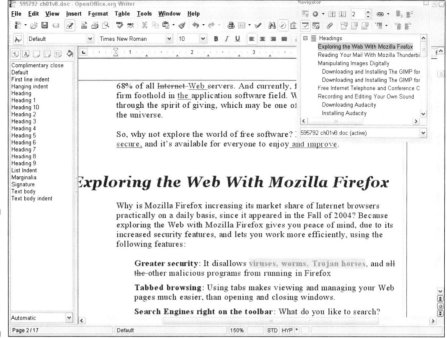

Figure 1-6:
OpenOffice.
org Writer is
useful for all
of your word
processing
needs.

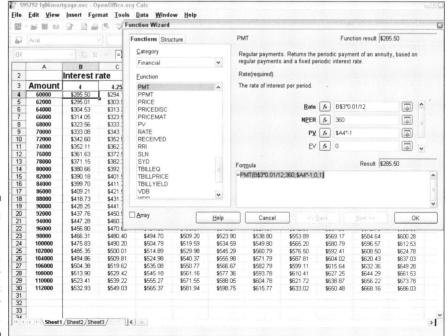

Figure 1-7:
OpenOffice.
org Calc
can handle
huge 2D or
3D tables
and over
65,000 lines.

Building databases

The newest member of the OpenOffice.org suite is OpenOffice.org Base, as shown in Figure 1-8. You can create new databases, complete with relational tables, using the Table Wizard. You can create links to other databases, such as dBASE, MySQL, Oracle, Access, and others, to enter data, query data, and generate reports using the Form, Query, and Report Wizards.

Figure 1-8:
Use the
Form, Query,
and Report
Wizards to
create a
database,
enter data,
find data,
and write
reports for
any Base
database,
or other
databases
such as
dBASE,
MySQL,
Oracle,
Access,
and others.

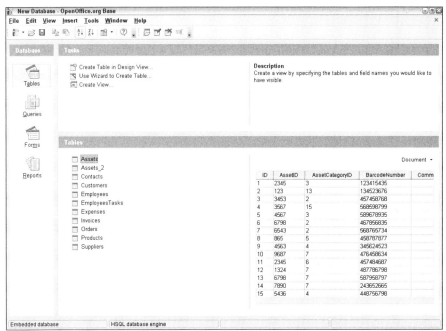

Creating Web pages

Using Writer's integrated HTML editor, you can create Web pages and Web sites right from Writer, as shown in Figure 1-9. You can create Web pages from scratch, using the Tables feature in Writer, and turn graphics or text into hyper-links that can link to other documents, other Web pages, and so on. You can position and wrap graphics and determine the size of your Web page. Or if you want to automatically create Web pages, using existing Writer documents, you can use the Web Page Wizard to publish them. The Web Page Wizard can automatically use headings as links, if you want.

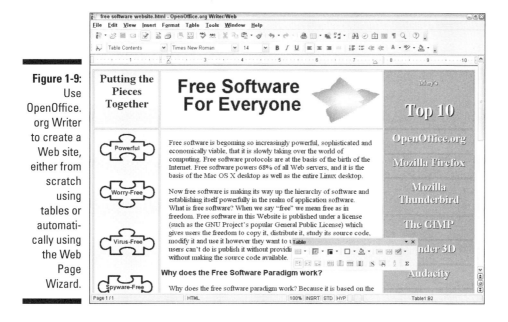

Figure 1-9:
Use
OpenOffice.
org Writer
to create a
Web site,
either from
scratch
using
tables or
automati-
cally using
the Web
Page
Wizard.

Drawing clip art and more

Draw is a vector drawing program that can make an artist out of anyone. You can create shapes, then combine them and pull points to transform simple shapes into recognizable drawings. Using Draw, you no longer have to wade through enormous amounts of clip art to find what's right for you — only to find that it's not available for commercial use. Try out the Duplicate feature to create elaborate designs, as shown in Figure 1-10. Simple drawing is not as hard as most people think. Draw also has a basic 3D art program that lets you create, rotate, position, light, and texture 3D objects.

Making presentations

Impress is a PowerPoint clone designed to help you create presentations, as shown in Figure 1-11. It imports and exports PowerPoint files, as well as Flash (SWF) files and HTML Web pages. You can create slide shows and add transitional effects, such as wipes and sounds. You can automatically advance slides at time intervals of your choosing, or you can advance slides manually with a single click or press of a key. You can also use the Navigator to choose the slide order as you go. Charts are simple to create, either 2D or 3D, and you can customize them. Creating a presentation is quick and easy with Impress because it uses basically the same menus and tools as Draw and Writer. The learning curve is quick.

Figure 1-10:
Draw 2D
or 3D clip
art with
OpenOffice.
org Draw.

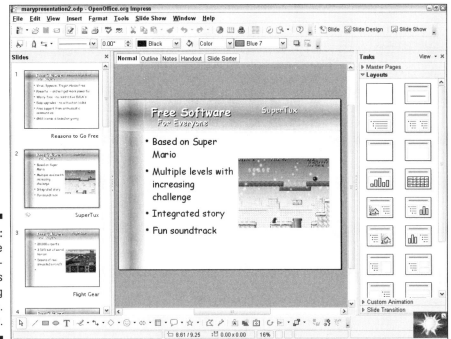

Figure 1-11:
Create
presen-
tations
easily using
OpenOffice.
org Impress.

Generating PDF documents

Another great feature of OpenOffice.org is that it can generate PDF documents from any of its modules. (It's funny that it can't read PDF documents, but that's okay. Adobe Acrobat Reader is free to use, even though it is not free as in the freedom to change it.)

Downloading and installing OpenOffice.org

OpenOffice.org 2.0 is available for Windows and GNU/Linux users. Mac OS X users currently have two options of earlier releases to choose from:

- ✓ **OpenOffice.org version 1.1.2:** This uses X11, a program that comes with Mac OS X.
- ✓ **NeoOffice:** This beta version currently runs like any Mac OS X program, as shown in Figure 1-12. By the time you read this, however, it may be available in a stable version. Even as a beta version, it's very handy.

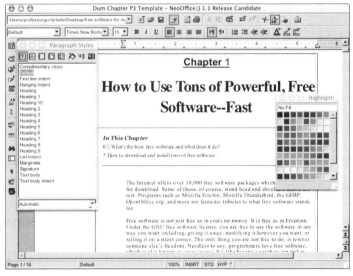

Figure 1-12: NeoOffice is one of the two Mac OS X versions of Open Office.org.

Downloading and installing OpenOffice.org for Windows and GNU/Linux

GNU/Linux users probably have OpenOffice.org as one of their applications. However, you may want to update it to the latest version. Windows or GNU/Linux users can follow these instructions to download OpenOffice.org:

1. Go to www.openoffice.org **and click on the Download tab.**

2. **Click on the OpenOffice.org 2.0 link.**

3. **In the pane that appears, select the language, operating system, and download site (any site near you is fine).**

   A window appears, informing you of the opportunities to contribute to the OpenOffice.org project.

4. **Click Continue to Download.**

   (You can always come back to this page to explore the opportunities to help OpenOffice.org grow.)

5. **Depending on your Web browser, a window may appear asking whether you want to save the program to the disk or open it. Choose Save To Disk.**

   This program takes about ten minutes to download on my computer, but your mileage may vary depending on the speed of your Internet connection.

After the files finish downloading, follow the instructions in the sidebar in the "Exploring the Web with Mozilla Firefox" section of this chapter to install programs with the following exception: In Step 7, you'll find that OpenOffice.org has more than one possible application program to click on. The program that you want to double-click on is called Setup.

After OpenOffice.org is installed, in Windows users can start OpenOffice.org by choosing Start ➪ All Programs ➪ OpenOffice.org ➪ (*select either Base, Calc, Draw, Impress, or Writer*). GNU/Linux users using the KDE desktop can choose K ➪ OpenOffice.org ➪ (*select either Base, Calc, Draw, Impress, or Writer*).

Downloading OpenOffice.org or NeoOffice for Mac OS X users

Mac OS X users can follow these instructions to download OpenOffice.org:

1. Go to www.openoffice.org **and click on the Download tab.**

2. **Click on the OpenOffice.org Mac OS X(X11) link.**

3. **Click either the NeoOffice Download Now link or the OpenOffice.org Download Now link. If you click OpenOffice.org, skip to Step 6.**

   NeoOffice is still a beta version, but may be easier and nicer to use, since it runs natively on Mac OS X. Although OpenOffice.org 1.1.2 using X11 is very stable and may provide more power. The choice is yours. Personally, I would choose NeoOffice and use that until I came across some problem that may require the other version. You can run both versions simultaneously on a Mac. If you choose OpenOffice.org 1.1.2, you also need to install X11 on your Macintosh if you haven't already, as described previously in this chapter in "Downloading and installing the GIMP for Mac OS X or GNU/Linux."

4. **If you chose NeoOffice, then be sure you have Mac OS X 10.2 or higher, 256 MB of memory, and 400 MB of free disk space on your computer.**

5. **Scroll down and click on a download link for any mirror. (If you want Openoffice.org in a language other than English, scroll down even further and click on the link for the language you want.) Save the download file to the hard drive.**

6. **If you chose OpenOffice.org in Step 3, then click in the URL column of a site near you and save the downloaded file to the hard drive.**

   It takes a few minutes to download.

After the files finish downloading, double-click on the downloaded file. If you downloaded NeoOffice, this should open a volume called NeoOfficej. Double-click on NeoOfficej to open a window with the NeoOfficej.pkg file. Double-click on the NeoOfficej.pkg file to start the Installation Wizard. Follow the instructions of the Installation Wizard.

To start NeoOffice click the Applications button in any folder window in the Finder, scroll through the applications until you reach NeoOffice, and double-click on it.

Downloading and installing Java 2 Runtime Environment

The Base database program in OpenOffice.org 2.0 does not run without a program called Java 2 Runtime Environment, which is a proprietary program by Sun Microsystems that is free to use. If you use Mac OS X, you don't need this program because at this writing Base does not run in Mac OS X. Also, for GNU/ Linux users, SimplyMEPIS comes with Java 2 Runtime Environment already installed, or you can download and install it yourself for other GNU/Linux desktops. To download and install Java 2 Runtime Environment, follow these steps:

1. **Go to** `java.sun.com/j2se/1.4.2/download.html`.

2. **Click on the Download J2SE JRE link.**

   A Terms of Use License Agreement window appears. (Basically, you're not allowed to modify, decompile, or reverse engineer the program. You're also not allowed to use it for the design, construction, operation, or maintenance of any nuclear facility.)

3. **Click Accept and then click Continue.**

4. **Click the Windows Installation, Multi-language link or click the link for your GNU/Linux operating system.**

5. **Save the program to the hard drive.**

6. **When installing Java 2 Runtime Environment, double-click on the downloaded file and follow the instructions of the Installation Wizard.**

3D Art and Animation

Blender is a powerful 3D animation program that allows you to do 3D modeling; add lights, textures, transparencies; and then animate your 3D world. You can create models from scratch, or you can type text and extrude it. It's handy if you want to create a 3D logo, as shown in Figure 1-13 — or even if you want to do a feature-length 3D movie. This program is designed for professionals, but the basics can be understood by novices, which is what I try to cover in Chapter 19.

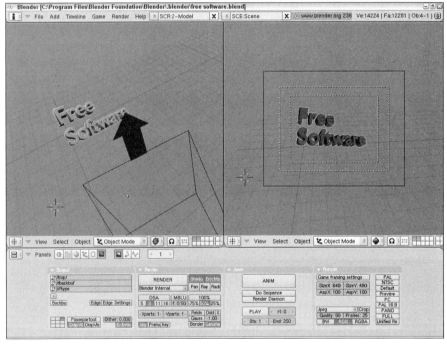

Figure 1-13: Create an animated 3D logo using Blender.

To download Blender for Windows or Mac OS X, go to www.blender3d.com and click on the Download Blender 2.36 link. In the table that appears, click the link for a continent — EU, USA, Australia — in the same row as the platform for the Blender version that you want to download. (Feel free to try any link, even if it's not your continent.) Save the program to the hard drive.

After the files finish downloading, Windows users can follow the instructions in the sidebar in the "Exploring the Web with Mozilla Firefox" section of this chapter to install Blender.

GNU/Linux users can download and install Blender using KPackage. See the Appendix for instructions.

Mac OS X users can install Blender by doing the following:

1. **Find the downloaded file without the file format .zip on the end. If you cannot locate the file, then double-click on the file with .zip on the end.**

   The file unpacks.

2. **Double-click on the downloaded folder blender-publisher-2.25-mac-osx-10.1 to open it.**

3. **Double-click on the blenderpublisher icon.**

4. **Drag the icon onto the Dock, if you want it to be there (which is handy).**

Creating Diagrams

Dia is a free diagramming program for Windows and GNU/Linux that is easy to use and versatile. You can use it to create flowcharts, IT networking diagrams (as shown in Figure 1-14) electrical diagrams, chemical engineering diagrams, civil engineering diagrams, maps, and more. It has tons of ready-made symbols, and all you have to do to create diagrams is basically just drag and drop. You can resize easily, move items around, add text, and more.

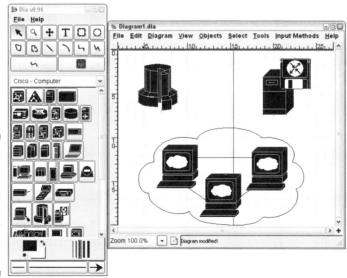

Figure 1-14:
Using Dia, you can create flowcharts and other diagrams quickly.

To download Dia for Windows, go to `http://dia-installer.sourceforge.net/` and click the link under the heading Latest Release. The Project: diaWin32 Installer: File List window appears with a list of files to download along with the file sizes beside each name. Click on one of the three filename links and click in the Download column for a site near you. Save the download to the hard drive and click the Back button to return to the previous window. Repeat the process to download all three files.

After the files finish downloading, follow the instructions in the sidebar in the "Exploring the Web with Mozilla Firefox" section of this chapter to install Dia using the dia-setup file.

GNU/Linux users can download and install Dia using KPackage, as described in the Appendix.

iPodder: The Podcast Receiver

The iPodder program lets you subscribe to your favorite Internet audio programs and listen to them at your convenience, not just when they happen to be broadcast. This gives you the power to listen to whatever you want, whenever you want. iPodder, shown in Figure 1-15, automatically downloads the latest programs of whatever you subscribe to, which you can then load onto your iPod or portable media player. You can also click on a program and hear it played on your computer's media player.

Windows users can follow these steps to download iPodder:

1. **go to** `http://ipodder.sourceforge.net`.
2. **Click on the appropriate Download link: Windows 2000 or XP; OS X 10.3 or Higher; or GNU/Linux.**
3. **Choose a mirror site near you and click in the Download column.**
4. **Save the file to the hard drive.**

After the file finishes downloading, Windows users can follow the instructions in the sidebar in the "Exploring the Web with Mozilla Firefox" section of this chapter to install iPodder.

Mac OS X users can install iPodder by doing the following:

1. **Find the downloaded file with the file format .dmg.** (If you can only find the file that ends with .dmg.gz, double-click on it; Stuff It Expander unpacks it and creates a file ending with .dmg.)
2. **Double-click on the downloaded file ending with .dmg.**
3. **Drag the application (the lemon icon) into the Applications folder.**
4. **Drag the icon onto the Dock, if you want it to be there (which is handy).**

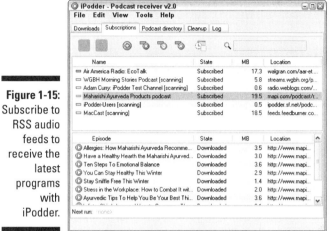

Figure 1-15:
Subscribe to
RSS audio
feeds to
receive the
latest
programs
with
iPodder.

Learning

Lots of free software is available for educational purposes. Chapter 21
includes a discussion of the following, as well as all the information on downloading and installing all of them:

- ✔ **Celestia:** Get an up close and personal view of the solar system, as shown
  in Figure 1-16, as well as explore hundreds of stars, including some with
  known planets. This program gives you the feeling of really touring
  around the universe. Budding astronomers will find it fascinating.

Figure 1-16:
Explore the
universe
with
Celestia.

✓ **Flight Gear:** This incredible program lets you pilot any one of dozens of aircraft to any one of 20,000 airports around the world, while automatically generating the terrain of the earth from a three-DVD set of terrain or from downloads. It also varies the time of day and weather conditions. Imagine flying around the world from the comfort of your home. You can even request instant online help. Mayday!

✓ **Gcompris:** Children may find Gcompris, a suite of colorful, educational games, to be lots of fun while learning the alphabet and more.

✓ **Solfege:** This ear-training software trains you to recognize musical notes, chords, pitches, and rhythm. The easiest level of this program is not all that easy, and the hardest is quite hard. You had better be serious about music to use this program.

✓ **Tux Paint:** This software is for children of all ages. Even the smallest can probably enjoy the stamps and paint tools, as shown in Figure 1-17. The interface uses large buttons and is easy to navigate using the mouse. Tux Paint doesn't require reading to understand how to use it.

✓ **Tux Typing:** This program teaches typing with fun game play. Fish drop from the sky with letters that you need to type before the fish hit the ground. Then Tux the penguin gets to eat them.

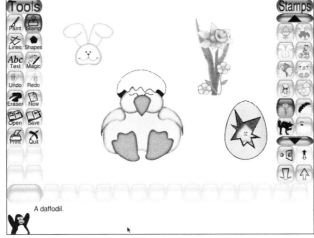

Figure 1-17:
Children
love the
Tux Paint
stamps.

Having Fun

Many great games are available as free software. Some are extremely involved and sophisticated, like Freeciv, a multiplayer, online, free software game similar to the popular Civilization game. Others are delightful, like SuperTux, the side-scrolling, jump-and-run platform game, shown in Figure 1-18, with lots of levels and a storyline to go with it. This is Super Mario in Antarctica. For more information about these games, including downloading and installation instructions, see Chapter 22.

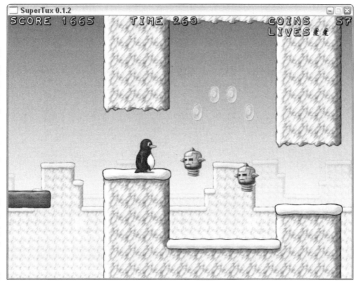

Figure 1-18: SuperTux is a delightful Super Mario-type side-scrolling, story-based game with lots of levels to keep every kid at heart busy for days!

Other great games include

- **BilliardGL:** A 3D pool game.
- **Circus Linux:** A clone of Circus Atari.
- **Crack Attack:** Similar to the Super Nintendo game, Tetris Attack.
- **Enigma:** A puzzle game with 700 different levels.
- **GlTron:** A clever game based on the game in the movie *Tron*.
- **GNU Chess:** Try to beat it!
- **Trackballs:** A marble game, shown in Figure 1-19, similar to the popular Marble Madness.

In Chapter 22, I describe how to download, install, and play the games — at least, how to start to play them — especially SuperTux, my favorite!

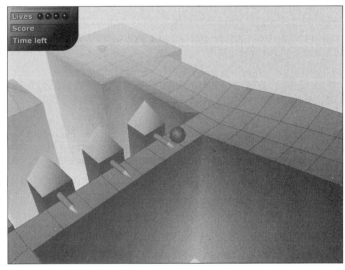

Figure 1-19:
Stay on
track with
Trackballs.

Powerful, Secure, Free: GNU/Linux Operating System

GNU/Linux operating systems come in all shapes and kinds, but the one generally rated as perhaps the easiest-to-use, most polished, and suitable for the newcomer is SimplyMEPIS, shown in Figure 1-20. SimplyMEPIS is very easy to install because it automatically determines what software drivers your computer hardware needs and installs them without your needing to bother about them. It also allows you to boot from a CD-ROM, if you want to just try out the program on any Windows computer just to see how you like it. Then when you reboot again without the CD-ROM in the drive, your computer reboots Windows, as usual.

SimplyMEPIS boots with a huge array of free software already installed, including Mozilla Firefox, OpenOffice.org, the GIMP, Audacity, and many more. And best of all, you don't need virus protection. The only protection SimplyMEPIS requires is the firewall it installs during the installation process. Viruses and other malicious software do not harm your computer when you run SimplyMEPIS, as is the case with other GNU/Linux desktops. For information on downloading and installing SimplyMEPIS, see Chapter 23.

Getting Support

The free software world doesn't leave you all to yourself with no recourse for support. In fact, often the opposite is true. Support forums for virtually every top free software application are brimming with activity. Hundreds of experienced users come to the aid of the free software newbies daily. And the searchable archives of these forums are a vast treasure chest of information.

Searching the support forum archives

Support forum archives for each major free software application are generally extensive and searchable. If you are using a stable version of a widely used program, and not a new beta, then it is likely that whatever question you have has already been asked by someone else. All you have to do is search the archives using keywords describing your problem. Normally, you can find the answer in less time than it takes to get a person on the phone using traditional phone support for proprietary applications. (And, guess what — the people answering your questions may be doing exactly the same thing! So, why not just do it yourself?)

Asking questions

If the answer to your question is not in the support forums, then go ahead, be brave, and ask the question on the forum. Be concise and brief, and title it descriptively. (Remember, this e-mail may be read by hundreds of people.) You can normally expect an answer in about 24 hours. Although, if your topic is hot, it may take as little as a few minutes.

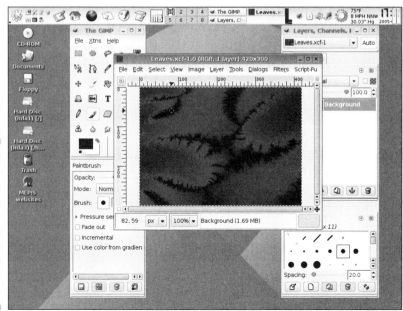

Figure 1-20:
The Simply-
MEPIS
desktop
installs
with tons
of free
software
and is
virus-free.

Where to go for support

Generally, all the home pages of the major free software applications have links for help and support. Check them out whenever you need advice. Here are a few examples of what's available and where.

- For OpenOffice.org, go to `www.openoffice.org` and click the Support tab. Then choose any of the following:

    - Click the Archives tab below the User Mail List heading, for a huge searchable archive.

    - Click the Subscribe tab below the User Mail List to subscribe to the User Mail List. You must be subscribed in order to send e-mail to it.

    - Click the User Help:User-FAQ Project link for a comprehensive list of well-organized FAQs.

    - Click Mac Support link for a Mac-related FAQs.

    - Click the OpenOffice.org Consultants Directory for paid email, phone, or on-site support.

- For support for Mozilla Firefox and Thunderbird, go to `www.mozilla.org` and click on the Support tab. Then choose any of the following:

    - Click on the Knowledge Base link for a searchable database of solutions.

    - Click on the link for Firefox Web Forum or Thunderbird Web Forum for e-mail support.

    - Click on the Third Party Phone And Email Support for phone support or email support for a small charge.

- For support for Skype, go to `www.skype.com` and click the Help tab. Then choose any of the following:

    - Type some key words into the Search Knowledgebase text box and click Search Knowledgebase.

    - Click Forum and the click the Search The Forums button to search all of the 13 active forums simultaneously.

    - Click the Users Guides link, if you think the answer to your problem may reside there.

    - Click the Submit Support Request for an e-mail form.

Chapter 2

The Best Places to Get Free Software

*T*he distribution and development of free software is taking place all over the Internet and all over the world. The largest Web repository of free software projects, SourceForge.net, has more than 95,000 projects and more than a million registered users. Because of the popularity of free software sites, having an idea of what's out there and where to go is a good idea. This chapter points you in the right direction by listing some popular sites you should check out early on in your software search.

Searching Out the Best of the Best for Windows

With thousands of free software packages out there, you probably don't want to spend time sorting through all of them. You just want the best. This book describes how to download and use the top free software applications, but many more excellent applications exist as well. The sites `www.winlibre.com/en/` and `www.theopencd.org` both offer a downloadable package of what these sites' authors consider to be the best free software for Windows. CD-ROMs that you can purchase are also available. Or you can download the applications individually from the Open CD project. The OSSwin project at osswin.sourceforge.net has links to hundreds of other free software applications that run on Windows. And My Open Source at `www.myopensource.org` offers links to the top free software packages for Windows, as well as rates them.

Also keep your eye on the GnuWin project, which is a Web site designed to help Windows users make the switch to free software. This terrific site is currently without a leading team, and until one is found, it is in danger of becoming out of date. Its URL is www.gnuwin.org.

 Another site that may be very useful when it is up and running properly is OpenSourceList.org (currently found at www.opensourcelist.org/oss/). This site is designed to be a comprehensive database for Windows open source programs but is currently still under construction.

WinLibre

WinLibre offers a CD-ROM that you can buy or a free download with a single installation program to install a whole collection of some of the best free software for Windows. You can download either a 151MB file with everything in it, or a much smaller 650KB file that downloads the programs from the Web one by one and installs them. The site also describes each free software application and has links to the home page of each application. The home page for WinLibre (in English) is www.winlibre.com/en/index.php (if you speak French you can go to www.winlibre.com).

Table 2-1 shows the free software programs included in the download or on the CD-ROM.

Table 2-1	The WinLibre CD-ROM and Downloads	
Free Software Name	*Function*	
OpenOffice.org	Word processing	Spreadsheet
	Database	Web site editor
	Drawing	PDF creation
	Presentation software	
PDFCreator	PDF creation	
Mozilla Firefox	Surfing the Net	
Mozilla Thunderbird	E-mail	
FileZilla	FTP client	
Nvu	Web site editor	

Free Software Name	Function
Gaim	Instant messaging
Zinf	MP3 and Ogg audio player
CDex	Sound file conversion
WinLAME	Encoder (for Audacity)
VLC Media Player	VideoLanClient
Video playerGIMP	2D image manipulation
Inkscape	Vector drawing
Blender	3D graphics and animation
Audacity	Audio creation
TightVNC	PC remote control
7-Zip	File compression and decompression
NetTime	PC date/time synchronization
ClamWin	Antivirus
Notepad2	A Windows Notepad replacement

The Open CD project

The Open CD project (www.theopencd.org) offers you the choice of buying a CD or downloading software for free, similar to WinLibre. This site also has a nicely designed interface that lets you read detailed descriptions of each program. And if you don't want all the programs, you can download just the programs you want. The Open CD project also offers downloads of the source code (which you don't want unless you're a developer). Table 2-2 lists the programs offered on the Open CD site.

Table 2-2	The Open CD Project
Program name	Function
OpenOffice.org	Office productivity suite
AbiWord	Word processor

(continued)

Table 2-2 *(continued)*

Program name	Function
PDFCreator	PDF creation
GIMP	Image manipulation
Blender	3D graphics and animation
Dia	Diagramming
Tux Paint	Paint program for kids
Firefox	Web browser
Thunderbird	E-mail
Mozilla suite	Web browser
	Web page composer
	E-mail & newsgroups
Gaim	Instant messaging
FileZilla	FTP client
TightVNC	PC remote access
WinHTTrack	Downloads Web sites
Audacity	Audio recording and editing
Celestia	Astronomical simulator
CDex	Sound file conversion
7-Zip	File compression and decompression
Notepad2	Windows Notepad replacement
SciTE	Source code editor
Sokoban	Puzzle game
Battle for Wesnoth	Fantasy/strategy game
Lbreakout	Arcade game

The OSSwin project

The OSSwin project at http://osswin.sourceforge.net contains hundreds of links to the home pages of free software programs that run on Windows. It offers 42 major categories of software applications, such as Audio editing tools, Graphics, Databases, Instant Messaging, Utilities, Webcam, Media players, Office tools, and more. This site is a great place to go if you're looking for something special. For example, students may want to explore the Math and Science links or the Encyclopedia links. The site's collection is huge but doesn't include any games.

My Open Source

My Open Source (www.myopensource.org) offers descriptions, links, and ratings of Open Source programs for Windows, divided into seven categories:

- ✔ Internet
- ✔ Utilities
- ✔ Multimedia
- ✔ Entertainment
- ✔ Office productivity
- ✔ Development
- ✔ Web scripts

You can sort programs by top-rated, most recent, most popular, and alphabetical. You can view screenshots and jump to the official page for each program. Plus, the site has links to other Open Source sites. This user-friendly site has a nice collection of most of the better programs.

Exploring tons of free software for Macintosh OS X

Most of the top free software applications are available for Mac OS X and have the look and feel of programs created for Mac OS X. But many other free software applications can also run on Mac OS X, using a program called X11, which has the look and feel of a Linux desktop. These free software applications can be found at the Fink Project which is a free software application project devoted to porting and packaging free software for the Mac, via X11.

The Fink project's home page is http://fink.sourceforge.net. The site contains details of what's available, how to download and run the free software applications, plus electronic mailing lists, documentation, news about the project, and an extensive FAQ.

Finding the Best Free Software for GNU/Linux

Most Linux operating systems come with the most popular free software packages already installed and ready to use. And the free software that does not come with it, is easily found, downloaded and installed using a program called KPackage. How to use KPackage is described in the Appendix.

The Mepis Linux site (www.mepis.com) offers an exciting, relatively new distribution of the Linux desktop called SimplyMepis, which appears to be wonderfully stable and up to date, and offers a large variety of free software. It is available by download or by purchasing a very inexpensive CD-ROM. The site also has links to very active forums and plentiful other sources of free technical support. To try out SimplyMepis, you can run it from the CD-ROM without having to download it to your computer. It installs with a lot of software, such as OpenOffice.org, the GIMP, Mozilla Firefox, Tux Racer, Frozen Bubble, Tux Paint, and many more. See Chapter 23 for more details regarding how to download and install SimplyMepis.

For All Platforms

Much of the best free software runs on all the major platforms: Windows, Mac, and Linux. The Web sites of these major projects offer downloads, information, and support to users as well as to developers:

- ✔ www.OpenOffice.org. This extensive Web site contains all the OpenOffice.org development Web pages as well as all the user support pages and downloads. You can go to this site to download the latest version of OpenOffice.org, or if you want to be wild, you can try out the newest development versions (that is, unfinished versions used for testing new features). You can also find active e-mail lists, tutorials, descriptions of the program, screenshots, the latest news, and more.

- ✔ www.Mozilla.org. The Mozilla Web site offers downloads of the Mozilla products, such as Firefox and Thunderbird. It also has news about the development of current projects and a store where you can buy Firefox T-shirts and more. It has support forums and online documentation, and lots of information for its developers. Mozilla is probably the best designed free software Web site I've seen. It is designed with both the user and developer in mind.

- ✔ www.Gimp.org. Gimp.org offers downloads of the most recent version of the GIMP, as well as past versions. It offers user support through active mailing lists and tutorials, as well as a link to free online access to the book, *Grokking the Gimp* published by Pearson Education. You can also find news and development information.

- ✔ www.Blender3d.org. The artistic and user-friendly Blender site offers the latest downloads of its 3D creation software suite as well as extensive tutorials and a link to active forums for support. It also has an amazing gallery and offers all the development information.

- ✔ www.Gnu.org. This site offers lots of information about the free software movement and a comprehensive directory of free software for a variety of platforms, including GNU/Linux (predominately), Windows, and Macintosh. It is the Web home page for the GNU Project, which develops the GNU system, a completely free UNIX-style operating system that together with the Linux kernel is the basis of what people call Linux (which probably should more properly be called GNU/Linux). The GNU Project also created the GNU General Public License, which is by far the most popular free software license.

- ✔ www.Freshmeat.net. Freshmeat.net is the Web's largest index of Unix and cross-platform software, updated daily. This site is especially useful for Linux users hunting for software. Its home page gives you a quick look at the latest new releases in the free software world, and the rest of the site also contains book reviews, project reviews, articles, and tutorials.

- ✔ www.Sourceforge.net. Sourceforge.net is the largest Web repository of free software projects. It has more than a million registered users and 97,000 projects, nearly all of which are available for free download. The home page offers news about the projects, and you can easily search the site for software you may want.

Part II

Using Powerful, Free Office Software

The 5th Wave   By Rich Tennant

©RICHTENNANT

"I love the way this program justifies the text
in my resume. Now if I can just get it to
justify my asking salary..."

In this part . . .

In this part, I describe how to use the powerful word processing, spreadsheet, and database programs of OpenOffice.org 2.0. Writer is a full-featured word processing program in which you can automatically generate indexes, footnotes, tables of contents, and more. You can create newsletters and templates, add graphics, and format your documents in a huge variety of ways. Using Writer, you can import Microsoft Word documents, modify them, and export them as Microsoft Word documents.

Then using Calc, the spreadsheet program, you can import Excel documents, modify them in Calc, and export them as Excel documents. Calc offers all the functionality you expect of a spreadsheet program: You can create 2D tables or 3D matrices; you can use any of hundreds of ready-made functions in different categories such as financial, statistical, database functions, and more.

And with Base, OpenOffice.org's database program, you can create databases, or link to many different database formats, such as MySQL, Access, dBase, Oracle, and more. You can use the Report wizard, Query wizard, or Table wizard to aid you with your database needs. You can also create form letters using Writer and link to your spreadsheet or database to perform mail merges quickly and easily.

Chapter 3

Word Processing with OpenOffice.org Writer

*W*hatever it is that you're looking for in a word processor, OpenOffice.org Writer 2.0 has it. Writer was created as a full-blown clone of Microsoft Word and has been endowed with virtually all the qualities and features found in Word. Writer's toolbars and menus were designed to facilitate an easy migration for individuals, businesses, and government offices from Word to Writer. If you're familiar with Word or any word processor, you will find Writer to be an easy switch. And if you're a novice to word processing, then you have no reason not to use Writer. It is a mature, full-featured word processor, for free! This chapter introduces you to Writer and its many features.

Getting Started

To use OpenOffice.org Writer, you first must install the program. This involves a simple downloading procedure from www.openoffice.org. OpenOffice.org (the program) consists of more than a million lines of code, yet it only takes about 10–20 minutes to download it using a DSL connection. For easy instructions on installing OpenOffice.org (the program, not the Web site) refer to "Processing Words" in Chapter 1.

Why is the program called OpenOffice.org — the same name as the Web site? Another organization already has dibs on the name OpenOffice, so calling the program OpenOffice.org keeps everyone's lawyers happy and simultaneously promotes the site where you may download the program.

Creating a new document

OpenOffice.org Writer opens with a new document. Writer allows you to open as many new documents as you want. To create a new document, choose File⇨New⇨Text Document. A new blank document appears, hiding the other document. To view whatever document you want, choose Window⇨(the name of the document window you want to view.)

The Standard toolbar, shown in Figure 3-1, provides handy buttons for many of Writer's functions, such as cutting, pasting, and undoing. The Formatting toolbar, also shown in Figure 3-1, offers buttons for formatting and selecting type size, style, and color. And the status bar at the bottom of the window gives you information on the status of your document, such as page number, page count, and zoom.

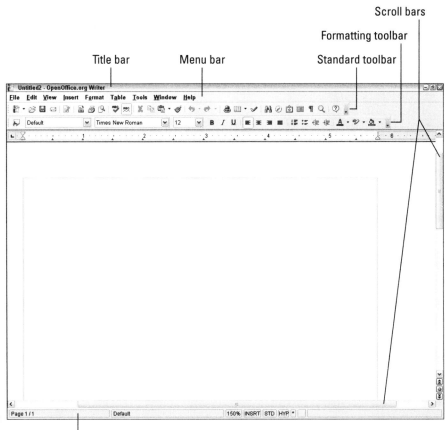

Figure 3-1:
The Writer
window.

Be sure that your two main toolbars are visible, as shown in Figure 3-1. If either or both are not visible, choose View⇨Toolbars⇨Standard or View⇨Toolbars⇨Formatting, so that each displays a check mark beside its name.

Writer offers a wide range of toolbars, as shown in the menu list in Figure 3-2. Many of these are floating toolbars, such as the Align toolbar and Insert toolbar, also shown in Figure 3-2. Some toolbars, such as the Drawing toolbar, appear at the top of the Writer window, as shown in Figure 3-2.

Opening documents and importing from Microsoft Word or other word processors

Writer is designed to import documents in the major popular word processing formats. Importing a file from another format is as easy as opening any Writer document. And Writer also exports a myriad of formats as well. In fact, if you want, you may read and write your files entirely in Word format (.doc) and never save as a Writer document at all!

Figure 3-2:
Writer offers many toolbars, such as Drawing, Align, and Insert.

To open or import a document, perform the following steps:

1. **Choose File➪Open.**

   The Open dialog box appears, as shown in Figure 3-3.

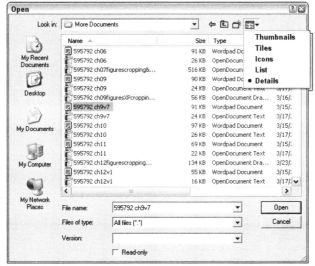

Figure 3-3:
The Open dialog box enables you to browse through your files and select the file you want to open.

2. **Browse through your files by double-clicking folder icons to open and view the contents of folders, or by clicking the Up One Level button to close a folder.**

   If you want to view only files of a certain type, such as just Text documents, or just Microsoft Word documents, choose the category you want to view from the File Type menu. The File Type menu lists more than 100 categories of files. If you want to view all of your files as you browse through your documents, then choose All files (*.*) from the list. This is the default. Selecting the File type is not required to open any document—it is simply an aid to finding the document you want to open.

3. **To select the file of your choice, click the filename, and then click the Open button to open the file.**

Word versus Writer compatibility

Generally, even large and complex documents appear identical when opened in Writer or Word. But a few exceptions exist. For example, some line spacings or row heights may create slightly different automatic paginations. Or small differences in margin settings may cause some words to wrap to another line in one program, but not the other. These incompatibilities are generally easy to fix, if they need to be fixed at all.

OpenOffice.org lists several attributes that may be affected when importing documents:

AutoShapes	Hyperlinks
Revision marks	Bookmarks
OLE (embedded) objects	WordArt graphics
	Animated text
Form fields	New chart types
Indexes	Tab, line, and paragraph spacing
Tables, frames, and columns	Grouped objects

In most cases, your imported AutoShapes, as well as everything else in the preceding list, will appear just fine. In some cases, however, they may appear different, so be aware.

Both Writer and Word have the capability to use macros, which are individual programs that run within the document. Macros perform specialized functions in a document, such as linking it to a database in a customized manner. Macros created in Word documents will not run in Writer, and macros created in Writer documents will not run in Word. Macros, however, can be reprogrammed to run in the other format.

Some Word documents have VBA (Microsoft Visual Basic) macros in them. These macros do not run in Writer, but they continue to reside in documents that are opened in .doc format and are saved by Writer when you save in .doc format. You have the option of not importing or resaving VBA macros if you're not planning on using them. VBA macros in the past have been linked to viruses on computers running Windows. To disallow VBA macros from being imported in a .doc file, choose Tools➪Options, and in the Load/Save dialog box that appears, choose ➪Load/Save ➪VBA Properties, and under Microsoft Word 97/2000, deselect Load Basic Code To Edit and also deselect Save Original Basic Code Again.

Editing Basics

Writer offers a myriad of basic editing options typical of all word processors, as well as advanced editing capabilities provided only by high-end word processors.

Choosing your text style, size, and color

The first step you probably want to take when starting a document is to choose the font, type size, and even the color of your type, if black is not your thing.

To choose the font type and font size for your entire new document, choose your font from the Font Name drop-down list on the Formatting toolbar. Then choose the size of the font from the Font Size drop-down list on the Formatting toolbar.

To change the font type, size, or color for a specific heading, paragraph, word, or group of words, first *select* the text that you want to change, then choose the Font Name and Font Size from the drop-down menus on the Formatting toolbar, or click the Font Color icon on the Formatting toolbar and choose a color from the floating Font Color toolbar.

Writer offers several ways to make a selection. You can select text in the following ways:

- ✔ **To select an area of text:** Click and drag the mouse over the text that you want to select.
- ✔ **To select a word:** Double-click anywhere in a word.
- ✔ **To select a sentence:** Triple-click anywhere in a line.
- ✔ **To select a large area of text:** Click at the beginning of the desired selection, then scroll down to the end of the desired selection and Shift+click.
- ✔ **To select the entire document:** Choose Edit➪Select All.

Using the ruler to set margins and tabs

Writer sets default margins for you, but you may want to change them. The easiest way to set left and right margins is to use the ruler, shown earlier in Figure 3-2. If your ruler is not visible, then choose View➪Ruler.

The top part of the two triangles on the left indicates the margin for the first line of your paragraph, and the bottom triangle indicates the margin for the next lines of your paragraph. The triangle to the right indicates the location of the right margin. Click and drag the margin symbols in your blank document to set the margins for your entire document.

You can specify different margins for different lines or paragraphs in your document. Just click in a paragraph or in a line (containing a return) and drag the margin symbols to wherever you want the new margins to be. When you release the mouse, the margins for that line or paragraph change accordingly.

This is an easy and simple use of tabs. (Writer also allows you to set margins with more detail. For more information regarding how to do so, see "Setting your margins" in Chapter 2.)

Aligning your text

Writer provides easy-to-find buttons on the Formatting toolbar that enable you to align your text in the following ways:

- ✔ **Align Left:** Aligns your text to the left margin.
- ✔ **Centered:** Centers your text between the right and left margins.
- ✔ **Align Right:** Aligns your text to the right margin.
- ✔ **Justified:** Aligns your text to both margins. (This option sometimes causes extra spacing between words to stretch the lines to both margins.)

To align your text in any of the preceding ways, first select the text that you want to align, then click one of the buttons: Align Left, Centered, Align Right, or Justified. (All the text is aligned in any paragraph that you select, even if you select just part of a paragraph.)

Cutting, copying, and pasting

After you're familiar with selecting text, then cutting, copying, and pasting any amount of text in any location is a breeze. Simply select the text you want to cut or copy, then click the Cut or Copy buttons on the Standard toolbar, choose Edit⇨Cut or Edit⇨Copy, or press Ctrl+X to cut or Ctrl+C to copy. Then click in your document at the location you want to paste, and click the Paste button, choose Edit⇨Paste, or press Ctrl+V. Whatever you cut or copied appears where you clicked.

Undo and redo

Writer offers both an undo feature and a redo feature. These features can be handy when your two-year-old comes to pound on your keyboard, or a million other times during the day when you just feel like backing up and starting again. To undo your previous edit, click the Undo button on the Standard toolbar, choose Edit⇨Undo, or press Ctrl+Z. To redo your undo, click the Redo button on the Standard toolbar, choose Edit⇨Redo, or press Ctrl+Y. (Have you ever wished the Undo button were available on places other than the computer?)

Inserting and overwriting modes

At the bottom of the Writer window is the status bar, shown earlier in Figure 3-2. The status bar offers information on what page number you're currently viewing, how many pages are in your document, how much you're zoomed in on your document, and whether you're in Insert mode (INSRT) or Overwrite (OVER) mode.

Generally, writers like to be in Insert mode, because when you insert text while in Insert mode, all text in the paragraph to the right of whatever text you insert moves to the right. In Overwrite mode, all text to the right of your insertion is overwritten character for character. So, if you don't want to accidentally lose any text, remain in Insert mode, which is the default. To switch from Insert to Overwrite mode or back again, click INSRT or OVER on the status bar.

Zooming

Often you may want to zoom in or zoom out in your document to get a better look at your page. Writer allows you to zoom in two ways:

- **Right-click the Zoom button on the status bar,** as shown in Figure 3-4, and choose the percentage or type of zoom from the Zoom pop-up menu. (If the Zoom pop-up menu does not appear, then see the tip below.) Choosing Optimal zooms in on everything in the current screen. Choosing Page Width zooms to the width of the page, and choosing Entire Page shows the entire page.

- **Click the magnifying glass on the Standard toolbar (or choose View⇨ Zoom) to bring up the Zoom dialog box.** In the Zoom dialog box, you may select the amount or type of zoom or choose any percentage of zoom from 20% to 599% by selecting Variable and choosing the percentage from the spin box.

If you are using Windows XP, right-clicking the Zoom button on the status bar may have no effect unless you hide the Windows XP taskbar. To do that, first unlock the taskbar by right-clicking an empty spot on the taskbar. A pop-up menu appears. If a check mark resides beside Lock The Taskbar, choose Lock The Taskbar to unlock it. Then position your mouse on the upper part of the taskbar so that the cursor turns into a double-arrow and click and drag the taskbar down until it disappears. You can always get it back by positioning your mouse at the bottom of the window, so that the cursor turns into a double-arrow and click and drag upward so that the taskbar reappears.

Figure 3-4:
Right-click
the Zoom
button on
the status
bar to
choose your
magnifica-
tion.

Finding and Replacing

Writer's finding and replacing capabilities are extensive. You needn't worry about losing anything in your document — even if your document is 1,000 pages long! Writer allows you to search for 31 attributes, such as font color or hyphenation, as well as lets you check for styles and matching case. You can also perform searches forwards or backwards, and add regular expressions, which enables you to use wildcards, and more. And the Find & Replace dialog box, as shown in Figure 3-5, is easy to use.

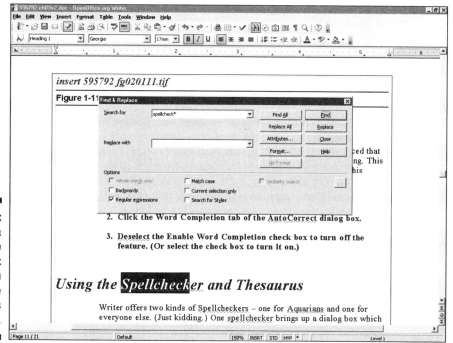

Figure 3-5:
The Find &
Replace
dialog box
allows you
to use
wildcards
and more.

To use the Find and Replace feature, click the Find On/Off button on the Standard toolbar, choose Edit⇨Find & Replace, or press Ctrl+F. Enter the text you want to find in the Search For input box and click the Find button. Writer finds the next instance of the word in the text. If you click the Find All button, Writer selects every instance of the text you are searching for.

If you want to replace text with other text, enter the text you want to replace in the Search For input box; then enter your replacement text in the Replace With input box and click the Replace button. Writer finds the next instance of the text matching the contents of the Search For box and replaces it with what's in the Replace With box. (Click Replace All to replace every instance of the text that it finds in the document.)

The Find and Replace feature has several options, as follows:

- **To apply your search to whole words only**, select the Whole Words Only check box. For example, if you search for "like," Writer won't return search results of "likes" or "dislikes."

- **To search backwards,** select the Backwards check box.

- **To match the uppercase and lowercase letters in the Search For input box,** select the Match Case check box.

- **To search in an area of selected text,** first select the block of text in your document, then click the Find On/Off button and when the Find & Replace dialog box appears, select the Current selection Only check box.

- **To add wildcards to your search,** select the Regular expressions check box, and use a "." wherever you want to insert a wildcard for a single character. For example, type "t.me" to find instances of time or tame. Or use "*" to insert any number of characters. Also, you may use any number of wildcards in your search. For example, in Figure 3-5, "Thes..rus" returns Thesaurus, or Thesuarus — for bad spellers, like me.

- **To search for words or expressions similar to what is in the Search For input box,** select the Similarity Search check box, and click the box on its right to bring up the Similarity Search dialog box to choose how many characters you want to allow the search to exchange, add, or remove from the text in the Search For input box. (I always use the Regular expressions option and wildcards to perform this task instead of this feature, because wildcards are quicker and more intuitive.)

- **To search for or replace styles,** select the Search for Styles check box. The Search For and Replace With input boxes transform into drop-down list boxes containing all styles in the document. Choose the desired style from either the Search for list or both the Search for and Replace With lists.

AutoCorrecting and Word Completing

The AutoCorrecting feature ensures that you will never see "t-h-i-e-r" instead of "their" or "t-r-u-e-l-y" instead of "truly" in your document — even if you type it wrong! Also, AutoCorrecting offers a Word Completion feature that can be handy or not, depending on how you like to write.

Adding words and shortcuts to the replacement table

If you downloaded the English language version of OpenOffice.org, then the AutoCorrect feature is loaded with great error-preventing items. However, you may want to add more words — such as the names of co-workers, clients, or bosses that you may want to ensure that you will never misspell. Or you can use it as a shortcut to eliminate typing long, frequently used words. For example, I added *ooo* to my AutoCorrect list to be replaced with OpenOffice.org. This way, whenever I type *ooo*, what appears in my document is OpenOffice.org.

To add or delete items from AutoCorrect, perform the following steps:

1. **Choose Tools⇨AutoCorrect.**

   The AutoCorrect dialog box appears.

2. **Be sure that the Replace tab is selected; then if the AutoCorrect dialog box is empty, choose English (USA) or the appropriate language from the Replacements and Exceptions for Language list box.**

   The AutoCorrect dialog box displays two lists, as shown in Figure 3-6. (Some languages do not have any AutoCorrect lists, but you can create your own.) The column on the left is a list of commonly misspelled words or abbreviations. The list on the right contains the correct spellings or correctly changed abbreviations. You can use AutoCorrect, for example, to get the circle around the *c* for the copyright symbol — which is not easy to do otherwise.

3. **To add an entry to the replacement table, enter the text that you want to replace into the Replace input box and enter the correct version in the With input box.**

   You probably need to delete whatever text already resides in the two input boxes, but don't worry; deleting whatever is in the boxes does not delete the items from the AutoCorrect list.

   After you enter your text, the New button to the right becomes enabled. (In Figure 3-6, the Replace box has ooo and the With box has OpenOffice.org.)

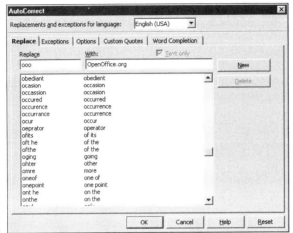

Figure 3-6:
The Auto-
Correct
dialog box.

4. **Click the New button.**

   The contents of the Replace input box and the contents of the With input box appear in the list.

5. **To be sure that your replacement table is turned on, click the Options tab and select Use Replacement Table in the (M) and (T) columns, if they are not already selected.**

   Selecting the (T) column enables Writer to autocorrect when you type new text; selecting the (M) column enables you to autocorrect the entire document when you choose Format⇨AutoFormat⇨Apply.

6. **Click OK.**

   The dialog box disappears, and now every time you enter what you added in the Replace box (for example, "ooo"), Writer changes it to what you added in the With input box (for example, OpenOffice.org).

Enabling or disabling Word Completion

The AutoCorrect feature has another aspect to it. You may have noticed that Writer sometimes likes to complete words for you while you type. This feature may be something you like, or it may drive you bananas. To enable or disable this feature, do the following:

1. **Choose Tools⇨AutoCorrect.**

2. **Click the Word Completion tab of the AutoCorrect dialog box.**

3. **Deselect the Enable Word Completion check box to turn off the feature. (Or select the check box to turn it on.)**

Using the Spellcheck and Thesaurus

Writer offers two kinds of spellcheckers — one for nitpickers and one for everyone else. (Just kidding.) The Spellcheck brings up a dialog box that identifies the misspelled word, suggests possible replacements for it, and allows you to choose and automatically insert the replacement. The other spellchecker, called the AutoSpellcheck, places a squiggly red line under misspelled words as you write them.

AutoSpellchecking

To use AutoSpellcheck, click the AutoSpellcheck On/Off button on the Standard toolbar. (It's the ABC button with the squiggly red line under it.) After you enable the AutoSpellcheck feature, Writer considers any words in your entire document that it does not find in your dictionaries to be misspelled and automatically places a squiggly red line beneath them.

Writer offers suggestions on how to fix your misspellings. To view the list of possibilities, right-click on the misspelled word, (or Alt+⌘+click on the Mac). A pop-up menu appears. You may choose one of the following options on the menu:

- **Choose the correct spelling** from the list of options.
- **Choose Spellcheck** to bring up the Spellcheck dialog box, as described in the following section.
- **Choose Add** to add the word that Writer thinks is misspelled to your dictionary, so that Writer no longer flags the word as misspelled in all documents.
- **Choose Ignore All** to cause the wavy red line to disappear under the word and under all the same words in the document.
- **Choose AutoCorrect** to add the misspelled word (as well as its replacement that you choose from the submenu) to the AutoCorrect feature so that every time you type the word, it is automatically replaced with the correct spelling.

Spellchecking

The Spellcheck is slightly different from the AutoSpellcheck — for one thing, it takes you to each word automatically that it suspects is misspelled. You needn't scroll through the document yourself, and it saves you a lot of right-clicking.

To use the Spellcheck feature to check the spelling of your document, click the Spellcheck button on the Standard toolbar or choose Tools⇨ Spellcheck⇨ Check. If nothing appears to be misspelled, then a dialog box appears with the message, "The spellcheck is complete." You just click OK. But if Writer finds a possible misspelled word, then the Spellcheck dialog box appears, as shown in Figure 3-7. The misspelled word is also highlighted in the document and usually is in view above or below the dialog box.

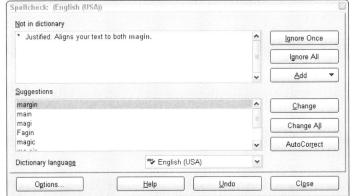

Figure 3-7:
The
Spellcheck
in action.

The Spellcheck dialog box allows you to choose from the following options:

- ✔ **Click Ignore Once** to make no change and proceed to the next possibly misspelled word.

- ✔ **Click Ignore All** to ignore every instance of the word in the document.

- ✔ **Click Add** to add the original word to the dictionary so that the spellchecker approves of it in all future spellchecking. (When you click Add, a drop-down menu appears of one or more dictionaries. Click on one of the dictionaries in the menu to add the original word to that dictionary.)

- ✔ **Select a replacement for the word in the Suggestions box and click Change** to replace the misspelled word in the document with the one you chose in the dialog box. (If you want to replace every instance of the word in the document, click Change All.)

- ✔ **Click AutoCorrect** to automatically replace the misspelled word in the document with the new word you chose from the list every time the word is typed in the future in any document.

- ✔ **Select a Language,** if it is not already suitably selected.

Finding the right words with the Thesaurus

Looking for the right word? You needn't worry. Use Writer's Thesaurus to find precisely the right words to say exactly what you mean. To use the Thesaurus, click in the word that you want to find possible synonyms for, and choose Tools➪Language➪Thesaurus to bring up the Thesaurus dialog box, as shown in Figure 3-8.

Using the Thesaurus dialog box, you can do any of the following:

✔ Scroll through the list of synonyms to choose the correct word. (If your word has more than one meaning, then click the appropriate meaning in the Meaning list to bring up the correct list of synonyms.)

✔ Select a synonym to replace your word and click OK.

✔ If you do not find the right synonym for your word, you can select a synonym and click the Search button to bring up synonyms for the synonym that you selected. (This gives you the freedom to really explore all options.)

Figure 3-8:
The
Thesaurus
dialog box.

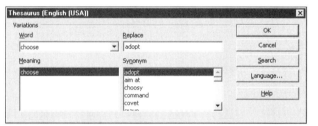

Recording Changes

Writer allows you to track the changes in your document. This feature may be useful if more than one person is working on the same document. Changes made by each individual are color-coded and recorded so that you can easily identify who changed what and where. Writer also gives you the option to view the changes or to hide the changes, so that they do not appear in your document until you want them to appear.

To record changes in your document, choose Edit➪Changes➪Record. Now whenever you add to your document or delete anything from your document, the added text appears in a new color, and the deleted text also appears in the same new color but with a strikethrough, as shown in Figure 3-9.

Deleted text   Inserted text

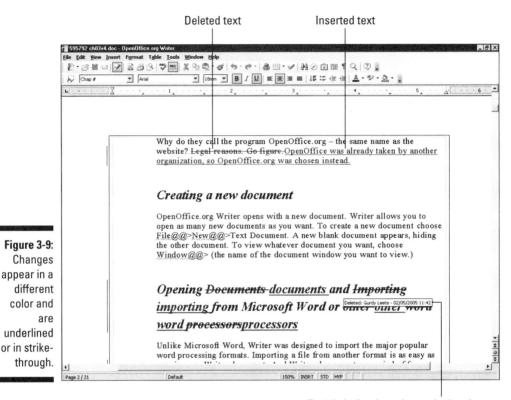

Figure 3-9:
Changes
appear in a
different
color and
are
underlined
or in strike-
through.

Tool tip indicating who made the change

Each separate OpenOffice.org Writer program (or Microsoft Word program, and others) that opens the document assigns a different color to any changes that are made so that you can easily look through a document to find the changes in different colored text. When you pass your cursor over the changed text, a balloon appears with the name of the person to whom the Writer application was registered, in the version of Writer in which the change was made, and the time and date of the change.

Showing and hiding changes

To show or hide the changes, choose Edit⇨Changes⇨Show. If the check mark appears beside Show, the changes are shown. Otherwise, they are hidden.

Accepting and rejecting changes

Often as you continue to work on a document, your changes may become numerous, and you may decide to accept or reject some or all of them. To do so, choose Edit⇨Changes⇨Accept or Reject to bring up the Accept or Reject Changes dialog box, as shown in Figure 3-10.

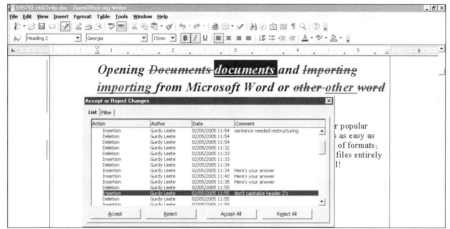

Figure 3-10: The Accept or Reject Changes dialog box.

In the Accept or Reject Changes dialog box, your changes are listed in the order in which they appear in the document. You can make a single change by clicking on it, or multiple changes by clicking and dragging the cursor over them, and then clicking the Accept or Reject button. Or you can click Accept All to accept all the changes or Reject All to reject the changes. Rejected changes revert to their previous state in the document, and accepted changes merge into the text, losing their color and underline, or disappearing if they are deleted.

Writer also allows you to filter your selection criteria in the Accept or Reject dialog box. You may want to do this to select only changes made by a certain author, or to select only deletions and not insertions, or to select only changes made before or after a certain date and time. To perform these tasks, click the Filter tab on the Accept or Reject dialog box. In the Filter tab, choose the Date, Author, Action, or Comment check box and choose your parameter from the drop-down list.

Adding comments to changes

Often, when you make changes to a document being worked on by more than one person, you may want to attach comments to your changes to explain why you made the change. To do this, click on the change in the document and choose Edit⇨Changes⇨Comment. In the Comment: Insertion dialog box, type in your comment and click OK.

To view comments, choose Edit➪Changes➪Accept or Reject and view the comments in the Comments column of the Accept or Reject dialog box, as shown in Figure 3-10. Or you can click on the change that you want to view the comment, and choose Edit➪Changes➪Comment to bring up the Comment Insertion dialog box where you can view the comment. You can also click the arrow buttons in this dialog box to view the next or previous comment in the document.

Working with Large Documents

How big is your book? 408 pages? More? Writer is an extremely robust program when it comes to dealing with lots of text, images, and large file sizes. You needn't worry about crashing your computer. Writer can handle it. But to preserve your sanity, you may want to separate your chapters into separate documents. Then you can link them using a master document — a single, read-only document that contains all of your linked documents.

Using a master document

Using a master document affords you the luxury of having smaller chapter documents, while still being able to view and print your complete document as a whole. This way, your page numbers are sequential from beginning to end, and you can create the table of contents and index for the whole kit 'n' caboodle. The master document allows you to read all the subdocuments that it contains, but does not let you change anything in the subdocuments. To do that, you have to change the original subdocument itself.

Creating your master document

To create a master document, first you need to create your subdocuments, which would be, for example, your separate chapter documents. (Any document can also be a subdocument.) Then do the following:

1. **Choose File➪New➪Master Document.**

   An untitled document appears within the Navigator window.

2. **In the Navigator window, click the Insert button and choose File from the pop-up menu.**

3. **Choose the file you want and click Insert.**

   The file appears in the master document, as shown in Figure 3-11.

Toggle   Update

Edit │ Insert

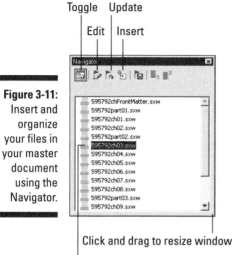

Figure 3-11:
Insert and
organize
your files in
your master
document
using the
Navigator.

Click and drag to resize window

Click and drag to reorder documents

4. **Repeat steps 2 and 3 for all the subdocuments that you want to insert into your master document.**

5. **To reorder your subdocuments, click and drag their names in the Navigator. (The order in which they appear in the Navigator is the order in which they appear in the master document.)**

6. **Save your master document by choosing File⇨Save, giving your master document a name, choosing your folder, and clicking Save.**

   For the File Type, Writer automatically chooses "Open Office Master Document" and gives it the file extension .odm.

Editing your master document

The files that are linked in your master document are read-only, so you need to edit the original documents if you want to change them. You can do that by doing the following:

1. **Select the document in the Navigator and click the Edit button.**

   Your original document appears.

2. **Modify your document (and choose File⇨Save, if you want) and then choose Window⇨*the name of your master document.***

   Your master document reappears.

3. **Select the name of the file you just edited (if it is not already selected).**

4. Click the Update button on the Navigator and choose Selection from the pop-up menu.

The change that you made in the linked document gets updated into the master document.

If you want to use the Navigator to navigate through your subdocuments, click on a subdocument name and click the Toggle button. The Headings, Tables, Text Frames, Graphics and other items appear in the Navigator for that document. Click on the Plus sign by Headings to see the headings and sub-headings, and then click on one of the headings or sub-headings, and that part of the document appears. To return to the list of subdocuments, click the Toggle button again.

Using the Navigator

The Navigator is a marvelous tool. You can use the Navigator as described in the preceding section to order and edit your subdocuments in your master document, but the Navigator also has many more uses. It is particularly wonderful to view your headings and subheadings at a glance, as shown in Figure 3-12. It's like an instant table of contents, in that when you click on a heading, the view instantly changes to that portion of the document!

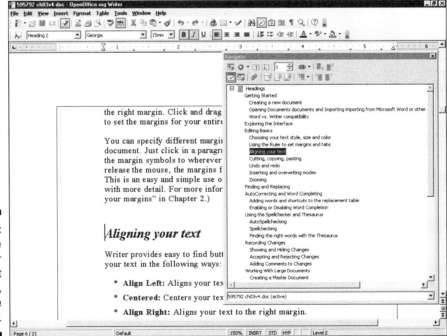

Figure 3-12: Navigate around your document with ease, using the Navigator.

The Navigator also contains expandable lists of your graphics, tables, hyperlinks, and more. Click on the little plus or minus sign in the first column to expand or collapse the lists. Click on any item, such as a heading, hyperlink, or graphic, to move the cursor to that heading, hyperlink, or graphic. Using the Navigator, you can jump all over your document quickly and easily.

Creating a table of contents

Writer automatically creates a table of contents wherever you specify by generating a list of the headings of your document along with their page numbers. Writer offers the heading styles Heading 1 to Heading 10 (see "Adding Style with the Stylist" in Chapter 4 for a description of how to apply and modify styles). After you apply the heading style, creating a table of contents is a simple procedure:

1. **In your document, click where you want the table of contents to reside. Or, if you're using a master document, click the Insert button, shown in Figure 3-13, choose Index, and skip to step 3.**

   No, this is not a typo; you really choose Index, even if you want a table of contents.

2. **Choose Insert⇨Indexes and Tables⇨Indexes and Tables.**

   The Insert Index/Table dialog box appears.

3. **Choose Table of Contents in the Type list box and choose Entire Document in the For list box.**

4. **Select the number of levels from the Evaluate Up To Level spin box.**

   By default, Calc assigns Header 1 through Header 10 as the ten levels. So, if you do not change the default and if you haven't assigned any headers above Header 3, for example, then even if the spin box says 10 levels, you will only have three levels. For details about how to assign headings, see "Adding Style with the Stylist" in Chapter 4.

5. **If you have assigned other styles to your headings, and not Heading 1 through Heading 10, select the Outline check box (if it is not already selected) and click the square box beside it. For each level, select the Level and Paragraph style that you want to assign to it. Repeat for each level to which you want a new style assigned.**

   In Figure 3-13, the top four levels have been changed to start with the Chap Title style and then continue down with the Heading 1, Heading 2, and Heading 3 styles. The other headings were not changed, because they were not used in the documents.

6. **Click OK.**

   Your table of contents appears in your document, or a new linked document entitled *Table Of Contents* appears in your master document.

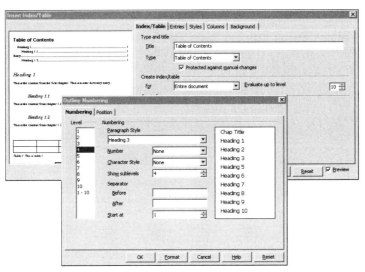

Figure 3-13:
Using the
Outline
Numbering
dialog box,
you can
assign the
style that
you want
Writer to
find in your
document to
generate
each level
of your table
of contents.

If you want to format your table of contents, you can select it and copy and paste it into your document, and then format it however you want. However if you do this, your new table of contents won't update the page numbers as your document changes. So, you may want to leave the formatting until the last step. (If you're using a master document, you'll want to copy the table of contents and paste it into a new document, and link the new document to the master document. After you paste your table of contents, you can edit it however you want.)

To delete your the automatically generated table of contents, right-click on it and choose Delete.

If Writer does not allow your cursor to appear in your table of contents, choose Tools➪Options➪Text Document➪Formatting Aids and select Enable the Cursor in Protected Areas check box.

Creating an index

Creating an index has two steps to it. First, you select the words that you want to appear in the index and mark them as index entries. Then you create the index.

Inserting index entries

To insert an index entry in your document, perform the following steps:

1. **Select the word or words and choose Insert➪Indexes and Tables➪ Entry.**

2. **In the Insert Index Entry dialog box that appears, choose Alphabetical Index from the Index list (this is the default) and do any of the following:**

    • **Type in a 1ˢᵗ key** (or choose one from the list box) if you want your selected item to be a subheading of another entry.

    • **Select the Main Entry check box** if you want the page numbers to appear in bold.

    • **Select the Apply To All Similar Texts check box** if you want all the pages on which the selected text appears to be listed in the index. Select Match Case or Whole Words Only if you want to be more precise about the text in the document that you match with your selected text.

3. **Click Insert.**

    Your new index entry appears highlighted in your document. You can leave this dialog box open and continue to select words in your document and click the Insert button. This method is handy for adding index entries quickly.

Creating your index

To create your index, do the following:

1. **Click in your document where you want the index to reside. Or if you're using a master document, click the Insert button, shown in Figure 3-11, choose Index, and skip to step 3.**

2. **Choose Insert⇨Indexes and Tables⇨Indexes and Tables.**

3. **In the Insert Index/Table dialog box, choose Alphabetical Index from the Type list box.**

4. **Select Combine Identical Entries, if it is not already selected, then deselect Combine Identical Entries with P or PP and select Combine With. Then deselect Case Sensitive (unless you want, for example, "Spreadsheet" to be a different entry than "spreadsheet").**

    If you don't deselect Combine Identical Entries with P or PP, then if you have two identical index entries on the same page for the phrase "free software" starting on page 22, for example, the entry appears as "free software 22p" (or "free software 22pp" if they are on consecutive pages). People aren't used to seeing that in an index, so you probably don't want that.

5. **Choose from the following options:**

    • **AutoCapitalize Entries:** Capitalizes the first letter of each entry

    • **Keys as Separate Entries:** Lists the page numbers for the keys as well as the subheadings of the keys

        A *key* is a heading in the index, under which are sub-headings.

- **Concordance File:** Lets you choose the name of a separate file for the index to reside in

- **Protected against Manual Changes:** Disallows any manual changes to your index in your document

6. **Click OK.**

   Your new index appears either in your document, in a separate document if you selected Concordance File, or as a separate subdocument of your master document.

If you want to format your index, you can select the index and copy and paste it into your document, and then format it as you want. If you do so, however, your new index won't update the page numbers as your document changes. So, you may want to leave the formatting until the last step.

To delete the automatically generated index, right-click on it and choose Delete from the pop-up menu that appears.

Saving and Exporting Your Document

Writer allows you to save and export your document in a wide variety of formats. It also offers an automatic saving feature that you can set to save your document automatically at specific intervals of time.

Saving as Writer, Microsoft Word, and more

To save your document, choose one of the following procedures:

- **To save a new document in any format for the first time:** Choose File⇨Save, click the Save Document button on the Standard toolbar, or press Ctrl+S. In the Save As dialog box that appears, as shown in Figure 3-14, open the appropriate folder, then fill in the file name and choose the file type, and click Save.

- **To resave a document previously saved in Writer format:** Choose File⇨Save, click the Save Document button on the Standard toolbar, or press Ctrl+S. The document will be saved in Writer format.

- **To resave a document previously saved in Word format:** Choose File⇨Save, click the Save Document button on the Standard toolbar, or press Ctrl+S. The document will be saved in Word format.

✔ **To resave a document with a new name or new file type, choose File⇨Save As** and in the Save As dialog box that appears, double-click the folder name to open the folder. Fill in the File Name and choose the File Type, and click Save.

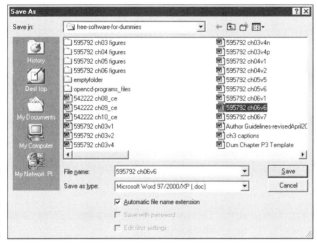

Figure 3-14:
The Save As
dialog box.

When you save, be sure the Automatic File Name Extension check box is checked; otherwise, you probably want to manually add the file extension to the end of the filename in the File Name input box (for example, Picasso report.odt).

Protecting your document

If you want to protect your document so that it can't be opened without a password, the first time you save your document, select the Save With Password check box in the Save As dialog box. Click Save, and a dialog box appears in which you need to type at least a five-letter password twice. After you type the password twice, click OK. Next time you open the file, you'll need to type the password, so don't forget it!

Exporting as PDF

At some time or another, you'll probably want to export documents to PDF. The PDF formats allows your readers to see your document formatted properly with all the font and layout information in your document even if they view your PDF file on a computer that doesn't contain the fonts in your document. A PDF document generally also cannot be changed in any way after it is created. This feature is useful for sending files over the Internet that you don't want modified by anyone. One small inconvenience with exporting to PDF, however, is that after you create your PDF file, you cannot open it in Writer. You need to use a PDF reader, such as the Adobe Reader or Xpdf to open it. (The Adobe Reader is available for a variety of platforms including Windows, Mac and GNU/Linux via a free download from `www.adobe.com`. Xpdf is a free software package for GNU/Linux.)

To export your PDF file, perform the following steps:

1. **If you want to export just a selection of your document, select the text that you want to export.**

2. **Choose File⇨Export As PDF.**

   The Export dialog box appears, which is similar to the Save As dialog box.

3. **Fill out the File Name and browse to the location where you want to export your file; then click Save.**

   The PDF Options dialog box appears.

4. **Choose All, Range, or Selection in the Pages section (and enter the range of pages if you chose Range).**

5. **Choose one of the three Compressions:**

   • **Screen Optimized** creates the smallest file size, but if you have graphics or charts or other objects requiring larger file sizes, some of the quality may be lost.

   • **Print Optimized** is optimized for printing, but still does not deliver the highest quality.

   • **Press Optimized** creates the highest quality PDF file, as well as the largest file size.

6. **Click Export.**

   A copy of your file is exported as a PDF file and placed in the folder you specified.

Chapter 4

Formatting Your Writer Documents

*O*penOffice.org Writer gives you the ability to format a document in multi-tudinous ways. You can customize page sizes, add columns to pages, or add a variety of borders around lines or paragraphs. You can add headers or footers to pages or add footnotes with ease.

You can also create, apply, and modify styles. Styles give you a consistent look for your document and the flexibility to change your document's appearance completely just by modifying the styles. Writer also allows you to create and use *templates*. Templates are documents that can contain layouts for pictures and text as well as formatting styles that you can reuse on other documents to ensure a consistent look and feel and save you time.

Formatting Pages

Do you want to set your page size for posters? Envelopes? Legal-sized paper? Do you want to create any number of columns in your pages? Or set precise margins? Writer enables you to set formatting options that apply to every page of your document in one stroke.

Setting page size, margins, orientation, and layout

When you create a new OpenOffice.org Writer document, the new document contains a default page size, default margins, and a white background. This default is geared for printing on normal-sized 8½" x 11" paper (U.S. version). But you may want to print on much larger or much smaller paper, or you may want to lay out your document to print sideways, which is known as *landscape* orientation. To modify the margins and paper format size and orientation, choose Format ⇨ Page to open the Page Style dialog box, and then click on the Page tab.

In the Page Style dialog box, you can do the following:

✔ **Choose the paper format.** The Format list box contains paper sizes, such as Legal and Tabloid, six different envelope sizes, and more. When you choose a format size, the Width and Height boxes automatically fill in the values of the format size, as shown in Figure 4-1.

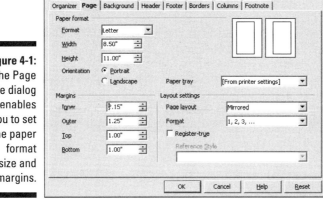

Figure 4-1:
The Page Style dialog box enables you to set the paper format size and margins.

✔ **Customize a paper format.** Click the up or down arrows of the Width or Height spin boxes to choose the size you want, or type the size along with your unit of measurement (inches or centimeters) in the spin boxes.

If your unit of measurement is inches, you can type cm to convert the amount you type into inches. For example: typing in 5.5 cm changes the value in the box to 2.17" as soon as you click in another input box. You can do the same for inches if your unit of measurement is centimeters.

When entering information into the spin boxes, be sure you don't press the Return or Enter key after typing in a spin box, unless you're finished with the dialog box. Writer interprets pressing Return or Enter the same as clicking OK.

- ✔ **Choose the orientation** by clicking either Portrait or Landscape. The image of the page layout changes in the dialog box accordingly.

- ✔ **Set the margins** using the Margins spin boxes, or enter values.

- ✔ **Choose the Page Layout settings.** Writer offers four Layout Settings that you can choose from:

  - **Right and Left:** Applies the same formatting to all the pages. (This is the default setting.)

  - **Mirrored:** Mirrors the formatting on the odd-numbered pages with the formatting on the even pages. (Use this option, for example, if you want a larger margin on alternate sides of your pages for note-book holes or binding purposes, as shown in Figure 4-1.)

    If you choose Mirrored for your Page Layout setting, you may want to click the Register-true check box, as well. This setting allows your type to line up the same on both pages as you open the book.

  - **Only Right:** Applies the format to odd-numbered pages only.

  - **Only Left:** Apples the format to even-numbered pages only.

- ✔ **Choose a paper tray.** Some printers allow you to choose a Paper tray to print from. If you're lucky enough to have such a printer available to your computer, the tray names should appear in the Paper Tray drop-down list. (If no tray names are listed, then you can cancel the dialog box and choose File ⇨ Printer Settings, then choose the printer from the Name list and click OK. To return to the Page Style dialog box, choose Format ⇨ Page.) Select the Paper Tray that you want to apply to this document.

Creating columns

Writer can automatically generate any number of columns on a page for you. You can let Writer choose the column spacing for you, or you can specify precise spacing yourself. Also, you can choose to insert a line to separate your columns or simply leave it out.

To generate columns for your document, choose Format ⇨ Page and click the Columns tab in the Page Style dialog box that appears.

In the Columns tab, you can do the following

✔ Choose from one of the five popular column style options in the Settings section.

✔ Choose the number of columns from the Columns spin box, which allows up to 99 columns! The result is shown in the image in the right third of the Settings section.

✔ Select the AutoWidth check box so that Writer automatically spaces your columns for you.

✔ Choose column spacings in the spin boxes to space your columns yourself. (Be sure you first deselect the AutoWidth check box.)

✔ From the Line list box, choose the size of line you want to separate your columns. Or choose None if you don't want a separator line.

✔ Choose the height and position of your separator line, if you have one, from the Height spin box and Position list box.

When you click OK, your new page format appears in your document.

Formatting Paragraphs

Writer offers a variety of formatting options for your paragraphs, such as line spacing, indenting, and borders. Before you apply any of these formatting options, first select the text you want to apply the formatting to. You can do so in the following ways:

✔ **For your formatting to apply to an existing paragraph or paragraphs within your document,** click anywhere in a paragraph, or click and drag to select the text you want to apply the formatting to. (Choose Edit ➪ Select All to select the entire document.)

✔ **For your formatting to apply to new paragraphs that you intend to write starting at the end of your document,** click at the end of your document.

Writer uses the word *paragraph* to refer not only to paragraphs, but also to lines of text. Any text between two returns (as well as before the first return and after the last return) is considered a paragraph.

Line spacing and paragraph indenting

To add line spacing or indentation to one or more paragraphs an entire document, perform the following steps:

1. **Click in the paragraph or select the text you want to apply the formatting to, or skip this step if your document is blank.**

2. **Choose Format ⇨ Paragraph and click the Indents & Spacing tab of the Paragraph dialog box, if it is not already selected.**

   The Paragraph dialog box appears, as shown in Figure 4-2.

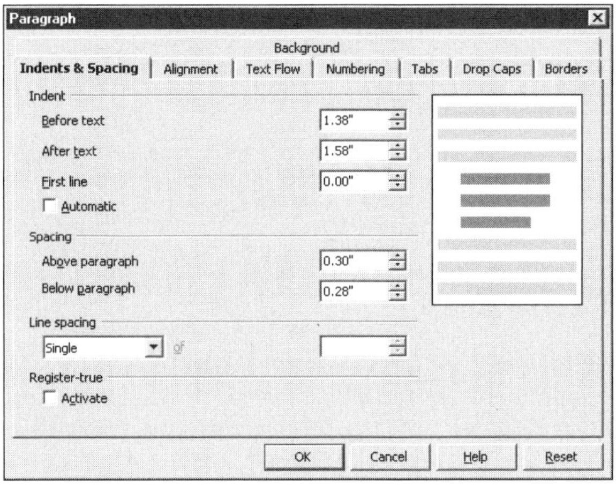

Figure 4-2:
Adjust margins and line spacing for paragraphs (and view a diagram of the result) in the Indents & Spacing tab of the Paragraph dialog box.

3. **Do any or all of the following:**

   Use the Before Text or After Text spin boxes to change the indentation before and/or after the text.

   Use the First Line spin box or select the Automatic check box to automatically or manually select the indent for the first line of a paragraph.

   Use the Above Paragraph or Below Paragraph spin boxes to add space above a paragraph and/or below a paragraph.

   Choose the Line Spacing from the drop-down list:

   - **Single:** Applies single line spacing to the paragraph or selection. This is the default.

   - **1.5 lines:** Applies one-and-a-half line spacing to the paragraph or selection.

   - **Double:** Applies double line spacing to the paragraph or selection.

   - **Proportional:** Enables you to select a proportion from the spin box in the Line Spacing section and applies a line spacing of the proportion that you choose (50%–200%). A proportion of 100% is the same as single spacing.

   - **At Least:** Applies a line spacing of at least the value that you set in the spin box in the Line Spacing section.

- **Leading:** Adds a vertical space between two lines. You set the size of the vertical space in the spin box in the Line Spacing section.

- **Fixed:** sets the text to the size you specify in the spin box nearby to the right. If you set the value low, it will crop the tops of characters.

Select the Activate check box in the Register-true section to activate the Register-true feature if you want the text in the paragraph or selected paragraphs to line up left and right pages of a book.

Notice that your new format appears in the image on the right-hand side of the Paragraph dialog box, as shown in Figure 4-2.

4. **Click OK.**

Whatever paragraphs you selected are now formatted in the manner you specified.

Adding borders

Writer enables you to spice up the appearance of your text by letting you add borders to your headings or paragraphs or even placing some lines above and below your book's figure captions. Or perhaps you would like to add drop-shadows behind your paragraphs? Writer lets you do all these things.

To add borders in your document, do the following:

1. **Click in the paragraph or select the text you want to add borders or backgrounds to.**

   If you select a partial paragraph, Writer adds the border or background to the entire paragraph.

2. **Choose Format ⇨ Paragraph and click the Borders tab of the Paragraph dialog box, shown in Figure 4-3.**

   The Borders tab of the Paragraph dialog box appears, as shown in Figure 4-3.

3. **You can do one of the following:**

   - **Choose a Default border:** Select one of the various Default borders from the Line Arrangement section of the Borders tab; the line arrangement appears in the User-defined area.

   - **Create a User-defined border:** Click on any or all of the sides in the User-defined box. When you click on a side of the box in the white area (not the gray area), a line appears on that side of the box. If you make a mistake, click the Set No Border box in the Default section; the lines disappear, so you can start over.

Figure 4-3:
You can
create a
border just
like the
border of
this figure's
caption
using the
Borders tab
of the
Paragraph
dialog box.

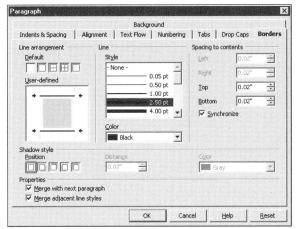

4. **You can select line styles and colors for your border in two ways:**

   • **Select different line styles and colors for different lines of your border:** If you click on a line in the User-defined section, a box appears around the line, indicating that the line is selected. After you select a line, you can choose a Line Style from the Style list box and a Color from the Color list box for that line. Do the same for each line you want to assign a Line Style or Color to.

   • **Select the same line style and color for all lines of your border:** If no line is selected in the User-defined area, then select a Line Style from the Style list box, and a Color from the Color list box. These options will apply to all the lines.

5. **Use the arrow keys in the spin boxes in the Spacing to Contents section to insert the desired spacing around your border. Click the Synchronize check box if you want the spacing to be equal on all sides.**

6. **If you want a shadow, click on one of the Position boxes in the Shadow Style section. In the Distance spin box choose the distance that you want your paragraph to appear to be floating above your document, and choose the color.**

7. **Click OK.**

   Sit back and admire your new bordered text.

Automatic Numbering and Bullets

Making lists is an essential and entertaining part of everyday life. If you make your list in Writer, you can add nice neat bullets to each item, or if you want a numbered list you can automatically add numbers. You can add numbers or bullets to your document in two ways:

✔ **To create a new bulleted or numbered list in your document,** click in your document where you want the list to start, then click the Bullets On/Off button or the Numbering On/Off button on the Formatting toolbar. Now, every time you press Return, a new number or a new bullet appears. Click the button again to turn off Bullets or Numbering.

✔ **To add bullets or numbers to a list that you already created in your document,** select the list and click the Bullets On/Off button or the Numbering On/Off button on the Formatting toolbar. Writer places a bullet or appropriate number beside each item of the list. Writer knows where the next bullet or number belongs because it places the bullet or number after the next Return.

To number with Roman numerals or find a different look for your bullets, you can choose from various types of bullets or numbers by choosing Format ⇨ Bullets and Numbering to bring up the Bullets and Numbering dialog box. Choose from the types of bullets or click the Numbering tab and choose from the types of numbers, and then click OK.

Formatting, Rotating, and Precisely Positioning Characters

The Formatting toolbar offers many formatting options for your characters, such as Font Type, Font Size, Bold, Italic, and Underline. But other options exist as well, which you can access by selecting your text and choosing Format ⇨ Character to bring up the Character dialog box. The Character dialog box has five tabs, which you can use for the following purposes:

✔ **Font:** Choose the Font, Typeface, and Size on this tab. (You can also make these choices using the Formatting toolbar.)

✔ **Font Effects:** In the Font Effects tab, shown in Figure 4-4, choose from six kinds of underlining styles and five kinds of strikethrough styles; choose the font color; give text an embossed or engraved look; change the selected text to all capitals or all lowercase; capitalize the first letter of each word; give the selected text an outlined look or shadow; or you can even make text blink! (Think twice about that!) Your selected text appears with the font effects applied to it in the preview pane.

✔ **Position:** In the Position tab you can raise or lower your selected characters to create a superscript or subscript look, or scale and rotate your characters.

✔ **Hyperlink:** In this tab you can change your selected text into a hyperlink, which can open a new Writer document when clicked on, or open a Web page on the Internet.

✔ **Background:** Choose a background color for the selected text in this tab.

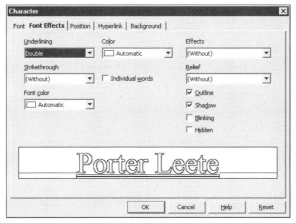

Figure 4-4:
Use the Font
Effects tab
of the
Character
dialog box
to add
assorted
effects to
text.

Adding Style with the Stylist

Any document appears much more professional and more artistic when you can maintain consistency in the formatting of your text for each heading and subheading, footnote, page header or footer, and more. Using styles allows you to ensure consistency, and it also gives you the flexibility to change your mind about the look of your document with no worries. For example, if you create a style for your main headings, and you suddenly decide that the font size of the headings is too large, or you want them all in bold, you can change them all in a single stroke. This feature may not seem like a big deal if you have two or three headings, but if you have hundreds of headings, it may suddenly seem worthy of veneration.

Touring the Stylist

To bring up the floating Stylist window, choose Format ➪ Styles and Formatting. The Stylist appears, as shown in Figure 4-5.

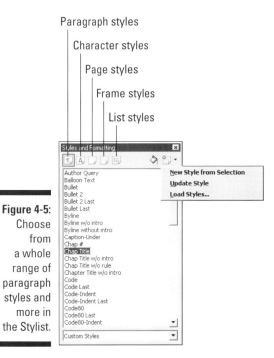

Paragraph styles

Character styles

Page styles

Frame styles

List styles

Figure 4-5:
Choose
from
a whole
range of
paragraph
styles and
more in
the Stylist.

The five buttons on the top row of the Stylist window represent the five major categories of styles, as follows:

- **Paragraph styles:** Styles that apply to whole paragraphs, such as Heading 1 through Heading 10, Caption, and Footer.

- **Character styles:** Styles that apply to words and characters found within a paragraph, such as Internet Link, Footnote Anchor, and Emphasis.

- **Page styles:** Styles that apply to pages, such as First Page, Left Page, and Right Page.

- **Frame styles:** Styles that apply to frames around text or graphics, such as Formula or Watermark

- **List styles:** Styles that apply to numbered lists and bulleted lists.

Most of the time, you'll probably want to select either the Paragraph styles or the Character styles.

Writer offers a list of types of Paragraph styles that you can choose from in the drop-down list at the bottom of the Stylist window. When you choose a category, the styles for that category appear in the Stylist list box. These Paragraph categories include the following:

- ✓ **HTML styles:** Displays a list of styles that are appropriate for using on Web sites.

- ✓ **Index styles:** Displays a list of styles normally used in creating indexes.

- ✓ **Applied styles:** Displays a list of styles applied in your document. (These are the styles that also appear in the Apply Style list box on the Formatting toolbar of your document.)

- ✓ **Custom styles:** Displays a list of styles you created for your document.

- ✓ **Automatic styles:** Displays a list of Writer's default styles.

- ✓ **All styles:** Displays a list of all the styles. (This option can be very confusing because you're inundated with an excessive number of styles, most of which you don't need for your document.)

Applying styles

The two easiest ways of applying styles are as follows:

- ✓ **If a paragraph style has already been used in the document**, you can simply click in the paragraph where you want to apply the style, and choose the style from the Apply Style drop-down list on the Formatting toolbar, shown in Figure 4-6.

- ✓ **If the style that you want to use is not a paragraph style, or if it has not been used previously in your document,** you probably want to apply your style using the Stylist.

Figure 4-6: Apply a paragraph style already in use in your document by choosing the style from the Apply Style drop-down list.

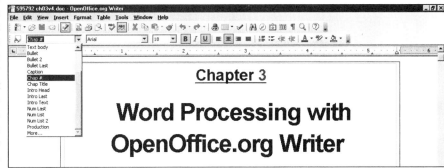

To apply a style using the Stylist, do the following:

1. **Click anywhere in the page, paragraph, numbered or bulleted list, border, or word that you want to apply the appropriate style to.**

2. **Choose Format ⇨ Styles and Formatting to bring up the Stylist window or press F11, if the Stylist is not already active.**

3. **Select the Page Styles button, the Paragraph Styles button, the Character Styles button, the Numbering Styles button, or the Frame Styles button to choose the appropriate style.**

4. **Select from the drop-down list of categories at the bottom of the Stylist to bring up a list of styles for either Pages, Paragraphs, Characters, Numberings, or Frames.**

   The list of styles that you choose appears in the Stylist list box

5. **Double-click on the style of your choosing.**

   For example, if you want to make your text into a heading, double-click one of the Heading styles (Heading or Heading 1–10).

   Your page, paragraph, word or character, frame, or list changes to the new style.

 If you want to apply the same style to several places in your document, click on the name of the style in the Stylist and then click the Fill Format Mode button (the paint can). The cursor turns into a paint can; now wherever you click in your document, the text transforms into the selected style. (Click the paint can again to turn it off.)

Adding a new style

You may or may not want to use Writer's default styles. At some point, you'll likely want to create your own styles to use in a document. You can add a new paragraph or character style by first applying a new style manually to a paragraph or character in your document. You can manually apply the new style from the following:

- ✔ Format menu options
- ✔ Formatting toolbar buttons
- ✔ The ruler

You can add a new style in two ways. You can right-click on the style in the Stylist that is most similar to the style you want to add and choose Add from the pop-up menu. The appropriate dialog box appears for formatting that style:

Paragraph, Character, Page, Frame, or Numbering. Type the new name for the style and use the tabs to choose whatever attributes you want for the new style, and then click OK.

You can also create a new look for a word or paragraph that does not already have a style applied to it, and do the following:

1. **Select the paragraph or character that you have formatted and want to represent your new style.**

2. **Choose Format ⇨ Styles and Formatting or press F11 to open the Stylist window, if it's not already active.**

3. **Click the Character Styles button or the Paragraph Styles button to open the appropriate Styles pane for the type of style you want to add.**

4. **Choose the list that you want your new style to be added to. (If you're not sure, you can probably just choose "Custom Styles.")**

5. **Click the New Style from Selection button in the Stylist window, as shown earlier in Figure 4-5.**

   The Create Style dialog box appears.

6. **Enter a Style Name into the input box. (Be sure your style name is not already used.) Click OK.**

   Your new style is added to the list you chose in step 4, as well as the Custom Styles list and the Applied Styles list.

Modifying a style

You can modify styles that you created or you can modify Writer's default styles. If you modify any of Writer's default styles, such as Heading 1, the style is changed only in your current document.

When you change a style, all instances of that style in your document also change. By modifying your styles you can give your document a whole new look instantly.

You can modify a style in two ways. You can right-click on the style in the Stylist, and choose Modify from the pop-up menu. The appropriate dialog box appears for formatting that style: Paragraph, Character, Page, Frame, or Numbering. Change whatever attributes you want in the dialog box or in any tabs in that dialog box, and click OK.

You can also apply a new look to a word or paragraph that already has a character or paragraph applied to it, and do the following:

1. **Select a character or paragraph containing the style that you want to modify and modify it to your liking.**

2. **Choose Format ⇨ Styles and Formatting or press F11 to open the Stylist window, if it's not already active. Click either the Paragraph Styles button or Characters Styles button to view the appropriate list of styles.**

   The style that you clicked in or selected in your document is highlighted in the list in the Stylist.

3. **Click the New Style From Selection button and select Update Style from the pop-up menu, as shown in Figure 4-5.**

   The style and all instances of that style in your document change to the new format.

Using and Creating Templates

When you create a new document, any customized styles you may have created in another document do not appear in the Apply Style drop-down list on the Formatting toolbar unless you have created and attached the template to your document. Styles, text, pictures, column layouts — whatever you want to use over and over in multiple documents — can all be saved as a template. Templates are ideal for the following uses:

✔ Personal or business letterhead, as shown in Figure 4-7

✔ A newsletter format

✔ A first page for your faxes

✔ A book format that's part of a series, such as the *For Dummies* template, complete with all the styles needed to format the book

✔ Greeting cards for you to personalize, plus a million more uses

Figure 4-7: Personal or business letterhead is commonly saved as a template.

Porter Enterprises
108 Sunshine Drive
Fairfield, Iowa 52556
(641) 555- 5555

You always have the option, of course, of simply opening a previous newsletter, deleting the text that you don't want, and keeping just the title, columns, and your styles. But using a template saves you the time of having to delete all the unwanted text every time you want to create a new newsletter, and it also ensures that nothing that you want to use over and over again accidentally gets deleted.

Creating a template

To create a template, follow these steps:

1. **Create a new document, such as an empty letterhead. Alternatively, if you have a document with lots of styles, such as a newsletter, then delete everything in your document except for the text you want to keep and formatting, such as columns and margins, that you want to use in the template.**

2. **Choose File ⇨ Save As.**

3. **In the Save As dialog box, give your template a name and browse through your folders to find the place you want your template to reside. Choose OpenDocument Text Template (.ott) as the File Type and click Save.**

   Your template is now saved.

Opening a template

To open a template, follow these steps:

1. **Choose File ⇨ New ⇨ Templates & Documents and, if you saved your template in your My Documents folder, click the My Documents button to view your files.**

2. **Browse through your files and select a template that you want to use — perhaps the one you just created?**

3. **Click Open.**

   Your template appears in the document, but the document is named "Untitled." Now when you change your document and save it with a new name, your original template remains unchanged, ready to reuse whenever you want.

Modifying a template

If you want to refine your template, open it using the steps in the preceding section, change it however you like, and choose File ⇨ Save As to save it again. Choose OpenDocument Text Template (.ott) from the File Type list box and save the file with the same name.

Inserting and Linking Pictures

Writer allows you to insert or link pictures into your document. Both methods appear the same in the document, but they differ in the resulting file size of the document and flexibility of changing the pictures, in the following ways:

- ✔ **Inserting pictures** increases the file size of a text document. When you change the original picture file, the inserted picture in your document does not change.

- ✔ **Linking pictures** does not increase the file size of a text document. However, if you send your document with linked pictures to another computer, you need to remember to send the linked picture files as well. The linked files need to reside in the same folder as your document or sub-folder, if they are to be moved. If you modify the content of the original linked picture file, that change also appears automatically in the document.

After your picture is either inserted or linked into your document, you can position it; resize it; crop it; adjust the color, brightness, or contrast; or give it any degree of transparency. You can add borders, or you can add a filter, for example, to change it into black and white. You can also specify how you want your text to wrap around the picture. (Did I also mention you could rotate your picture?)

To insert or link a picture into Writer, perform the following steps:

1. **Click in the text where you want to locate the picture, and then choose Insert ⇨ Picture ⇨ From File.**

   The Insert Pictures dialog box appears, as shown in Figure 4-8.

2. **Browse through your files to find the picture that you want to insert into your document. You may also do the following:**

   - **To see a preview of your picture in the preview pane,** select the Preview check box.

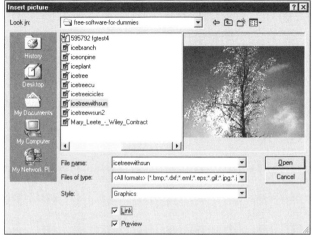

Figure 4-8:
Use the
Insert
Pictures
dialog box
to insert
pictures
into your
document.

- **To limit your search for a picture of a particular type,** select the type from the File Type list box, which includes a list of the 28 file graphic file formats that Writer can open. The 28 formats are BMP, DXF, EMF, EPS, GIF, JPG, JPEG, JFIF, JIF, MET, PBM, PCD, PCT, PCX, PGM, PNG, PPM, PSD, RAS, SGF, SGV, SVM, TGA, TIF, TIFF, WMF, XBM, and XPM.

3. **If you want to link your file instead of inserting it, select the Link check box.**

4. **Click Open.**

   Your picture appears in your document.

Resizing and positioning a picture

When your picture appears in your document, two other items also appear:

✔ Your Formatting toolbar changes to the Pictures toolbar, as shown in Figure 4-9.

✔ Your picture has eight small green squares around it — three on each side — called *handles.*

If the Picture floating toolbar does not appear, then choose View ➪ Toolbars ➪ Picture to open the toolbar, as shown in Figure 4-9.

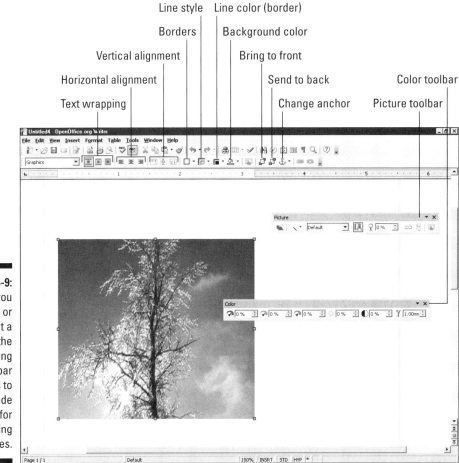

Line style   Line color (border)

Borders   Background color

Vertical alignment   Bring to front

Horizontal alignment   Send to back   Color toolbar

Text wrapping   Change anchor   Picture toolbar

Figure 4-9:
When you open or select a picture, the Formatting toolbar changes to include buttons for formatting pictures.

The two most popular ways to resize and position a picture are as follows:

- **Clicking and dragging:** To resize an image, click on and drag a handle. (To resize it without changing its proportions, hold down the Shift key while you click on and drag a handle.) To position an image, click anywhere in the picture (except on a handle) and drag the picture anywhere on the page.

- **Using the Picture dialog box.** This gives you more precise control over the size of your image. To do this, choose Format ➪ Picture. The Picture dialog box appears as sown in Figure 4-10.

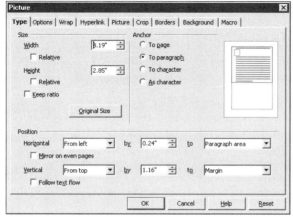

Figure 4-10:
In the Type
tab of the
Picture
dialog box,
you can
resize,
anchor, and
reposition
your picture.

Click the Type tab of the Picture dialog box if it is not already active. In the Type tab, you can do the following:

- ✔ **Resize the picture using the Width and Height spin boxes.** Be sure to select the Keep Ratio check box if you want to maintain your picture's proportions. Select the Relative boxes to see the percentage of change.

- ✔ **Revert the image to its original size** by clicking the Original Size button. This button resizes your image to its true size, which may be larger or smaller than it previously appeared in your document.

- ✔ **Precisely position the picture using the drop-down list boxes in the Position section.**

- ✔ **Anchor the picture.** See the following section for details.

If you lose the proportions of your picture, perhaps by dragging a handle, you can click the Original Size button to get the proper proportion once again and resize it with the Keep Ratio box selected.

Anchoring a picture

What happens when you insert a picture and then add paragraphs of text above the picture? Should the picture move to accommodate the new text, or should it stay put? What happens in this situation is determined by how you anchor your picture. Writer allows you to anchor a picture in four ways:

- ✔ **To Paragraph:** Anchors a picture to a paragraph so when the paragraph changes its position on a page, the picture moves along with it. (This option is the most commonly used.)
- ✔ **To Page:** Fixes a picture's position on the page.
- ✔ **To Character:** Anchors a picture to a character.
- ✔ **As Character:** Changes the line height of the text to the height of the image. (This option doesn't change the text size; it generally just puts a lot of empty space in the same line as the picture.)

To anchor your picture, click on the picture; then click and hold the Anchor symbol on the Formatting toolbar, shown in Figure 4-9, so that a menu drops down. Then choose one of the four previously mentioned options.

Aligning a picture

You can align your picture by selecting the picture and clicking one or two of the following buttons on the Formatting toolbar: Align Left, Center Horizontal, Align Right, Align Top, Align Vertical Center, or Align Bottom. These buttons produce different effects depending on how your picture is anchored. For example, if your picture is anchored to a paragraph, then the vertical alignment button aligns your picture vertically within the paragraph, not the page.

If you use any of the alignment buttons when your picture is aligned To Page, it probably will align to the edges of the page and not the margins. This may not be what you want. To remedy the situation, be sure your picture is selected; then choose Format ➪ Picture to open the Picture dialog box. In the Position section of the Type tab, you can choose the horizontal or vertical alignment from the Horizontal and Vertical drop-down list boxes, then choose Page Text Area from the To list. You could also specify your image's precise location by choosing From Left or From Top in the Horizontal or Vertical lists, and then choosing the precise measurements in the By spin box, and in the To box selecting what it is measuring to.

The easiest way to position a picture anchored to a paragraph or character is by clicking and dragging it in the document.

Wrapping text around a picture

When you read a magazine or even a newspaper, you may notice that the text "wraps around" the pictures. With Writer, you can lay out your pages like a pro, too. You can wrap text around your image to the right, left, on both sides, or even through the image. Writer also allows you to specify the amount of white space that you want around the image. This feature is particularly handy in reports where you need to use visual aids to illustrate your point, or in newsletters where you want to spice things up a bit.

To wrap your text, select your picture and click the Page Wrap button or Wrap Through button on the Formatting toolbar. Your text now wraps around or through your picture.

 For more control over how your text wraps, select your picture and choose Format ➪ Picture to open the Picture dialog box. Click the Wrap tab. Choose the type of wrap you want from the six icons in the Settings section. Choose your Spacing from the spin boxes in the Spacing section, if you want, and then click OK.

Adjusting color, brightness, contrast, and transparency

You may want to make the colors in a picture brighter, give them more contrast, or adjust the green, blue, or red values in them. To make these adjustments, select the image and click the Color button of the Picture floating toolbar to open the Color floating toolbar, shown in Figure 4-9. Then use the spin boxes on the Formatting toolbar to adjust the image. (If the Picture toolbar is not visible, choose View ➪ Toolbars ➪ Picture.)

If you want to overlap two pictures and make the top one slightly transparent, you can use the transparency spin box on the Picture toolbar to give an picture any level of transparency. Then drag the partially transparent image over another image.

 If you want to select an image that is covered by another image, click the top image and click the Send To Back button on the Formatting toolbar (when a picture is selected). The image on the bottom becomes the top image, which you can now click to select.

Filtering a picture

Writer supplies eleven filters for pictures: Invert, Smooth, Sharpen, Remove Noise, Solarization, Aging, Posterize, Pop Art, Charcoal Sketch, Relief, and Mosaic. Almost all of these filters have adjustable parameters and offer you a nice variety of effects. To use these filters, click on your picture and click on the Filter button on the Picture floating toolbar to open the floating Filters toolbar, shown in Figure 4-11. Click on the filter of your choice, and choose the parameters from any dialog box that appears and click OK.

Figure 4-11:
You can apply filters to an image to achieve interesting effects.

Adding Headers and Footers

Headers are lines of text that appear on the top of the pages of a document, such as the chapter name, book name, or page numbers. For an example of a header, check out the top of this page. Footers appear at the bottom of each page, such as page numbers. Writer can automatically generate headers and footers for your pages; you just specify what you want in them.

Creating headers and footers for every page in a document

If you want each header or footer to be the same on every page of a document, choose Insert ⇨ Header ⇨ Default or Insert ⇨ Footer ⇨ Default. A text box appears at the top of the page for headers, as shown in Figure 4-12, or at the bottom of the page for footers. Whatever you fill in either text box appears as a header or a footer on every page.

Figure 4-12:
Type a header into the text box at the top of the page.

Inserting fields into headers and footers

In the header or footer, you may want to use special fields, such as page number, page count, date, time, subject, title, or author. To insert any of these fields, click in the header or footer where you want to insert the field; then choose Insert ⇨ Field and choose from the list of fields.

Adding Footnotes

Typing footnotes into a term paper used to be the most painful part of twelfth-grade English. Fortunately, Writer lets you do it with ease. It automatically places that small. slightly raised number, in the correct sequence, and creates a footer text box containing the number. All you have to do is type the footnote information. Writer even formats your information into a special footnote style.

To add a footnote, follow these steps:

1. **Place the cursor at the place in the text you want the footnote number to appear and choose Insert ⇨ Footnote.**

   The Footnote dialog box appears.

2. **Select Automatic, if it is not already selected, or click Character and type a character into the input box. Click OK.**

   A small raised number (or character) appears in the text. If you chose Automatic, then the number increments automatically with each foot-note, starting with number 1. The same number (or character) appears in a text box at the bottom of the page with the cursor beside it, ready for you to type in the footnote details.

3. **Click in the footnote text box at the bottom of the page and type in your footnote details.**

   Writer formats the footnote in the appropriate style.

Printing

Paper and ink are not cheap, nor do we want to fill up the landfills with mis-printed documents, so you probably want to look carefully at your pages before you print them.

Using Page Preview to preview a document

To see how a document is going to look on paper, choose File ⇨ Page Preview. Your document appears in the Page Preview format, as shown in Figure 4-13. Use the buttons on the page preview toolbar as follows:

- ✔ **Arrow buttons:** Use these buttons to turn pages.

- ✔ **Zoom buttons:** Use these buttons to zoom the view in and out in a document.

- ✔ **Two Pages, Multiple Pages, or Book Preview buttons:** Use these buttons to view two pages or more than two pages in the window at the same time.

- ✔ **Full Screen On/Off button:** Use this button to fill up the screen of your monitor with the document window.

- ✔ **Print Page View:** Click this button for the Print dialog box to appear.

- ✔ **Print Options Page View:** Click this button if you want to print more than one page on a single sheet of paper.

- ✔ **Close Preview:** Click this button to return to the normal page format.

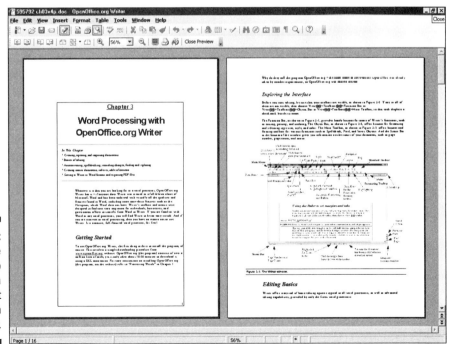

Figure 4-13: Use Page Preview to see how a document will look on paper.

If a document doesn't look the way you want it to, you may need to add page breaks. To do so, close Page Preview and place the cursor in the document where you want a page break to occur. Choose Insert ⇨ Manual Break, choose Page Break, and click OK in the dialog box.

Setting printing options and printing

To print a document choose File ⇨ Print, or (if you are in Page Preview mode) click the Print Page View button on the Page Preview toolbar. The Print dialog box appears.

Writer allows you to print from the following choices:

- **All pages:** This option is the default.

- **A range of pages:** Select Pages and fill in a range; for example, 1–5.

- **Selected text:** Select text in your document before choosing File ⇨ Print. Then select the Selection option.

- **Right pages:** Click the Options button, select Right Pages, and deselect Left Pages.

- **Left pages:** Click the Options button, select Left Pages, and deselect Right Pages.

- **Brochure:** To print both right and left pages on the same sheet of paper in landscape format, click the Options button and select Brochure.

- **Reversed order:** Click the Options button and select Reversed.

- **Scale a printout:** Click the Properties button and choose a percentage from the Scale spin box.

- **Print in Landscape format:** Click the Properties button and choose Landscape from the Orientation drop-down list.

If your printer has more than one tray, you may need to specify the paper size. To do so, choose the Properties button in the Print dialog box and choose the paper size from the drop-down list.

After you choose your settings, click OK to print.

Chapter 5

Creating Spreadsheets with OpenOffice.org Calc

*O*penOffice.org Calc spreadsheets can hold and process enormous amounts of information. Imagine a piece of paper with 65,536 rows and 256 columns. If each row is half an inch high, your paper would be as tall as a 40-story building. If you add functionality to that piece of paper, such as sorting, searching, and numerical manipulations, you get a Calc spreadsheet.

Getting Started

A single installation procedure installs Writer, Calc, Draw, Impress, and Writer's HTML editor, all at the same time. No extra procedure is needed to install Calc. Refer to Chapter 1 for easy instructions on downloading and installing OpenOffice.org.

Creating a new Calc spreadsheet

To open a Calc spreadsheet, from your Writer document, choose File⇨New⇨ Spreadsheet. A new spreadsheet appears, as shown in Figure 5-1.

Active cell   Title bar   Menu bar   Formula bar   Standard toolbar   Formatting toolbar   Scroll bars

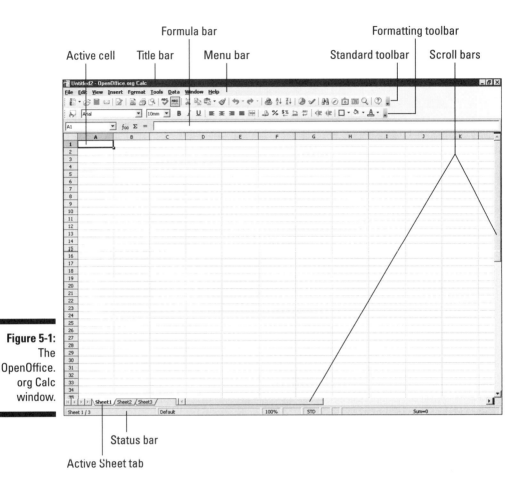

Figure 5-1:
The
OpenOffice.
org Calc
window.

Status bar

Active Sheet tab

Opening and importing spreadsheets

Open an existing Calc spreadsheet by choosing File➪Open, and browse through your files in the Open dialog box by double-clicking on folder names or using the Up One Level button. Select the spreadsheet file, which can be in Calc's .ods or .sxc format, Excel's .xls format, or a number of other compatible formats. You don't need to select from the File Type list box, unless you want to view only spreadsheet files, for example, in your search. Calc automatically determines the file type and imports the file appropriately.

Excel versus Calc compatibility

Just as Writer is compatible with Word, Calc is probably even more compatible with Microsoft Excel. The numerical formulas, sorting, filtering, and everything else are almost 100 percent compatible with Excel. Some incompatibility may exist — especially with some functions, formulas, or Excel Pivot tables. You can generally adjust these items without much difficulty.

Also, like Writer, Calc cannot process Microsoft macros. Any macros written in a Microsoft Excel document need to be rewritten in Calc in order to function. The people at OpenOffice.org predict that about 1 percent of Excel users have too many macros in their spreadsheets to make immigration to Calc feasible.

Getting to Know Your Calc Spreadsheet

Your spreadsheet has lots of little boxes in it called cells — about sixteen million or so. Each cell is identified with the column name (A, B. C. . .) and row name (1, 2, 3. . .). Thus, cell B5 is in the second column, fifth row. (Columns are named from A to Z and then AA to AZ, then BA to BZ and so on, until Column IV.) Every cell can contain anything you want — from emptiness to an entire book. Generally, cells are combined into rows and columns, and these combinations are called tables. For example, your checkbook register can be a table with the check number, date, recipient, amount, and balance as your columns. You can place tables in your spreadsheet anywhere you want and give them names. A single spreadsheet can have as many tables in it as you like — as long as they fit. After you create tables, you can manipulate them by sorting, filtering, adding, or whatever you want to do.

And, if over sixteen million cells are not enough for you on a single spreadsheet, you can also have more than one spreadsheet, called sheets. Sheet names appear in tabs in the lower right-hand corner of your spreadsheet (refer to Figure 5-1). New spreadsheets offer three sheets, but you can choose Insert⇨Sheet to add as many sheets as your computer has room to process. When you have many sheets, you can scroll through them using the arrow buttons to the left of the sheet name tabs. Using sheets, you can create not just tables of data, but matrices, which are 3D tables. Calc can store and process data in matrices as well as tables.

Like Writer, your Calc window has a Standard toolbar for functions like opening documents, creating new documents, or viewing the Find & Replace dialog box or the Navigator. It also has a Formatting toolbar for formatting type and numbers, as well as adding borders and alignment. It has floating toolbars for inserting graphics, columns, rows, and more, which you can access by choosing View⇨Toolbars, as shown in Figure 5-2. And it also has the Formula Bar for selecting ranges, inputting data, and creating formulas.

Figure 5-2: Calc offers an assortment of toolbars for use in your spreadsheet.

Entering data

When you type in Calc, whatever you type appears in the active cell of your spreadsheet, which is the cell with the bold border around it, as shown in Figure 5-1. If you press Return, the data that you typed stays in the cell, and the active cell moves to the next cell below. Generally, data is stored in a single line in each cell, although having line breaks within a cell is possible, by pressing Ctrl+Return instead of Return. For example, the heading, "Digital Technology Budgets for the 2005-2006 school year" has a line break in it, as shown in Figure 5-2.

To edit data in a cell, you can either double-click in the cell so that a cursor appears, or you can single-click in the cell and click in the Input Line on the Formula Bar so that a cursor appears. If the Formula Bar is not visible, choose View⇨Toolbars⇨Formula Bar.

If Calc is capitalizing the first letter of each word in your cells, then you may want to choose Tools⇨AutoCorrect, and select the Options tab of the AutoCorrect dialog box. Deselect Capitalize First Letter Of Every Sentence and click OK.

Changing column widths and row heights

You may want to change the width of your column if your numbers or dates are too large to fit in a cell. (If a cell is too small to hold a number or date, the symbol ### appears in that cell.) Or you may want to change the width of your column to hold more text in the cells. No matter what the size of the column is, you can type as much text into a single cell as you want; if the cell is not big enough to hold your text, it visually spills over into the cell to the right of it, provided that cell is empty. Otherwise, the text appears truncated in your spreadsheet, although this is only an appearance. If you change the width of the column that the cell resides in to encompass all the text, the entire text of your cell always appears.

To change the width of your column, click anywhere in your spreadsheet; then move your cursor to the row with the column names and place it over the line separating the column that you want to make wider or smaller and the next column to the right, as shown in Figure 5-1. When the arrow changes to a double-arrow, click and drag the column to whatever width you want. Dragging to the right makes it bigger. Dragging to the left makes it smaller and can even hide it.

To restore a column that is hidden, double-click on the line separating the column names — and be sure that the double arrow is slightly off-center toward the right!

Inserting and deleting columns and rows

As you enter data into your spreadsheet, you may find that you need to insert a column or row here and there — or perhaps many columns or rows. When you add columns or rows, Calc renames all the columns or rows to the left or beneath the columns or rows that you add.

To add columns and rows, click a column or row name to select the column or row, or just click in any cell of that column or row. Then choose View⇨ Toolbars⇨Insert Cell to bring up the Insert Cell floating toolbar (refer to Figure 5-2). Click the Rows or Columns button in the Insert Cell toolbar. A new row or column appears above or to the left of the row or column that you selected or your active cell. (If you click in a cell and drag to select more than one cell, that many new columns or rows will appear when you click the Rows or Columns button.)

Selecting ranges

You can format the numbers or text in your cells by clicking in a cell and choosing any of the formatting options on the Formatting toolbar, such as Font Name, Font Size, the Alignment buttons, the Number Formatting buttons, and more. But often, you'll want to format more than one cell at a time — perhaps a whole table or the entire spreadsheet. To do that, you need to select ranges of cells. A range is simply a group of cells. Selected cells in a range appear shaded. You can select a range in various ways:

- **To select a small range of cells,** click and drag your cursor from one corner cell of a range to the opposite corner.

- **To select the entire sheet,** choose Edit⇨Select All (or press Ctrl+A), or click the Select All button (the square above the row names and to the left of the column names).

- **To select an entire row or column,** click on a column name or row name.

- **To select several entire columns or rows,** click and drag from one column name or row name to another column name or row name, as shown in Figure 5-3.

- **To select a very large range, do one of the following:**

  - Click one corner cell of the range you want to select, then Shift+click the cell in the opposite corner of the range. (You can use scroll bars to scroll to the corner cell for large ranges.)

  - Type the cell range in the Sheet Area input box on the Formula Bar. (Type the address of the upper-left corner cell of your range, followed by a colon, and then the cell address of the lower-right corner cell of your range, and press Return.)

- **To select a table,** press Shift+Ctrl+arrow (up, down, right or left) to do the following:

  - **If your active cell is not empty,** this command selects all contiguous non-empty cells in the direction specified, stopping just before the next empty cell. (One exception to this is when the adjacent cell in the direction of your arrow is empty; Calc then treats the active cell as if it were empty, too. Yes, this sounds confusing, but intuitively, it works.)

  - **If your active cell is empty,** this command selects all contiguous empty cells in the direction specified, including the next non-empty cell.

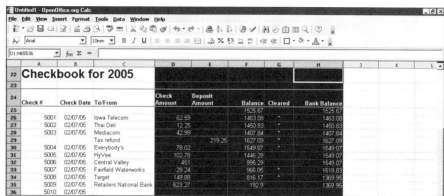

Figure 5-3:
Select many
columns at
once by
clicking and
dragging
column
headings.

✔ **To select non-contiguous ranges,** click the Selection mode button on the status bar repeatedly until it says "Add" and click and drag any number of times in the document to select ranges. Then click the Selection mode repeatedly again until it says "STD." (If you are running Windows XP and the Selection mode button on the status bar does not change when you click it, you may need to hide the Windows XP taskbar for this to work.)

✔ **To select a 3D range,** select a range of cells in your worksheet using one of the aforementioned methods; then Shift+click the sheet tabs for the sheets in which you want to select the same range. The tabs of selected sheets appear white.

If you select sheets other than the active sheet, don't forget to deselect them after you finish formatting. Otherwise, any entries you make to any cells in the active sheet are also made to the same cells in the selected sheets, which may or may not be your intention.

Formatting Cells and Tables

Calc offers a wide variety of formatting options. You can format individual cells, ranges of cells, or your entire spreadsheet by using the buttons and list boxes on the Formatting toolbar to choose your fonts, alignment, borders, backgrounds, number of decimal places for your numbers, and more. And you can use the Cell Format dialog box to format your dates, time, currency symbols, and more precisely format your numbers.

Formatting text

After you select a range of cells, you can format the text and numbers in that range just like you would format the text or numbers in a single cell. The Formatting toolbar, as shown in Figure 5-1, offers a number of formatting options, including the following:

- ✔ **Choose your font** from the Font Name and Font Size list boxes. Your cell height automatically changes to accommodate a larger size font.

- ✔ **Choose your font color** by clicking the Font Color button to show the floating Font Color toolbar and clicking on any color that you want.

- ✔ **Choose a background color or border** by clicking their respective buttons to show their floating toolbars, and then click on a background color or a border for your selection.

- ✔ **Format the alignment of the contents of your cells horizontally** within the individual cells by clicking Align Left, Align Centered Horizontally, Align Right, or Justified. (These alignment buttons operate in the same manner as in Writer, except the margins that they align to are the margins of the individual cells, not the margins of the document.)

Formatting numbers

Spreadsheets have a lot to do with numbers, so the fact that Calc allows you to format numbers in a myriad of ways is not surprising. For example, do you want to enter "1" and have it show up as "1.00"? Or do you want dollar signs in front of your numbers? Or percentage signs after your numbers? The Formatting toolbar, as shown in Figure 5-1, contains five handy buttons for formatting numbers. To format numbers, first select a cell or range of cells; then click one of the following buttons:

- ✔ **The Number Format: Currency button** puts a dollar sign (or other currency sign) in front of the number and adds two decimal places, if needed. For example, 1 becomes $1.00.

- ✔ **The Number Format: Percent button** changes your number into a percentage with two decimal places.

- ✔ **The Number Format: Standard button** resets the number format to Calc's default number format.

- ✔ **The Number Format: Add Decimal Place button** adds a decimal place to your number.

- ✔ **The Number Format: Delete Decimal Place button** deletes a decimal place from your number. For example, click this twice to get rid of the two decimal places inserted by the Number Format: Percentage button.

Formatting dates, currency, and more

Numbers, dates, currency, time, scientific notation, and Boolean values can all be formatted in Calc. You can automatically format a cell or range of cells so that, for example, if you type **1/29/05**, Calc automatically changes your date to January 29, 2005; Saturday, January 29, 2005; or any number of formats, including zaterdag 29 januari 2005 (if you prefer Dutch). Also, you can change your currency signs to British pounds, Spanish pesos, or whatever.

To format your numbers, dates, currency, and so on, follow these steps:

1. **Select the range of cells or individual cell that you want to format.**

2. **Choose Format➪Cells.**

   The Format Cells dialog box appears, as shown in Figure 5-4.

3. **Choose the Category that you want to format.**

4. **If you want to choose a language other than your default language, select one from the Language drop-down list.**

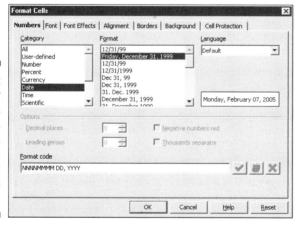

Figure 5-4: Format your dates, currency, numbers, and more with the Format Cells dialog box.

5. **Choose the format that you want from the Format list box.**

   Your result appears in the Preview Field, showing the formatted version of whatever data resides in your active cell.

6. **Choose any options in the Options section.**

   • **Decimal places:** Displays your number with the number of decimal places you specify in the spin box. If your number contains more decimal places, Calc rounds it.

   • **Leading zeros:** Adds the number of leading zeros that you specify in the Leading Zero spin box.

- **Negative numbers in red:** This option can be scary in your checkbook spreadsheet. Use with care.

- **Thousands separator:** These may not always be commas in every currency.

7. Click OK.

Now whenever you type in a cell that has been formatted, your number or date transforms into whatever format you assigned.

Moving Around in Your Spreadsheet

Small spreadsheets are easy to get around in, just by using the arrow keys. However, when your spreadsheets get large, getting to row 65,536, for example, just by using the arrow keys, could take quite a while. Here are some techniques for getting around:

- **Ctrl+Home:** Moves the active cell to A1.

- **Ctrl+End:** Moves the active cell to the last cell on the spreadsheet containing data.

- **Home:** Moves the active cell to column A of whatever row the active cell was on when you pressed Home.

- **End:** Moves the active cell to the last non-empty column of whatever row the active cell was on when you pressed End.

- **Ctrl+left arrow:**
  - If the active cell is in a table, the active cell moves to the first column of that table, (as long as no empty cells exist in the same row between the active cell and that first column).
  - If the active cell is empty or in the first column of a table, the active cell moves to the next non-empty cell to the left. If all the cells to the left are empty, the active cell moves to the first column of the sheet.

- **Ctrl+right arrow:** Does the same as Ctrl+left arrow, except in the other direction. (Substitute "last" for "first" and "right" for "left.")

- **Ctrl+up arrow:**
  - If the active cell is in a table, the active cell moves to the topmost row of that table (as long as no empty cells exist in the column between the active cell and the topmost cell).
  - If the active cell is empty or in the topmost row of a table, the active cell moves to the next non-empty cell above it.

- **Ctrl+down arrow:** Does the same as Ctrl+up arrow, except it goes down. (Substitute "bottom" for "topmost" and "below" for "above.")

- **Alt+Page Down:** Moves the active cell one screen over to the right. (For example, it moves the cursor from A1 to K1 if column J was the last column visible in your window.)

- **Alt+Page Up:** Moves the active cell one screen over to the left, which is the reverse of Alt+Page Down.

- **Ctrl+Page Down:** Moves the active cell one sheet to the right.

- **Ctrl+Page Up:** Moves the active cell one sheet to the left.

- **Ctrl+Backspace:** If your active cell is not visible in your window, use this command to find your active cell.

In an empty worksheet, press Ctrl+down arrow to see the last row available to you (row 65,536). Press Ctrl+right arrow to see the last column available to you (column IV).

Autofilling Cells

Calc provides an easy way to automatically create a column or row of numbers in any sequence you specify. This is useful for creating numbered lists or filling out column and row headings of tables, such as mortgage tables, where each column and row heading specifies a new numerical value. And you can also use the autofill feature to copy and paste a value other than a number, such as text or a formula, into many cells.

Generating a consecutive sequence

To create a consecutive sequence (1, 2, 3, and so on), click in the cell where you want your sequence to begin, type the first number of your new sequence, and press Return. (You can start at any number you want.) Click in the cell again and then pull the small square below the lower right-hand corner of your active cell, as shown in Figure 5-5.

You can pull this square up, down, or sideways in either direction, creating the following results:

- Pulling down or right results in a column or row of consecutive numbers starting with the number in the active cell.

- Pulling up or left results in a column of consecutive numbers in reverse order, starting with the number in the active cell.

Drag the Autofill tab to create a sequence

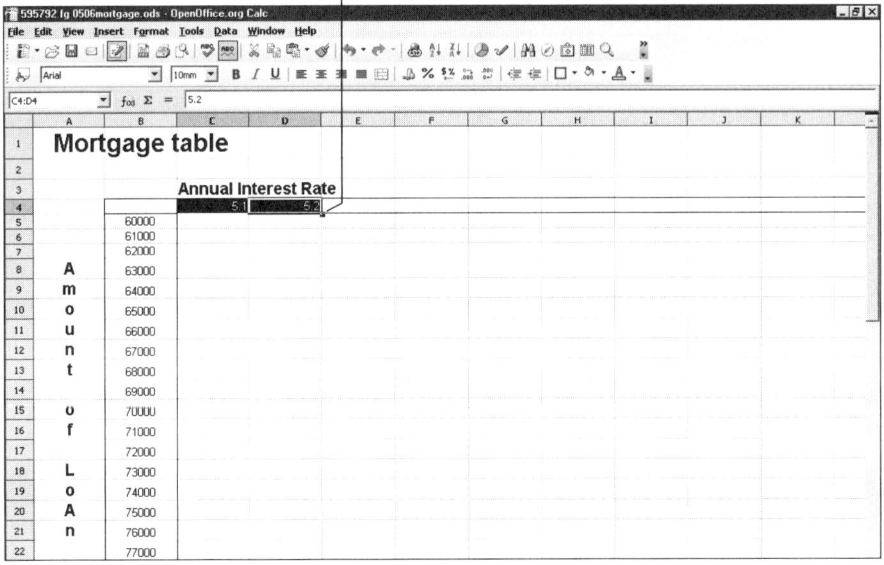

Figure 5-5:
Use the
Autofill
tab to auto-
matically fill
your cells
with a
sequence of
numbers.

Generating any sequence

You can generate any sequence of numbers such as (1, 5, 10, 15, and so on or
.001, 002, .003, and so on) using this autofilling feature. To automatically generate any sequence in a row or column of cells, do the following:

1. **Type two numbers of the sequence in conseccutive cells, such as 6000
   in F20 and 6050 in F21.**

2. **Click in the first cell of your sequence; for example, either F20 or F21,
   depending on the direction you want to go, and drag to select the
   second cell.**

3. **Drag the autofill square either up or down, in the same direction as
   your sequence.**

   The cells fill automatically in the sequence you typed in the original
   two cells. For example, selecting F20 and then F21 and dragging down
   creates a sequence of 6000, 6050, 6100, 6150, 6200, and so on.

Autofilling with text or a formula

If you drag the autofill square on the active cell border, if the contents of your
active cell is not a number, whatever resides in the active cell will be copied
into all the cells that you autofill. For example, if you type "A" into the active

cell and then drag the autofill square, "A" will be pasted into all the squares that you drag over. This feature is really handy for pasting formulas, for example, if you have a formula creating a sum of one column and then drag the formula with the autofill square across all the columns, Calc will insert the sum for each individual column. (For information on creating a sum, see Chapter 6.)

Turning Off the Grid

When you print your spreadsheet, Calc does not print the grid by default. However, you may also want to turn off the grid when you view your spreadsheet on the screen. To do so, choose Tools⇨Options. In the Options dialog box that appears, expand the OpenOffice.org Calc menu by clicking the plus sign beside OpenOffice.org Calc in the list on the left, and click View. In the Options-Spreadsheet-View pane that appears to the left, deselect the Grid Lines check box. (Or if you want, you can change the color of your grid lines from light gray to something more fun!) Then click OK.

Naming Tables

Calc offers many benefits to anyone who takes the time to name the tables in his or her spreadsheets. Table names appear in the Sheet Area list box on the Formula Bar, so anytime you want to select the entire table after it is named, you can select the name from the Sheet Area list. This feature can be very helpful, even if you just use it to find your table in a large spreadsheet.

To name your table, follow these steps:

1. **Choose Insert⇨Names⇨Define.**

   The Define Names dialog box appears, as shown in Figure 5-6.

2. **Type a descriptive name for your table.**

   Your name cannot contain blanks.

3. **Click the Shrink button, which is the small square button to the left of the More button.**

   The Define Names dialog box shrinks to just the title bar, the Assigned To input box, and Shrink button.

4. **Click in the upper-left corner cell of your range and drag to the lower-right corner cell of your range that you want your name to define.**

   A blue border surrounds your selection, and the range appears written in the Assigned To input box.

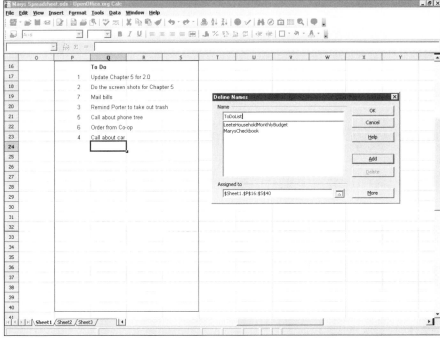

Figure 5-6:
You can use
the Define
Names
dialog box
to name
your ranges.

5. Click the Shrink button.

The Define Names dialog box reappears, as shown in Figure 5-6.

6. If you want to change your address from Absolute to Relative (see the explanation, discussed next), delete the dollar signs from the Assigned To box.

Notice that the address of your table is in the Assigned to input box. The address appears with dollar signs in front of the sheet name as well as each row and column name in your range. Dollar signs indicate an *Absolute address,* which basically means that the range does not change even if you cut and paste the data in your table elsewhere. If you want to have the flexibility to move your range anywhere and still keep its name, you need to delete the dollar signs. Cell addresses without dollar signs are known as *Relative addresses.* For more information, see Chapter 6.

7. Do one of the following:

- **Click Add** to add the name to the list and then repeat steps 2 through 7 to continue defining names for your ranges of cells.

- **Click OK.**

  The Define Names dialog box disappears and whatever name or names you added now appear in the Sheet Area list.

Sorting

Calc also offers Sort Ascending and Sort Descending buttons on the Standard toolbar to quickly sort your table on a single key. Or you can use the Sort dialog box, which provides options that enable you to sort tables in more complex ways.

Using the Sort Descending or Sort Ascending buttons

To use these buttons, select the table that you want to sort. Be sure that the key that you want to sort on is in the first column. Also, be sure not to select any column headings because they might get sorted along with everything else! Then click the Sort Ascending button or Sort Descending button. Your table reorganizes itself sorted in ascending or descending order.

Using the Sort dialog box

Calc also offers a much more powerful sort than the Sort buttons can provide. The Sort dialog box allows you to sort your table using up to three keys. Or you can sort your columns instead of your rows. And you can copy your results to another area on your spreadsheet — which is highly recommended, so that you don't lose the order of your original data.

To perform a more powerful sort, do the following:

1. **Select the table that you want to sort.**

   Select column and row headings, as well. If you named a table, you can select your table from the Sheet Area list.

2. **Choose Data⇨Sort.**

   The Sort dialog box appears.

3. **Click the Options tab.**

   The Options tab appears, as shown in Figure 5-7.

4. **If you want to sort your columns instead of rows, choose the Left to right (sort columns) button in the Direction section.**

5. **If the table that you selected has column headings in it, then select the Range contains column labels check box (or Range contains row labels if you are sorting columns).**

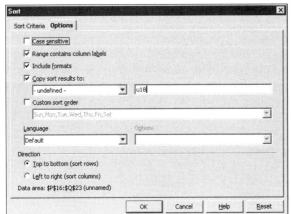

Figure 5-7:
The Options
tab of the
Sort dialog
box.

6. **Select the Copy sort results to: check box and in the input box below it and to the right, type in a single cell address, such as Z1, that you want to become the upper left-hand corner cell for your new sorted table.**

   (But first be sure that your new sorted table will not overwrite your selected table or any other data in your spreadsheet.)

7. **Click the Sort Criteria tab and choose the Sort By column or row heading from the list box, and select Ascending or Descending order. Then, if you want, you can do the same in the Then By sections below for up to three keys.**

8. **Click OK.**

   Your table is copied in sorted order with its upper-left cell located at the address you specified. Your original table is left unchanged.

Filtering

When the tables in your spreadsheet get quite large and you need to find a record fast, filtering is a great way to find whatever you're looking for. Calc offers several filtering options, including the AutoFilter and the Standard Filter.

AutoFiltering

To use the AutoFilter, select your table, including your column headings, and choose Data➪Filter➪AutoFilter. Your column headings all have drop-down lists containing each unique data item in each column, as shown in Figure 5-8. You can choose any data item from any drop-down list as your filter criteria.

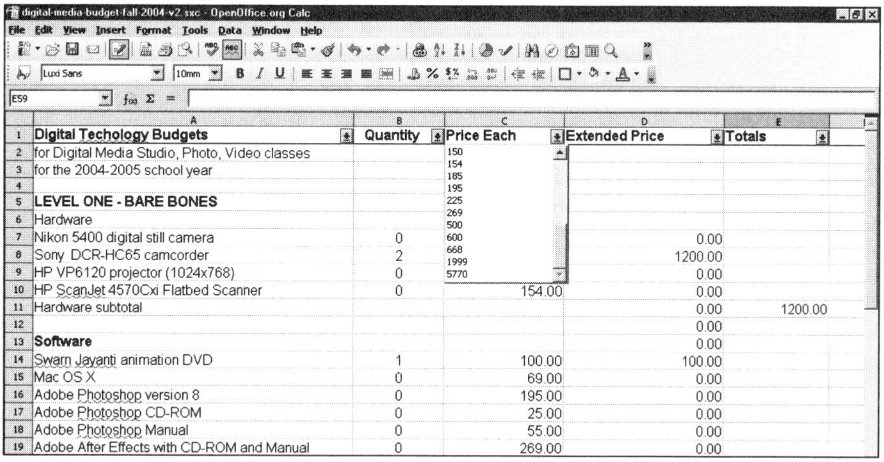

Figure 5-8:
Use the
AutoFilter to
locate
information
in your table
quickly.

To turn off AutoFiltering, click anywhere in the table and choose Data⇨ Filter⇨AutoFilter.

Using the Standard Filter

The Standard Filter is similar to the AutoFilter, except it allows you to filter using conditional criteria, such as greater than, less than, largest, smallest, and more. It allows up to three filtering criteria, which can be combined using And or Or. Also, the Standard Filter allows you to use wildcards. (For details about wildcards, see Chapter 3.)

To filter your data using the Standard Filter, do the following:

1. **Select the table that you want to filter, including column headings.**

2. **Choose Data⇨Filter⇨Standard Filter.**

   The Standard Filter dialog box appears.

3. **Click More.**

4. **Select the Range Contains Column Labels check box.**

5. **Check the Copy Results To check box and in the input box beneath it and to the right, type in a single cell address, such as Z1, that you want to become the upper-left corner cell for your filtered results.**

6. **Check the Regular Expression check box if you plan to use wildcards.**

7. **Select the No Duplication check box if you have duplicate records in your table and you don't want to view them all.**

   (A record is database lingo for a row of data in your table.)

8. **In the top Field Name list box, choose the column that you want the filter to apply to. In the top Condition list box, choose the condition. Then choose a value that the condition applies to in the Value list box, as shown in Figure 5-9.**

9. **If you want more than one filtering criteria, choose And or Or from the Operator list and choose the Field Name, Condition, and Value for your second criteria. Do the same for a third criteria, if you need another one.**

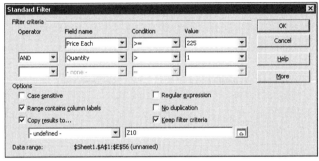

Figure 5-9:
The
Standard
Filter allows
you to filter
your
records.

In the example in Figure 5-9, the records in the table are filtered to show only records with items costing $225 or more that have a quantity greater than 1. The results are copied to a new table with cell Z1 as the upper-left corner cell of the table.

10. **Click OK.**

Your filtered results are copied to the location you specified and your original table is left unchanged.

Saving and Exporting a Document

To save your document, choose one of the following procedures:

✔ **To save a new document in any format for the first time:** Choose File⇨ Save, click the Save Document button on the Standard toolbar, or press Ctrl+S. In the Save As dialog box, open the folder that you want to save your document in, then fill in the File Name and choose the File Type. The default File Type is OpenDocument Spreadsheet (.ods). Click Save.

✔ **To resave a document previously saved in Calc format:** Choose File⇨ Save, click the Save Document button on the Standard toolbar, or press Ctrl+S. The document is saved in Calc format.

✔ **To resave a document previously saved in Excel format:** Choose File⇨ Save, click the Save Document button on the Standard toolbar, or press Ctrl+S. The document will be saved in Excel format.

✔ **To resave a document with a new name or new file type:** Choose File⇨ Save As. In the Save As dialog box that appears, open the folder that you want to save your document in, then fill in the File Name, choose the File Type, and click Save.

When you save, be sure the Automatic File Name Extension check box is checked, otherwise you need to add the file extension to the end of the file-name in the File Name input box (for example, mySpreadsheet.ods).

Protecting your document

If you want to protect your document so that it can't be opened without a password, the first time you save your document, select the Save With Password check box in the Save As dialog box. Click Save, and a dialog box appears in which you need to type at least a five-letter password twice. After you type the password twice, click OK. Next time you open the file, you'll need to type the password, so don't forget it!

Exporting as PDF

Before you export to PDF, you may want to adjust your page breaks. To do so, see Chapter 6.

To export your document as PDF, select the range of cells that you want to export, then choose File⇨Export As PDF. In the Save As dialog box that appears, double-click the folder name to open the folder, fill in the File Name, and click Save. In the PDF Options dialog box that appears, if you selected a range, click Selection. If you did not select a range, you can click Pages and fill out a page numbers in the input box, or you can click All to export all pages. Then choose the type of Compression that you want, as described in Chapter 3.

Chapter 6

Juggling Numbers in Calc

. . . .

. . . .

*N*othing is better than a spreadsheet for storing and manipulating numbers in tables. The uses for spreadsheets are infinite. Accountants, businessmen, statisticians, scientists, government officials, and many others use spreadsheets extensively in their daily work.

Using Calc, you can explore "what if" scenarios. For example, you can enter formulas into your cells that can refer to other cells, which can refer to other cells, and so on, so that when you change a value in one cell, your whole spreadsheet instantly changes to reflect the new value. This flexibility enables you to explore a multitude of financial, scientific, or statistical scenarios, and more. Exploring the "what if's" can give you an edge in the business world.

Okay, so you may not need to use spreadsheets in your business or your work. But everybody needs to budget their finances. Everyone needs to balance their checkbooks. Even for everyday uses, Calc can be extremely helpful. This chapter builds on Chapter 5 by showing you how to fine-tune Calc for optimum use.

Adding and Subtracting

Adding a column or row of numbers is exceedingly simple in Calc. Just click in the empty cell below the column (or to the right of the row), click the Sum button on the Formula Bar, and click the Accept button on the Formula Bar. The total appears in the cell.

When you use the Sum button, Calc assumes that all contiguous cells with numbers above the active cell, below it, to the right of it, or to the left of it are to be added. Which direction does it choose? It guesses. If your column or row of numbers has a break in it, then Calc only adds up to that break. This simple method of adding has its limitations, but Calc provides three easy ways to precisely specify what you want added and where you want your total to reside:

✔ Use the Sum button and drag the border around your column or row.

✔ Use the Sum button and type the range of cells to be added.

✔ Type your formula manually into the cell.

Dragging the border

To some people, defining your summation range by dragging the border may seem a little more complicated than just typing in the range. But in the long run, you'll probably find that this method is much quicker and easier to use than manually figuring out a range. And it's not just useful for adding. The ranges for all formulas and functions in Calc can be specified in this visual way. To add up the contents of a column or row, using the border to specify the range, perform the following steps:

1. **Click in the empty cell that you want the total to reside in.**

   This cell does not have to be at the end of any row or anywhere near the numbers you want to add.

2. **Click the Sum button.**

   The formula =SUM() appears with the range of cells in the Input Line; for example =SUM(C6:C24). A blue border appears around the range of cells that Calc guesses that you want to add, as shown in Figure 6-1.

3. **Move your mouse over the border until your cursor turns into a hand. Then drag the border so the upper left-hand corner of the border fits over the top cell or leftmost cell of the column or row you want to add.**

4. **Move your mouse over the small square on the bottom right-hand corner of the border until the hand or white arrow cursor turns into a plus sign. Then drag the border down the column or across the row that you want to add or even across an entire table or part of a table.**

   If you place the border around a table, Calc adds all the cells in that table and places the total in the active cell.

Accept button

	A	B	C	D	E	F
28						
29	Software					
30	Swarn Jayanti animation DVD	1	100.00	100.00		
31	Mac OS X (for faculty -- for class preparation)	3	69.00	207.00		
32	Adobe Photoshop version 8	10	195.00	1,950.00		
33	Adobe Photoshop CD-ROM	10	25.00	250.00		
34	Adobe Photoshop Manual	10	55.00	550.00		
35	Adobe After Effects with CD-ROM and Manual	15	269.00	4,035.00		
36	Adobe After Effects site license	15	150.00	2,250.00		
37	Adobe After Effects CD-ROM	15	25.00	375.00		
38	Adobe After Effects Manual	15	55.00	825.00		
39	Troikatronix Isadora (interactive software for video/pe	5	225.00	1,125.00		
40	SIGGRAPH animation DVDs	3	44.00	132.00		
41	Quark Xpress	17	99.00	1,683.00		
42	Macromedia FreeHand, Dreamweaver, Flash upgrad	17	185.00	3,145.00		
43	Corel Painter 9	17	71.00	1,207.00		
44	Corel Painter 9 CD	3	25.00	75.00		
45	Final Cut Express HD	10	79.00	790.00		
46	Final Cut Express HD CD set	2	15.00	30.00		
47	Final Cut Express HD manual	1	20.00	20.00		
48	join siggraph $27			27.00		
49	Software subtotal				=SUM(D30:D48)	
50	Hardware and software subtotal				39,046.00	
51						
52	Supplies			.00		
53	Printer cartridges, paper, etc.	1	500.00	500.00		
54	Subtotal			.00	39,546.00	
55						

Figure 6-1:
The steps
for visually
defining
your range
for the Sum
(or any)
function.

5. **Click the Accept button on the Formula Bar.**

   The total of all the cells within the border appears in the empty cell you
   clicked in step 1. The border disappears. Calc assigns a value of zero to
   all blank cells or cells with text.

Canceling your formula

If you change your mind before completing your addition and want to forget
about it, you need to know how to cancel it; otherwise, you may find yourself
in a wonderland of endless blue or red borders. You can cancel your addition
(or any function or formula that you may be in the middle of) by clicking the
Cancel button on the Formula Bar. The Cancel button appears only on the
Formula Bar when you're creating or editing a formula.

Typing in your range

Instead of dragging the border around the cells you want to add, you can sum a range of cells by doing the following:

1. **Click in the empty cell that you want the total to reside in.**

   This cell does not have to be at the end of any row or anywhere near the numbers you want to add.

2. **Click the Sum button.**

   The formula =SUM() appears with the range of cells in the Input line; for example, =SUM(A1:A12). A blue border appears around the range of cells that Calc guesses that you want to add.

3. **Click in the Input line and type a new range of cells in the formula. Then click Accept.**

   The total for the range you typed appears in the active cell.

Inserting your formula manually

You don't need to use the Sum button to create totals. You can type the same formula that the sum function would insert into any cell you want a total to reside in. For example, if you type =sum(A1:A12) into cell B12 and click the Accept button on the Formula Bar, Calc puts the sum of cells A1 through A12 into cell B12.

Entering Mathematical Formulas

All formulas in a cell in Calc begin with an equal sign. Calc recognizes mathematical operators, such as +, -, *, /, %, and ^ (exponentiation). So you can type into your active cell such equations as =a1+b1+c1+4 to add those three cells together plus the number 4. You can also use parentheses; for example, =(c1+c2)/6 yields a result different from =c1+c2/6, (with a few exceptions, such as when c1=0).

Calc allows you to include the following in your formulas:

- ✔ **Numbers or text:** You enclose text in quotations.
- ✔ **Arithmetical operators:** +, -, *, /, %, and ^ (exponentiation).
- ✔ **Comparative operators:** =, >, <, >=, <=, or <> to return the values TRUE or FALSE. For example: =A1>B1 returns TRUE if the value in A1 is greater than the value in B1.

✔ **Parentheses:** To separate operations.

✔ **Cell references and ranges,** which can include:

  • **A single cell:** For example, A1.

  • **A range of cells:** You may use the addresses for the range or the name of the range; for example, (A1:B12) or (myTableName).

  • **A matrix:** This is a range spanning sheets; for example, (Sheet1.A1:Sheet3.B12).

  • **An intersection of two ranges:** Use an exclamation point between two ranges to indicate this. For example, (A1:C5!C4:D6) yields cells C4 and C5.

✔ **Function names:** Calc provides 365 ready-made functions (one for each day of the year?), such as SUM, which are discussed in the next section.

You can create a formula as simple as =A,1 which places the value of the cell A1 into the cell that this formula resides in. Or you can create a more complicated formula, such as =F11+D12-E12, where F11 could be a running balance of your checkbook, D12 could be deposits, and E12 could be withdrawals. Or, if you want to really go wild, you could have a super-complicated formula that's over 200 characters long in a single cell! (This situation is not uncommon with spreadsheet super-users.)

Cutting, Copying, and Pasting Cells, Ranges, and Formulas

What happens when you refer to a cell in a formula and then that cell address changes, either because you cut and paste the cell elsewhere or because you insert rows or columns above or to the right of the cell, which changes its address? And what happens when you move a formula itself to another cell? Should the addresses in the formula change to reflect the new location of the formula? Or should they refer to the original cells? Calc deals with these issues by providing more than one way to address a cell.

Absolute and relative addressing

Calc gives you the choice of referring to a cell or range of cells in a formula using three different types of addresses:

✔ **Relative address:** A relative address changes to reflect any new location of its data when it is moved by cutting, copying, and pasting the cell or by inserting cells to the right or above it. An address with no dollar signs in front of it is a relative address; for example (C5).

✔ **Absolute address:** An absolute address does not change, regardless of whether the data in the cell remains in the cell or moves elsewhere. This address is indicated by using dollar signs in front of the row and column name. For example, a formula that refers to the cell C5 always refers to that particular cell and never any changed location of the data previously in that cell.

✔ **Part relative and part absolute:** You can also indicate a row as an absolute address and a column as a relative address (or vice versa) by placing a dollar sign in front of either the row or column name. For example, $C5 anchors the column as C but enables the row to change. This partial relative address is useful when creating tables of functions, such as the mortgage table in Figure 6-5.

Copying and pasting formulas

If your cell contains a formula, any relative address in that formula changes when you paste the formula into a new location. This may seem annoying at first, but actually, it's great! If you want to total a table, just type your formula into a single cell, copy (Ctrl+C) and select the cells that you want to paste the formula into, then paste (Ctrl+V). That same formula will change in each cell to reflect its new location, and this way you can create a whole row or column of totals for your table in one stroke, as shown in Figure 6-2.

In Figure 6-2, the new totals were copied from cell H3 into cells H4–H12 by clicking in H3 and dragging the autofill tab, located at the bottom right-hand corner of the active cell.

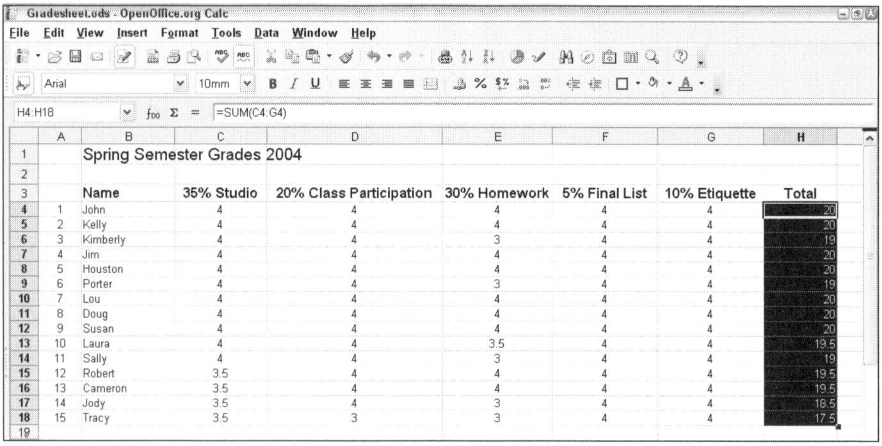

Figure 6-2: Create a column of totals by copying and pasting or dragging the autofill tab to paste a single formula into a column.

Using Functions

Calc offers many ready-made functions that you can pick and choose from or combine and nest to suit your purposes. These functions are divided into eleven categories as follows:

12 Database functions

30 Date and Time functions

59 Financial functions

18 Information functions

6 Logical functions

62 Mathematical functions

14 Array functions

77 Statistical functions

19 Spreadsheet functions

28 Text functions

40 Add-in functions

Inserting functions with the Function Wizard

To view and insert the names and descriptions of the different functions that Calc provides, follow these steps:

1. **Click in an empty cell.**

2. **Click the Function Wizard button on the Formula Bar.**

   The Function Wizard dialog box appears.

3. **Choose the category from the Category drop-down list, and then click on the name of the function in the Function list.**

   A description of the function appears in the pane to the right of the Function list, as shown in Figure 6-3. Repeat this step, if necessary, until you find the function that suits your needs.

4. **Double-click on the function that you want to use.**

   The Function Wizard dialog box displays input boxes for the arguments (the values) that the function requires, as shown in Figure 6-4. Many functions require several *arguments* or values to determine a result. The function WEEKDAY, which returns the day of the week, requires only one argument, which is Number. (Even though it says Number, it is looking for a date, such as 11/15/05.) The Type argument is optional.

   In general, you can use the following as arguments for your functions, as appropriate:

   • **Values:** A value refers to a number, a date, or text. When you enter values, the result appears in the Result box in the Function Wizard, as shown in Figure 6-4.

- **Cell addresses or ranges:** Sometimes an argument requires a range of cells; at other times, a single cell. For example, you can type a date, such as 05/07/05 into cell A1 and your function, =WEEKDAY(A1) returns the number 7, which stands for "Saturday."

- **Formulas:** Wherever a function requires a numerical value, you can also type a formula (without the leading equal sign).

- **Functions:** Using a function as an argument is called *nesting functions.*

Figure 6-3:
The Function Wizard dialog box allows you to view descriptions of each function in each category as well as select a function and enter it into your active cell.

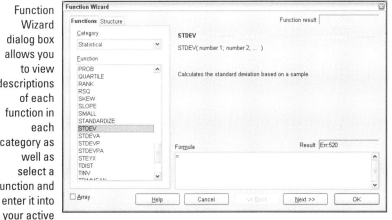

Figure 6-4:
You can input your values, ranges, formulas, or functions into the input boxes of the Function Wizard.

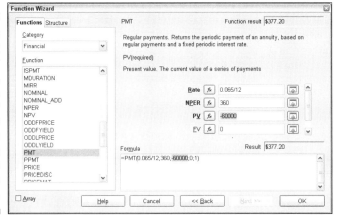

5. **Click in an empty input box and do one of the following:**

   - **If you want your function's result to be based on a value or for- mula,** type the value or a formula (with no equal sign in front of it) into the input box.

   - **If you want your argument to reside in a cell or range of cells,** type the address as shown in Figure 6-4. You can also click the Shrink button on your Argument dialog box to shrink the Function Wizard dialog box and click the cell or drag in the range of cells that you want your data to reside in, and a colored box appears around the cell or cells. Then click the Shrink button on your Argument dialog box to return to the Function Wizard dialog box.

   - **If you want your argument to be the result of another function,** click the Function button to the left of the input box. In the new Function Wizard dialog box, perform steps 3 through 6, then click the Back button to return to the current function. For example, to use TODAY() as your argument for WEEKDAY(), click in the Number input box, click the Function button, double-click TODAY, in the function list, and click the Back button.

6. **Repeat step 5 until all required input boxes are assigned.**

   If a scroll bar appears beside the argument input boxes, be sure to scroll down and fill in all the required fields.

   Be sure you don't prematurely press Return after entering a value, cell address, or range into your input box. Calc interprets it as clicking the OK button, and the Function Wizard dialog box disappears.

7. **Click OK or press Return or Enter.**

   The result of your function appears in the active cell and the function appears in the Input line of the Formula Bar.

You can also get the same results without nesting functions by assigning a function in one cell, then assigning a second function in another cell, using the cell address for the first function as your input in the second function. I find this method to be easier than nesting functions in the Function Wizard.

Troubleshooting functions

If an error message appears in your cell instead of the result that you expected, do the following:

- ✔ **Count your semicolons.** Is the number of arguments (which are sepa- rated by semicolons) the same as the number of arguments required by the function in the Function Wizard dialog box? (Don't forget to scroll down if a scroll bar appears beside the argument list! And no need to include optional arguments, if you don't want to.) If not, delete or add the extra or needed arguments.

✔ **Check to be sure that if the function requires a cell range for an argument, that you did not assign it a value or single cell.** (And check the reverse, too!) This is a common source of errors in spreadsheets.

✔ **Be sure that the cells that the function refers to are not empty, unless they are permitted to be.**

If your function is still misbehaving, do everything you can to simplify it until you get it to work in some way. Then one-by-one assign the cell ranges or values to each argument, testing that a result appears after each entry. When you get an error message, you've found your culprit. Try different values and different cell ranges in that argument. If you're stuck, get support! See Chapter 1.

Editing functions and formulas

Editing formulas and functions are easy and fun in Calc. It is all color-coded. Because functions are a type of formula, I'll use the word *formula* to describe both in the following steps. To edit a formula, perform the following steps:

1. **Click in the cell containing the formula that you want to edit.**

   The formula appears written out on the Input line.

2. **Click on the Input line.**

   Your formula appears color-coded in your cell. Each range for each argument has a different color. These colors correspond to borders on your spreadsheet.

3. **You can edit your formula in the following ways:**

   • **To change any cell address or range in the formula,** click and drag the border with the same color as the range and reshape it or move it. The range changes accordingly in your formula. Conversely, you could edit the cell ranges in the Input line, which changes the locations of the borders.

   • **To change anything else in your formula,** click in the Input line or in the formula in the cell and type in your changes.

4. **To stop editing, click the Accept button on the Formula Bar. Or, if you want to cancel your edits, click Cancel on the Formula Bar.**

   Don't forget this step; otherwise, whenever you click in your spreadsheet, a colored border will probably appear, driving you crazy!

Using Date and Time functions

Using Date and Time functions in combinations with themselves can be useful for a myriad of scheduling purposes and administrative applications. For example, you can calculate the number of days between the current date and whatever date you place into cell A1 by using the function =DAYS(TODAY();A1). Place your deadline in A1 for a rush of adrenaline — only three more days before the book is due!

To update Date and Time functions, such as =NOW() and =TODAY() so that they reflect the current time and not the time that they were inserted into the cell, you need to choose Tools⇨Cell Contents⇨Recalculate or press F9.

Using Financial functions

Financial functions provide you with all the functionality you would expect from a financial calculator, but having these functions on a spreadsheet gives you the power to see everything at a glance. You can generate whole tables of financial information, if you want. For example, you can use the PMT() function to determine a mortgage payment for a specific amount borrowed and a specific interest rate. Then you can create a table of payment amounts using a series of borrowed amounts for column headings and a series of interest rates for row headings, as shown in Figure 6-5.

Using Database functions

Database functions are handy to use when you need to extract information from a large table. (The word *database* here refers to any table with column headings in your spreadsheet.) These database functions all use search criteria that allow you to search your table in various ways.

In the search criteria table, you can list as many criteria as you want. Search criteria on a single line are linked by AND. If you want to link your criteria using OR, place the criteria on a separate line, and be sure the border defining your search criteria includes that line as well.

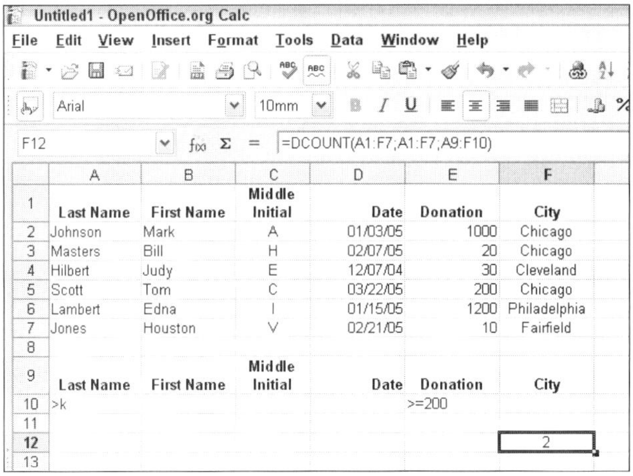

Figure 6-5:
Database
functions
use search
criteria, as
shown here
in cells
A9:F10, to
determine
their results.

Some other database functions are as follows:

- **DAVERAGE** finds the average of a field in your table for records that match the search criteria. For example, to find the average amount of donations given by people from Chicago, in the example shown in Figure 6-6, you could type Chicago in F10 and use the Function Wizard or type =DAVERAGE(A1:F7;E1;A9:F10) into any cell. This returns a value of 406.67.

- **DGET** returns a value for a single cell in your database. For example, if you type a last name, such as Johnson, into A10 in the example shown in Figure 6-5, and use the Function Wizard dialog box or type DGET(A1:F7;E1;A9:F10) into a cell, the value 1000 is returned. (You could also type "Donation" instead of using E1.) If your search criteria has more than one matching record, DGET displays an error message.

- **DMAX and DMIN** return the maximum or minimum values for a field in the records matching the search criteria.

- **DSUM** adds all the values in a field for all records matching the search criteria.

- **DSTDEV and DSTDEVP** determine the standard deviation in two ways using the values from cells matching the search criteria.

- **DCOUNTA** appears (to me, at least) to be exactly the same as DCOUNT. DCOUNT returns the number of cells that match your search criteria, and DCOUNTA returns the number of non-blank cells that match your search criteria. I guess there could be instances where those two results could differ.

Using Logical functions

Logical functions deal with whether something is true or false, and they have a multitude of uses. For example, if you keep track of your checkbook information in a spreadsheet, you may want to have a column for noting checks that have cleared. Maybe you want to note that with an asterisk. Then in the column "Balance for Cleared Checks" you want to subtract the check, but only if it is cleared. To do this, you can enter an IF statement, such as =IF(E5="*";F4-D5;F4) which means in English, "If '*' is in cell E5 then subtract D5 (the check amount) from F4 (the running balance of cleared checks) from and enter that amount as the new current running balance for cleared checks; otherwise enter F4 (the former running balance of cleared checks) into the cell."

Preparing to Print

If the data in your spreadsheet fits into a single page, or if you want to select a small range of cells that would fit on a single page, you probably don't need to preview your printout, and you can skip to the last section, "Printing Your Spreadsheet." Or you may want to skip ahead to the section, "Adding Headers and Footers" before heading to "Printing Your Spreadsheet." Otherwise, read on.

Previewing your printout using Page Preview

Before you print, viewing your pages in Page Preview mode is always a good idea. To do this, choose File⇨Page Preview. The first page of your document appears as it would look on a printed page. Use the Previous Page and Next Page buttons on the toolbar to page through your document. Click the Zoom In or Zoom Out buttons to zoom in and out of your document. Notice that Calc inserts a default header at the top of each page, which is the name of the sheet. You may want to change the header to your liking or add a footer as well.

Also, Calc assigns automatic page breaks if your spreadsheet is too large to fit on a single page. If these page breaks are not acceptable to you, you can do one of the following (each of which I describe in more detail later):

- **Change the size of your page to reflect a different size of paper that you plan to print on.**
- **Adjust automatic page breaks.**
- **Insert manual page breaks.**

Inserting headers and footers

To insert your own header or footer into your spreadsheet, or to delete the default header, follow these steps:

1. **In Page Preview mode, click the Page Format button on the Page Preview toolbar. (If you're not in Page Preview mode, choose File⇨ Page Preview.)**

   The Page Style dialog box appears.

2. **Click the Header or Footer tab and do one of the following:**

   - **To turn on or off the header or footer,** select or deselect the Header On check box or Footer On check box.

   - **For a different header or footer on the left than on the right page,** deselect the Same Content Left/Right button.

   - **Choose the margins, spacing, and height from the spin boxes, if you want.**

3. **If you turned off the header or footer, go to step 9; otherwise, click Edit.**

   The Headers Edit dialog box appears (or Footers Edit dialog box) with three input boxes: Left Area, Center Area, and Right Area. These boxes represent the alignment for the text that you type in them.

4. **Click the Text Attributes button to choose your Font, Typeface, and Size in the Text Attributes dialog box. Click OK.**

5. **Type the text for your header into any of the input boxes.**

6. **To insert a field, click in an input box and click any of the buttons:**

   - File Name
   - Sheet Name
   - Page
   - •Pages (total page count)
   - •Date
   - •Time

7. **Repeat step 6 for as many fields as you want to add. When your header or footer is complete, click OK.**

8. **If you want a border around your header or footer, click the More button in the Header or Footer tab, choose the design of your border, and click OK.**

   (For more details about inserting borders, see Chapter 4.)

9. **In the Header or Footer tab, click OK.**

   Your header or footer appears in the Page Preview.

Changing the page size

To change the page size so that Calc automatically positions the page breaks to reflect the proper paper size, click the Page Format button on the Page Preview toolbar. The Page Style dialog box appears. (You can also use this dialog box to add borders, backgrounds, and more to your pages.) In the Page tab you can choose your new page size and margins. When you click OK, Calc readjusts the automatic page breaks and the Page Preview changes to reflect the new size of your page.

Adjusting automatic page breaks

If your spreadsheet is more than a single printed page, you probably want to see how Calc intends to insert automatic page breaks. You can do so by choosing File➪Page Preview. You can click the Next Page button and see how your spreadsheet will look as a printed document, or you can just click Close Preview, if you look carefully, you see that and Calc automatically inserts thicker grid lines in your document where the page breaks will occur.

If you want the page break lines to stand out in your document, try hiding your grid lines, so that only the page break lines appear. Choose Tools➪ Options and in the left-hand pane of the dialog box that appears choose OpenOffice.org Calc➪View, deselect Grid Lines and then click OK.

Viewing the page breaks in your document gives you the option of watching them change as you do any of the following:

- **Adjust the width of your columns or rows** so that they fit within the automatic page breaks, by clicking and dragging the line separating one column name from another or one row name from another.
- **Delete columns or rows.**
- **Add columns or rows.**

You can also hide columns or rows that you don't want to appear in your printout. For instructions for hiding cells, see Chapter 5.

If adjusting the automatic page breaks does not produce the desired effect, try adding manual page breaks.

Inserting manual page breaks

To manually insert a page break into your document, click in the cell to the right or below the column or row where you want to add a page break, and choose Insert➪Manual Break➪Column or Insert➪Manual Break➪Row. A blue line appears in your spreadsheet indicating the page break.

To delete this page break, click in any cell below or to the right of it, and choose Edit➪Delete Manual Break➪Row Break or Edit➪Delete Manual Break➪Column Break.

Using Page Break Preview

You can get a good look at your page breaks by choosing View➪Page Break Preview. Your spreadsheet appears zoomed to 60% with the page breaks appearing as blue lines and the page numbers in large, light gray text on the background of each page.

You can do everything in Page Break Preview that you can do in the normal view of your spreadsheet, but it also allows you to drag your page breaks to wherever you want them to reside. But you have to be careful doing this, because you don't want to drag a page break beyond what can fit on the printed page — unless you don't care about shrunken data. If you have too much on a page, Calc won't hesitate to shrink everything down to fit.

Dragging a page break in Page Break Preview may result in your data shrinking to fit the page.

You can zoom in or zoom out in Page Break Preview by right-clicking the zoom button and selecting the amount of zoom from the menu.

To turn off Page Break Preview, choose View➪Normal. Your spreadsheet then returns to normal.

Printing a Spreadsheet

Once you know that your spreadsheet is going to look fine on paper, you can choose File➪Print; in the Print dialog box that appears, do the following:

1. **Select the Printer from the Printer Name list box.**

2. **Choose one of the following from the Print Range section:**

   • **All:** Prints every page in all the sheets.

   • **Pages:** Type in the page number or range of pages; for example 1-5. (Generally, Calc assigns page numbers sequentially down the first column of pages in the spreadsheet, then moves to the next column of pages, and the next, and so on.)

   Selection: Choose this option to print a selected a range of cells in your spreadsheet.

3. **Choose the number of copies from the Number of copies spin box.**

4. **Click OK, and you're done.**

Chapter 7

Building Databases with OpenOffice.org Base

* *

* *

*B*ase is a full-featured database that allows you to create your own database, complete with tables, forms, queries, and reports. Base guides you through each step with four wizards that you can access whenever you want. Also, Base allows you to *register* another database, such as dBASE, MySQL, Oracle, and so on, so that you can access data and input information as if it were a Base database. This chapter introduces you to Base and shows you how to get started using it.

Getting the Basics of Base

Base is an extensive database program that lets you easily store, enter, and access information as well as create reports from it. Base stores data as *tables*, which are like spreadsheets with columns and rows of information. Each row is called a *record* and each column is called a *field*. The columns and rows are generally not always visible as they are in a spreadsheet. Also, generally more than one computer can input or read data from a database at the same time.

Base is a *relational database,* which means you can create relationships between tables. For example, if your business is a delivery service, you may have a table with the items that each customer wants you to deliver for the week. You may have another table of your customers' names and addresses. These tables are obviously related, and you can create a relationship between them by specifying either your customer name or a customer number as a *key*. A key is the link between the records in one table and the records in another. After your tables are related, you can more easily create your forms, queries, and reports.

You are not alone! Base to the rescue

Base doesn't leave you alone to muddle through the world of databases; it actively guides you through every step:

- ✔ **Creating tables:** When setting up your database, Base provides lots of ready-made tables. All you have to do is select them and choose from lists of suggested fields. For example, if you have a business and choose a table for Employees, you'll want fields such as Last Name, First Name, Home Phone, Social Security Number, and so on.

- ✔ **Generating queries:** This means generating useful subsets of the data in the database. Using the Query Wizard you can search and group subsets of data to get just the records that you want to deal with.

- ✔ **Designing forms:** You can design forms for inputting data or for viewing information in records one at a time using the Form wizard.

- ✔ **Generating reports:** You can create useful reports from the information in your database using the report wizard.

Using Base with MySQL, dBase, and more

Creating databases is only part of what Base can do for you. What's really exciting about Base is that it allows you to connect to other databases on your PC or over a network and use forms and queries to access them. Base can also import from address books, spreadsheets, or text files. Connections can then be saved by *registering* them.

Databases that Base can open directly are:

- ✔ **dBASE**
- ✔ **Microsoft Access**
- ✔ **MySQL**
- ✔ **Oracle**

Base can connect to these and other networked databases using JDBC, ODBC, and ADO. Base can also create databases from the following:

- ✔ **Address books:**
  - • **Mozilla**
  - • **LDAP**

- • **Microsoft Outlook**

- • **Windows Address Book**

✔ **Spreadsheets:** Base can input data from spreadsheets but cannot write to spreadsheets like it can to databases.

✔ **Text files:** When data is organized in a specific way in a text file, Base can read it as though it were in a simple database.

To connect to any of the preceding databases, or address books, spreadsheets, or text files, you need first to register the database, address book, or text file with Base. That basically means telling Base what type of database it is and how to connect to it. For more information on registering databases, see Chapter 8.

Creating a New Database

To create a new database, follow these steps:

1. **Start OpenOffice.org Base by either:**

- • **Choosing Start➪OpenOffice.org 2.0 Base.**

- • **Or, if you are in any other module of OpenOffice.org, choosing File➪New➪Database.**

The Database Wizard appears, as shown in Figure 7-1.

Figure 7-1:
The
Database
Wizard.

2. **Choose Create a new database and click Next.**

   The Save and Proceed step of the Database Wizard appears.

3. **If you want to be able to access your database from OpenOffice.org Writer (for Mail Merges and so on) or OpenOffice.org Calc, click Yes, register the database for me.**

   You can always register your new database later, if you want, but why not do it automatically now?

4. **Click Open the Database for Editing and click Finish.**

   (You can click Create Tables Using the Table Wizard, but either way is fine because starting the Table Wizard is simple, too.) The Save As dialog box appears.

5. **Give your database a name in the File Name input box and open the folder that you want it to reside in (anywhere is fine) and click Save.**

   The Base window opens as shown in Figure 7-2. This is where you can choose what mode you want to work in: Tables, Queries, Forms, or Reports. Just click one of the four buttons on the left. Any existing tables, queries, forms, or reports are listed in the pane below the Tasks pane.

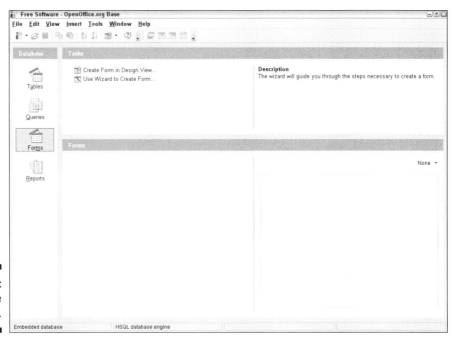

Figure 7-2:
The Base
window.

Setting up your tables

The first thing you need to do after you create a database is create your tables. You can create as many tables as you want and link them together using keys and relations. If your database is going to be extensive and include lots of tables and relationships, you may want to map out everything on paper first.

Base gives you the choice of using the Table Wizard to create your tables, or you can use the Design View to create your tables.

To create a new table using the Table Wizard, you can do the following:

1. **Click on the Tables button on the left side of the database window, shown in Figure 7-2. Then click on the Use Wizard to Create Table link.**

   The Table Wizard appears, as shown in Figure 7-3.

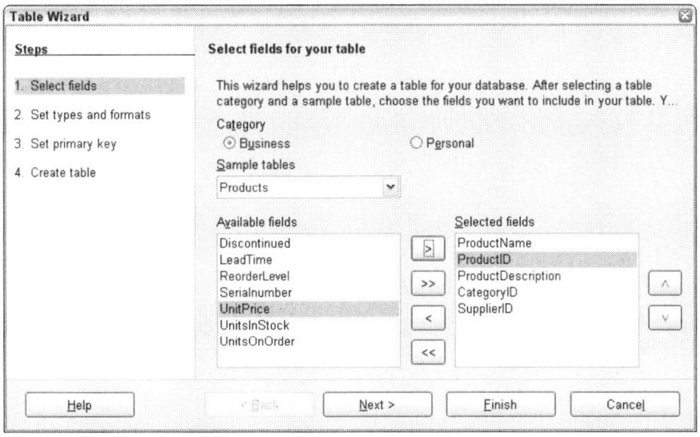

Figure 7-3:
The Select
Fields
window of
the Table
Wizard.

2. **Choose a category, either Business or Personal, and choose a table from the Sample Tables list box.**

   Choose a table with fields similar to what you want your table to contain. For example, I chose Business as a Category and Products as a sample table, because I wanted to make a table of the available free software, which is like a product.

   The available fields are listed in the Available fields list box.

3. **Select a field that you want in your table, and click the right arrow button.**

   The field appears in the Selected fields list box.

4. Repeat step 3 for all the fields that you want in your table.

5. Make sure the order of the fields in the Selected fields list box is how you want them to appear in the database. If you want to reorder them, select a field and click the up arrow or down arrow button.

The field moves up or down in the Selected fields list.

6. Click Next.

The Set field types and formats dialog box of the Table Wizard appears, as shown in Figure 7-4.

Figure 7-4:
The Set field types and formats window of the Table Wizard.

7. In the Set field types and formats window, you can customize your fields by selecting a field in the Selected fields list and doing any of the following:

- **Rename the field** by clicking in the name on the right and typing a new name.

- **Choose a new Field Type** from the Field Type list box.

- **Choose Yes or No from the Entry Required list box.** (If your field is a key, this needs to be Yes.)

- **Type a new length in the Length box.** (This is the maximum length of the field.)

- **Add a field** by clicking the plus sign button.

- **Delete a field** by selecting the field you want to delete and clicking the minus sign button.

- **To change the position of the field in the table**, select it and choose the up arrow or down arrow to move it through the Selected fields list box.

8. **Repeat step 7 until all your fields are just as you want them; then click Next.**

   The Set primary key window of the Table Wizard appears, as shown in Figure 7-5.

Figure 7-5:
The Set primary key window of the Table Wizard.

9. **If you want to assign a primary key to your table, select the Create a primary key check box. This option gives you three choices:**

   • **Choose Automatically add a primary key** if you want Base to insert a new field for the primary key.

   • **Choose Use an existing field as a primary key.** Now you're talking! This is the normal procedure. Select the field that you want to establish as your primary key. (If you want Base to automatically generate data in the field, select the Auto value check box.)

   • **Choose Define primary key as a combination of several fields.** For example, with this option you could choose the LastName, FirstName, and MiddleInitial fields to serve as your primary key. This option can come in handy.

10. **Click Next.**

    The Create Table window of the Table Wizard appears.

11. **Type a name for your table into the input box, and under What do you want to do next?, choose one of the following:**

    • **Insert data immediately** opens a spreadsheet-like window for you to insert data into your fields.

    • **Modify the table design** opens a Design View window for you to modify your table.

- **Create a form based on this table** opens the Form Wizard, if you want to create a form immediately.

If you want to further modify your table, then instead of clicking the Modify the table design button, you can choose step 1, 2, or 3 from the list of steps on the left side of the Table Wizard.

12. **Click Finish.**

    Your table is created and one of three windows opens, depending on what option you chose in step 11.

If you end up either in Table Design View or in a window that allows you to enter your data, you can close them by clicking on the close box to get back to the main Base window. You can also choose the name of your database from the window menu.

Designing and using forms

Base offers you the choice of entering data into cells like a spreadsheet or the more traditional way of entering data into a database by using forms. Forms have the advantage that you can enter data from more than one table into the same form and it will be saved in the proper table. Also, the appearance of forms is more appealing than a spreadsheet. It allows you to focus just on the current record without having data of other records clutter your window.

The example that follows uses two tables I created: the Products table (which I created previously) and a Categories table. The Categories table just has a Categories-ID field (which is the primary key) and a CategoryName field.

To create a form, you can do the following:

1. **In the Base window, shown earlier in Figure 7-2, click the Forms button.**

   The Tasks pane changes to include two links: Create Form in Design View and Use Wizard to Create Form.

2. **Click Use Wizard to Create Form.**

   The Form Wizard appears, as shown in Figure 7-6.

3. **Select the table that you want to use for your form from the Tables or queries list box.**

   The fields of the table appear in the Available fields list box.

4. **Select a field that you want in your form, click the right arrow button, and repeat until all the fields that you want are in the Fields in the form list. If you want all the fields in your form, click the double right arrow button; all the fields move to the Fields in the form list.**

Figure 7-6:
The Form
Wizard.

5. Click Next.

The Set up a subform window of the Form Wizard appears.

6. If you want to add fields that are in a different table into your form, select the Add subform check box and click Next.

The Add subfield fields window of the Form Wizard appears.

7. Choose the table for your subform from the Tables or queries list, select a field, and click the right arrow for each field that you want in your form. Click Next.

8. Select the fields that will join your tables together from each table. Click Next.

For example, I chose Category ID, as shown in Figure 7-7, because it's the key of the Categories table, and it exists in the Products table. When you click Next, the Arrange Controls window appears.

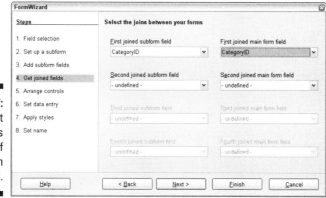

Figure 7-7:
The Get
joined fields
window of
the Form
Wizard.

9. **Select an arrangement for your form and subform from the four options and click Next.**

   The Set data entry window appears.

10. **Choose how this form is to be used by doing the following:**

    • **If you want to just add new records and not see any old records**, click the button for The form is to be used for entering new data only.

    • **Otherwise**, click The form is to display all data button.

11. **If you chose to display all data, select any of the following:**

    • **Do not allow modification of existing data.** If you select this option, you can view all the forms, but you can't change any existing form, just new ones.

    • **Do not allow deletion of existing data.** This option prevents you from deleting any existing records.

    • **Do not allow addition of new data.** Select this option if you want to prevent new records from being added.

12. **Click Next.**

    The Apply Styles window of the Form Wizard appears.

13. **Click on any of the styles in the Apply Styles list, and the background changes accordingly. You can also choose a 3D look, Flat look, or No Border. Click Next.**

    The Set name window of the Form Wizard appears.

14. **Enter a name for your form.**

    For example, I chose Enter Products as a name.

15. **Choose either Work with the form or Modify the form.**

    If you want to modify the form, you can do it right in the Form Wizard by clicking on one of the steps on the left side of the dialog box and changing whatever you want.

16. **Click Finish.**

    Your form may appear automatically, or it may be listed in the Database window ready for you to double-click and use. Figure 7-8 shows an example of a form created using the Form Wizard.

To use your form, click on the form button in the database window; then double-click on the Form name in the Forms section. The Form appears. You can do the following with the form:

✔ **Enter data into the form,** if you want, and if you specified that you could enter data into it in the Form Wizard.

✔ **Save the form,** by clicking the Save button on the Form Navigation bar, as shown in Figure 7-8.

✔ **Navigate through your records,** by clicking the arrow buttons on the Form Navigation bar, or typing in a record number in the Record input box.

✔ **Sort your records,** by clicking one of the Sort buttons on the Navigation bar.

✔ **Delete a record,** by clicking the Delete button on the Navigation bar.

✔ **Insert a new record,** by clicking the New Record button on the Navigation bar.

✔ **Refresh your records,** by clicking the Refresh button on the Navigation bar. You can use this to view all the forms, if people other than you are entering records at the same time.

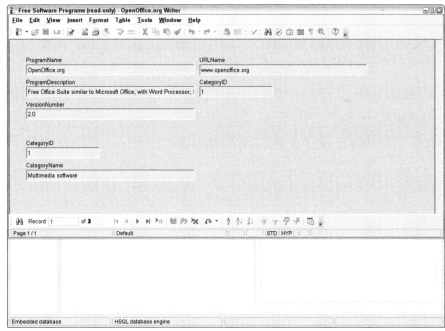

Figure 7-8: A form created by the Form Wizard.

Querying your database

Queries are subsets of the data in your tables that you can use to view forms or write reports. Queries can be simple, extremely complex, or anything in between. For example, I created a simple query for the Free Software database to show me only records having the Category ID of 3, which is free multimedia software.

To query your database, you can do the following:

1. **In the Database window, shown in Figure 7-2, click the Queries button.**

   The Tasks pane changes to include three tasks:

   - **Create Query in Design View:** Select this option if you're familiar with Design View, and prefer this method of querying.

   - **Use Wizard to Create Query:** Select this option for an easy way to create a wide variety of powerful queries.

   - **Create Query in SQL View:** Select this option for advanced queries written in SQL (a programming query language for database programmers).

   Also, any previously created queries are listed in the Queries pane.

2. **Click the Use Wizard to Create Query link.**

   The Query Wizard appears, as shown in Figure 7-9.

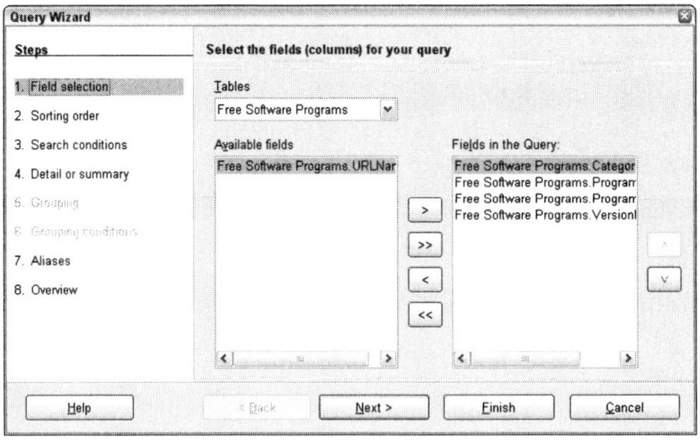

Figure 7-9:
The Base
Query
Wizard.

3. **Select the table that you want to include in your query, select the fields that you want to use one by one, and click the right arrow to move them from the Available fields list to the Fields in the Query list.**

4. **If you want to re-order your fields in the Fields in the Query list, you can click on a field and click the up or down arrow to move any field up or down in the list.**

5. **Click Next.**

   The Sorting order window of the Query Wizard appears.

6. **Choose the first field that you want to sort on from the drop-down list and indicate whether you want to sort ascending or descending. Then repeat if you want more sort fields. Click Next.**

   The Search conditions window appears, as shown in Figure 7-10. This is where you specify your query.

Figure 7-10:
The Search conditions window of the Query Wizard.

7. **Choose a field from the Fields drop-down list, choose a condition from the Condition drop-down list, and type a value in the Value input box. Repeat up to two times for each condition you want to set. If you set more than one condition, select either Match all of the following or Match any of the following, near the top of the window. Click Next.**

   For example, I wanted a query of just the free multimedia software, so I chose Category ID as the Field, Is Equal To as the Condition, and typed 3 into the Value text box, because that is my code for Multimedia. (A query is similar to the Standard Filter in Calc that is discussed in Chapter 5.) When you click Next, the Select the type of query window appears.

8. **Choose one of the following:**

   • **Detailed Query:** Choose this option to show all of your records. Unless you're doing accounting, this option is probably what you want; click Next and go to step 10.

   • **Summary Query:** If you have fields with numeric values, such as currency values, you can choose this option to generate subtotals for categories. Choose the Function (Sum, Average, Minimum, or Maximum) and a field. Repeat for as many functions as you want; then click Next.

9. **If you chose Summary Query in step 8,** do the following:

   1. In the Grouping window, choose the fields one by one that you want to group by in the Available fields list, and click the arrow button to move them to the Group By list box. Click Next.

   2. Select your grouping condition in the Grouping conditions window, which is similar to what you perform in step 7. Click Next.

10. **If you want to change your field names to something different, just for the sake of the query, type a new field name in the Alias text boxes for any field. Click Next.**

    The Overview window appears.

    If you want to modify your query, click on any of the steps in the left pane of the Query Wizard to return to them and modify them.

11. **Choose how you want to proceed after finishing the query by choosing either Display Query or Modify Query (which opens the Query Design View).**

12. **Change the name of your query in the Name of Query text box, if you want.**

13. **Click Finish.**

Chapter 8

Creating Reports from Your Database

· ·

In This Chapter

▶ Generating reports with your database using the Report Wizard

▶ Registering your database, address book, or spreadsheet

▶ Defining tables in spreadsheets

▶ Mail merging

· ·

*O*penOffice.org lets you access and enter data from many different kinds of data sources, including the following:

✔ **Databases:** Such as Base, dBASE, MySQL, Microsoft Access, and Oracle.

✔ **Address books:** Microsoft Outlook, Mozilla Thunderbird, and many other mail clients.

✔ **Spreadsheets and text files:** These can be accessed by Base in read-only format.

It also gives you the ability to use the data from the databases or other data sources in many ways. In this chapter we discuss two major ways of using your database information:

✔ Generate reports from your data sources using the Report Wizard. I describe how in this chapter.

✔ Create form letters using OpenOffice.org Writer and merge data, such as names and addresses, into the letters. Find out how in the later "Mail Merging" section.

Generating Reports Using the Report Wizard

Generally, creating a report using the Report Wizard consists of three steps (which are explained in detail in the following sections):

1. **Register your database, address book, or spreadsheet.**

   You need to tell OpenOffice.org what kind of database it is, or whether it's an e-mail address book or spreadsheet, and where it is located (see the following section).

2. **Create a query.**

   This step is optional and described in Chapter 7. If you want to use a subset of the records in any table of your database, address book, or spreadsheet, you need to create a query, which is like a new table generated by Base that contains the fields and records you want in your report.

3. **Create your report using the Report Wizard.**

   The Report Wizard leads you step by step through the process of creating reports, as described later in the section "Creating a report using the report wizard."

Registering your database, address book, or spreadsheet

OpenOffice.org Base lets you register a database, address book, or spreadsheet, so that the data in it is available to be used or even updated using OpenOffice.org Writer, Calc, or Base. For example, you may want to use Writer to do mail merges, Calc to add your data to a spreadsheet, or Base to use the Form Wizard, Query Wizard, or Report Wizard. Any database that you created using Base is probably already registered, as long as you did not specify not to register it when you created it. If you register a spreadsheet, the data in it is in read-only format when being used as a data source.

To use a registered database in Base, just open it and it opens in Base. To access it in Calc or Writer, click the Data Sources button on the Standard toolbar; then navigate through your databases, tables and queries by clicking the plus and minus signs in the list of databases, queries and tables. The buttons on the Data Source toolbar allow you to sort, filter, find, cut, copy and more similar to a Calc spreadsheet,

To register a database, spreadsheet, or address, follow these steps:

1. **Start OpenOffice.org Base by either**

    • **Choosing Start⇨OpenOffice.org 2.0 Base.**

    • **Or, if you're in any other module of OpenOffice.org, choosing File⇨New⇨Database.**

    The Database Wizard appears.

2. **Choose Connect to an existing database, and choose the database type from the Database type drop-down menu, as shown in Figure 8-1.**

    Depending on your choice of data source, the steps pane changes to reflect different steps.

    The Mozilla Address Book refers to the other Mozilla mail client and not Mozilla Thunderbird.

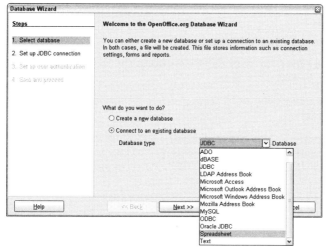

Figure 8-1:
Choose the database type to register a data source.

3. **Click Next.**

    The pane on the right changes, requesting new information. If you selected a database, spreadsheet, or text, the pane changes to requesting information about where it resides. If you selected an address book, OpenOffice.org Base may or may not need any additional information to figure out where it is.

4. **If a pane appears requesting information about the location of your database, spreadsheet, or text file, enter the information or click the Browse button and select the filename. Click Next.**

5. **If the Set Up The User Authentication pane appears, which may occur even if you choose a spreadsheet, you can type the User Name or whatever other information it requests and click the Test Connection button, if one appears.**

   A dialog box appears, informing you that "The connection was established successfully." (I left the User Name blank, and it still worked.) However, if the dialog box indicates otherwise, try a different User Name or other information that it requests and click Test Connection again. You may need to contact the database administrator for the required information to connect to the database.

6. **Click Next.**

   The Save and proceed pane appears.

7. **Be sure that Yes, register the database for me is selected, and click Finish.**

   The Save As dialog box appears.

8. **Type a name for your database, open the folder that you want it to reside in and click Save.**

   This is where you save your queries, forms, and reports, if you want to create any.

   The Base window appears, ready for you to create forms, queries, or reports using the database. Or you can close the Base window and use the registered data source in Writer or Calc.

Creating a report using the Report Wizard

To create a report, you can first create a query, as described in Chapter 7, if you want to use a subset of the data in your table. Alternatively, if you want to include your entire table in the report, you can skip the query and do the following:

 As of this writing, OpenOffice.org Base is still a beta version and the Report wizard does not always work properly. It is scheduled to be completed in a matter of months, but if you need an alternate way to create reports, feel free to create them in OpenoOffice.org Calc. In Calc, click the Data Sources button on the Standard toolbar, then navigate to your query or table. Double-click on the query or table to bring it up in the Data Source view, then you can select the data in your query or table by Shift+clicking the column headings and copy and paste the query or table into your spreadsheet where you can create your report.

For an updated details on the status of the Report wizard, check out
www.infinityeverywhere.net/free.

1. **In the Database window of OpenOffice.org Base, click the Reports button.**

   The Tasks pane changes to include the Use Wizard to Create Report link. Any previously created reports are listed in the Reports pane.

2. **Click the Use Wizard to Create Report link.**

   A new Writer document appears as well as the Report Wizard, as shown in Figure 8-2.

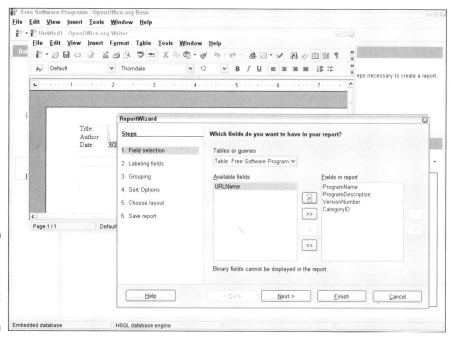

Figure 8-2:
OpenOffice.
org Base's
Report
Wizard.

3. **Select the table or query that you want to include in your report, select the fields that you want to use one by one, and then click the right arrow to move them from the Available fields list to the Fields in report list.**

4. **If you want to re-order your fields in the Fields in report list, you can click on a field and click the up or down arrow to move any field up or down in the list.**

5. **Click Next.**

   The Labeling Fields window of the Report Wizard appears.

6. **Type the labels that you want for your fields in your report, and click Next.**

   The Grouping window of the Report Wizard appears.

7. **Select any field that you want to group your report by, and click the right arrow button to move the field into the Groupings list. Repeat for as many fields as you want to group, and click Next.**

   The Sort options window of the Report Wizard appears.

8. **Choose the fields that you want to sort by and choose either Ascending or Descending. Click Next.**

   The Choose layout window of the Report Wizard appears.

9. **Choose from an assortment of layouts and layouts of headers and footers.**

   When you select any of them, the Writer document behind the Report Wizard changes to reflect the selection. (You may need to increase the size of the Writer window to view the selection fully.)

10. **Click Next.**

    The Save report window of the Report Wizard appears.

11. **Type the main title of your report and choose one of the following:**

    • **Static report:** This kind of report does not change when the data in your database changes.

    • **Dynamic report:** This kind of report changes when you click the Refresh button to reflect any changes in your database.

12. **Click Finish.**

    Your report appears, and every time you want to see the report again, just click on the Reports button in the Base window and click on the name of the report in the Reports pane.

Mail Merging

Mail merging is the process of creating a form, such as a letter that you want to send out to many individuals, and then merging with it the names and addresses of the recipients to personalize the letter. Mail merges are performed in OpenOffice.org Writer, using information from a registered database. Creating a mail merge has four steps:

1. **If you want to put your names and addresses or other information in a spreadsheet, you can follow the instructions in the next section. (Otherwise, you can use any data source that you can register using**

the instructions found earlier in this chapter.) If you want to select a subset of your data, whether in a spreadsheet, address book, or database, you can create a query, as described in Chapter 7 and use that to generate your mail merge.

2. **Register your database, spreadsheet, or address book.**

   This is described earlier in the section "Registering your database, address book, or spreadsheet."

3. **Create a form letter.**

   You can create any kind of document you want. Don't be concerned with inserting any fields when you first create your document. Just leave some space where you want the names and addresses to go or for whatever fields you plan to use from your database. Then insert your fields into the form letter, as described later in the "Creating a form letter" section.

4. **Perform the mail merge.**

Creating a spreadsheet for your mail merge

Choose File➪New➪Spreadsheet to open up OpenOffice.org Calc. For your mail merge, you have the choice of having a single table in your spreadsheet or multiple tables.

✓ **To create a spreadsheet with a single table to be used as a data source,** you can put your column headings in Row 1, and Base will register the entire spreadsheet as a single table.

✓ **To create a spreadsheet with more than one table to be used as a data source,** you create your tables anywhere in the spreadsheet, and name them using Data➪Define Range to define the name of your table, as described in the next set of steps.

To define the name of your tables to be used as data sources, perform these steps:

1. **Select a table in your spreadsheet, including the column headings.**

2. **Choose Data➪Define Range.**

   The Define Database Range dialog box appears, as shown in Figure 8-3.

3. **Type a name for your table.**

4. **Click More.**

   The Define Database Range dialog box expands.

5. **If you want the defined range of your table to grow or shrink as you insert or delete rows, select Insert or Delete Cells.**

6. **Click OK.**

Repeat these steps for each table you want to name. Then register the spreadsheet using the above instructions, "Registering your database, address book, or spreadsheet."

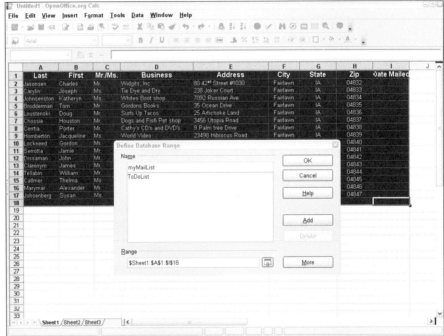

Figure 8-3:
You can use the Define Database Range dialog box to name tables, which is handy when using your spreadsheet as a data source.

Creating the form letter

To create a form letter, you can do the following:

1. **In OpenOffice.org Writer, type the content of the letter and leave space for where you want names, addresses, and whatever other fields you want to add from your data sources.**

   An example of a form letter is shown in Figure 8-4.

2. **Choose View⇨Data Sources.**

   The Data Source pane appears. You can adjust the pane with the list of data sources by clicking and dragging to the right of the scroll bar to expand or contract the width of the data source list box.

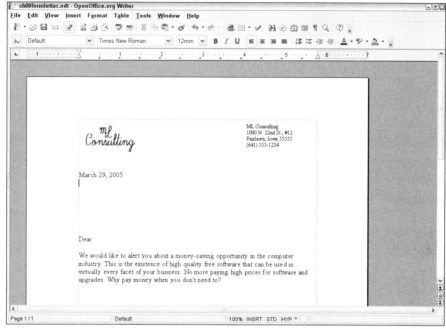

Figure 8-4:
To perform a
mail merge,
first create
a form letter
with blanks
where you
want to
insert fields.

3. Click the plus sign next to the data source containing the table that you need for your mail merge.

Two items appear beneath the data source name: Queries and Tables.

4. If your mail merge data resides in Queries, click the plus sign to view the names of the queries. If you did not create any queries and your mail merge data is in a table, click the plus sign next to Tables to view the names of the tables.

The names of the tables that you defined in your spreadsheet or created in your database, or that you are accessing from a database, spreadsheet, or address book, are listed.

5. Click the name of the table containing your data.

The table of data appears in your Data Source View, as shown in Figure 8-5.

6. Drag the Column Headings one by one to the locations that you want them to appear in the form letter. You can add text or spaces or punctuation before or after the headings.

The column headings appear in the document where you drag them. They appear shaded, as shown in Figure 8-6.

7. Choose File⇨Save to save your document.

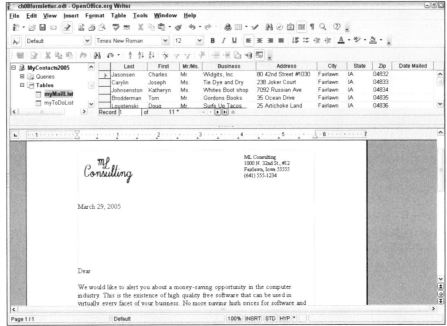

Figure 8-5:
The Data
Source
View and
form letter
ready to
insert fields.

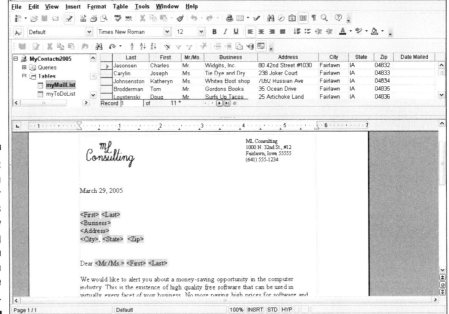

Figure 8-6:
A form
letter
with fields
inserted by
dragging
them from
the Data
Source
View.

Generating the mail merge

You have the choice of printing the letters or saving them to a file. To merge your letters with your data source, you can perform the following steps:

1. **Choose Tools⇨Mail Merge Wizard.**

   The Mail Merge Wizard appears, as shown in Figure 8-7. Yes, OpenOffice. org has a Mail Merge Wizard, but in its current incarnation I believe it's more trouble than it's worth, and the way I describe to perform a mail merge is easier, as well as more flexible.

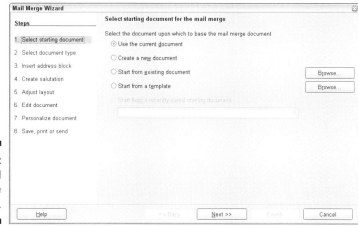

Figure 8-7:
The Mail
Merge
Wizard.

2. **Be sure that the Use the current document radio button is selected (this is the default). Click Next.**

   The Select a document type pane appears.

3. **In the Steps panel, click the link for 8. Save, print, or send.**

   Yes, we are going to bypass most of the Mail Merge Wizard. If you want, you can check it out on your own. You may decide it's perfect for you.

   A Mail Merge window appears, displaying the status of your mail merge, and disappears when your mail merge is complete. The Save, Print, or Send pane appears in the Mail Merge Wizard.

4. **To save your merged document as a single document, click Save Merged Document.**

   The Save Merged Document Settings pane appears.

5. **Choose one of the following:**

   • **Save as a Single Document:** This option saves each letter as a new page in a single document.

   • **Save as Individual Documents:** This option automatically appends a number to the end of the filename and increments it for every letter it saves.

   • **From:** This option also saves each letter as an individual document. Type in the starting page number and ending page number to save only that specific range of pages.

6. **Click the Save Document button.**

   The Save As dialog box appears.

7. **Open the folder where you want your document to reside, fill in a File Name, and click Save.**

   Your mail merge file appears, as shown in the example in Figure 8-8. It is saved and ready to print whenever it's convenient for you. You can also edit it however you like.

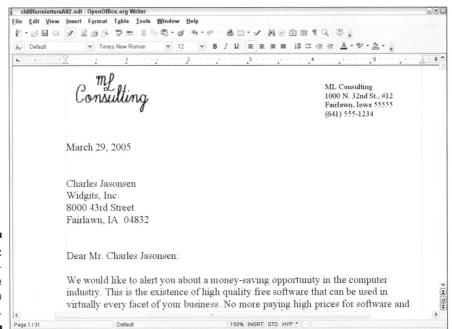

Figure 8-8:
A mail-merged file ready to print.

Part III

Exploring the Internet — More Easily, More Securely, and More Featurefully

The 5th Wave   By Rich Tennant

"You should check that box so they can't profile your listening and viewing habits. I didn't do it and I'm still getting spam about hearing loss, anger management and psychological counseling."

In this part . . .

In this part, we explore the reasons why Mozilla Firefox is gaining market share in the Internet browser market on a daily basis since its release in Fall 2004: because it offers greater security than Internet Explorer, the current leading Internet browser, and because it offers a full range of great features. Using Firefox, you can access a menu of search engines, including Google, right in the browser window. You also have easy RSS integration, as well as a super Find feature. Chapter 9 describes in detail the features of Mozilla Firefox and how to use them.

Mozilla Thunderbird is another remarkable newcomer to the Internet scene. Chapter 10 explores this e-mail program that is top-rated for its greater security and leading-edge features, such as an intelligent junk mail filter, a smart address book, RSS integration, and more.

If you want to create your own Web pages, you may want to check out the HTML editor in OpenOffice.org Writer. You can design your own look, add graphics, create links, or if you want to publish your Writer documents, you can use the Web wizard to publish them automatically for you.

One of the newest innovations to affect the Web is the portable media player, such as the iPod, that you can load with music downloaded from the Internet and play wherever you like. Chapter 12 describes how to subscribe to podcasts using iPodder and hear them on your computer's media player. And Chapter 13 tells how to transform your computer into a phone using Skype. You can use Skype to talk over the Internet for free with crystal clear reception. You can even have conference calls with up to four computers (and people, too).

Chapter 9

Surfing and Searching the Web with Mozilla Firefox

* *

* *

*O*nly 100 days after it was released, Mozilla Firefox was downloaded 25 million times and gained 4.8 percent of the market share for Internet Web browsers, compared to Internet Explorer's 92.7 percent.

People are jumping on the Firefox bandwagon for many reasons, among them that Firefox was designed from the start with security in mind and has security features unmatched by its peers. Firefox is designed to disallow Web sites from downloading, installing, or executing programs on your computer without your permission. Firefox also gives you more privacy by blocking pop-up ads, if you want them blocked, allowing you to surf the Web without annoying and time-consuming commercials.

Firefox is trim and fast and offers great features, such as tabbed browsing, Google search (and other search engines) in the toolbar, RSS news feed integration, and easy downloading, as well as all the basic features of any Web browser. In this chapter, I explain how to use the many of the latest Web browsing features that Firefox offers.

Using Tabs, Bookmarks, and Other Basics

To use Firefox, you first need to download and install the program, as described in Chapter 1. To navigate to a Web site, type the address in the input box, shown in Figure 9-1, and press Return (or Enter, depending on your keyboard).

For Web sites with addresses ending in .com, you can type just the name of the site, such as **yahoo** or **google**, and press Return. Firefox automatically adds the `http://www.` in the beginning and the `.com` at the end.

You can increase or decrease the size of the text by pressing Ctrl++ or Ctrl+- (or ⌘++ or ⌘+- for the Mac). Firefox increases and decreases the text size at smaller increments than most other mail clients, giving you lots of control over the size of text that you view.

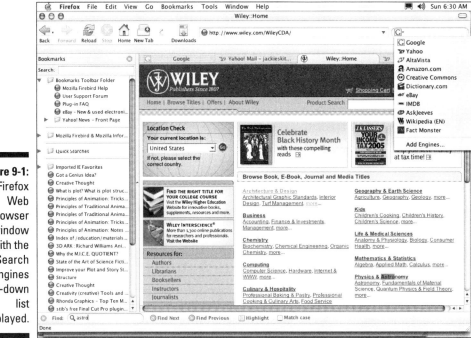

Figure 9-1:
The Firefox Web browser window with the Search Engines drop-down list displayed.

Using tabs for convenience

If you want to open more than one Web page at a time, you have the choice of opening them as windows or as tabs. Tabs are very handy because they don't clutter up your computer screen like a bunch of open windows do. The names of the pages appear on tabs on the bar above the viewing pane, as shown in Figure 9-1. You can click on a tab to view the page instantly.

Here are some instructions for using tabs:

- **To open a new tab,** press Ctrl+T (⌘+T for Mac) or choose File⪤New Tab; a new blank tab appears.

- **To open a link in a new tab,** right-click the link and choose Open Link in New Tab. If you have a three-button mouse, you can middle-click the link.

- **To open the next tab,** on Windows and Mac, press Ctrl+Tab.

- **To close a tab,** right-click on the tab and choose Close Tab, or click on the tab (if it is not already your current tab) and choose File⪤Close Tab.

- **To reload a tab,** right-click on the tab and choose Reload Tab, or click on the tab (if it is not already your current tab) and click the Reload button, shown in Figure 9-1.

Bookmarking

Bookmarks help you remember the location of Web pages that you've visited, and they also let you go there fast, without having to type in a long and cryptic URL. You can add bookmarks one at a time, or bookmark all the tabs in a window at once. You can organize your bookmarks into folders and find them easily from the Bookmark menu. If you imported bookmarks from Internet Explorer when you installed Firefox, they will be in a folder called Imported IE Favorites.

Finding and using bookmarks

To use your bookmarks most efficiently, you probably want to first view them in a sidebar, shown in Figure 9-1. You can view your bookmarks in a sidebar by choosing View⪤Sidebar⪤Bookmarks or pressing Ctrl+B (or ⌘+B for the Mac).

In the sidebar, you can do the following:

- **Scroll through your bookmarks** and open and close folders by clicking on their disclosure triangles

- **Open the page in the current tab or window** by clicking on the bookmark

✔ **Search your bookmarks** by entering a search criteria in the Search box

✔ **Resize the sidebar** by clicking and dragging its right-hand border

✔ **Close the sidebar** by clicking the Close button at the top right of the sidebar

Creating bookmarks one at a time or for all tabs at once

To create a bookmark for your current page, or for all the tabs in your window, follow these steps:

1. **Choose Bookmarks⇨Bookmark this page.**

   The Add Bookmarks dialog box appears. The Name input box automatically lists the title of the page. You can change this name, if you want to, which may be instructive if the title of the page is something exciting like "Welcome."

2. **Select the folder that you want the bookmark to reside in from the Create In drop-down list. Or if you want to create a new folder, click the Show All The Bookmark Folders button (the triangle button).**

   If you clicked the Show All The Bookmark Folders button, then the dialog box expands, as shown in Figure 9-2.

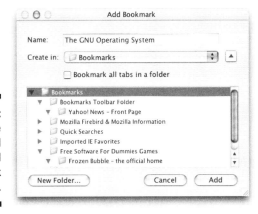

Figure 9-2: The expanded Add Bookmark dialog box.

3. **If you want to add a new folder, click the New Folder button, type a folder name, and click OK.**

4. **If you have more than one tab open in your Web browser window and you want to bookmark all those tabs and place them in the folder that**

you selected or created, select the Bookmark all tabs in a folder check box.

5. Click Add.

Your bookmark (or bookmarks) is added to the folder that you specified.

Managing your bookmarks

The Bookmark Manager lets you organize your bookmarks in the most functional way for you. To open the Bookmark Manager, choose Bookmarks⇨ Manage Bookmarks. In the Bookmarks Manager, as shown in Figure 9-3, you can do the following:

- ✔ **Reorganize your bookmarks into different folders:** Select the bookmark, click the Move button, select the folder, and click OK.

- ✔ **Give your bookmarks different names or assign them searchable keywords:** Select the bookmark, click the Rename button, and change the bookmark's name in the dialog box or type in a keyword and click OK.

- ✔ **Create new folders:** Click the New Folder button and type the name of the folder and a description, if you want, and click OK.

- ✔ **Create new separators:** Select the bookmark or folder below where you want a new separator to appear and click New Separator.

- ✔ **Delete bookmarks (or separators):** Select the bookmark or separator and click the Delete button.

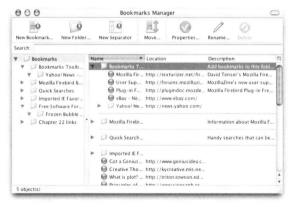

Figure 9-3:
The
Bookmarks
Manager.

Seeing and searching your History

Firefox remembers your visited pages for a certain number of days, and you can increase or decrease this number of days by choosing Tools⇨Options

(Windows) or Firefox⇨Preferences (Macintosh) or Edit⇨Preferences (GNU/Linux), clicking on the Privacy button, expanding the plus sign (Windows) or disclosure triangle (Macintosh) beside History, and typing in a new number. Firefox allows you to do the following with your History:

- ✔ **View the History in a sidebar** on the left side of your browser window, shown in Figure 9-4, by choosing Go⇨History.

- ✔ **Resize the History sidebar** by dragging its right border to make it wider or narrower.

- ✔ **Sort the History** by Date and Site, by Date, by Site, by Most Visited, and by Last Visited by choosing the appropriate option from the View drop-down menu on the History sidebar.

- ✔ **Search the History** by entering your search criteria in the Search box. (To see your entire history again, just delete what's in the Search box.)

- ✔ **Close the History sidebar** by clicking the Close button at the top right of the side bar.

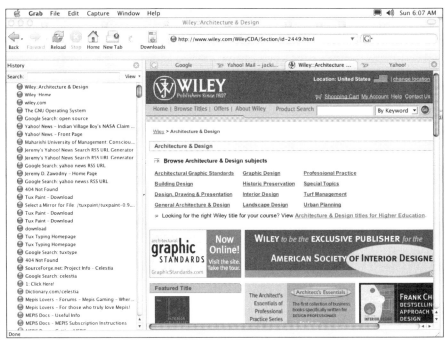

Figure 9-4:
You can view, sort, and search your History in a sidebar.

Setting Your Preferences

Firefox has many preferences that you can set to configure your Web browser the way you want it to work. To open the Preferences dialog box, choose Tools➪Options (Windows) or Firefox➪Preferences (Macintosh) or Edit➪ Preferences (GNU/Linux). The dialog box appears, as shown in Figure 9-5. Some of the preferences you can set are as follows:

- ✓ **Select your home page:** See the instructions later in this section.

- ✓ **Select your language:** Click the General button, then click the Languages button, select your language from the drop-down list of countless languages (24 beginning with A alone!), and click OK.

- ✓ **Blocking or selectively allowing pop-ups:** See the instructions later in this section.

- ✓ **Assign the location for your downloads:** Click the Downloads button, choose either Ask me where to save every file or Save all files to this folder, and select the folder.

- ✓ **Choose whether you want to view the Download Manager:** Click the Downloads button and select either, neither, or both of the following: Show Download Manager window when a download begins or Close the Download Manager when all downloads are complete.

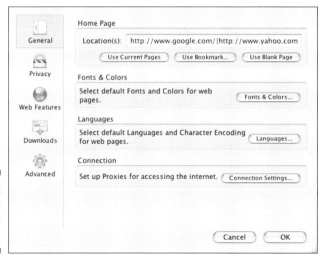

Figure 9-5:
Firefox's
Preferences
dialog box.

Assigning your home page or home pages

When you start up Firefox, you may want it to automatically open a particular page, such as the main page for Google or Yahoo!. Or you may want several pages to open in their own tabs all at once. To specify the page or pages that you want Firefox to open when you start Firefox, do the following:

1. **Open the page or pages that you want Firefox to open with.**

2. **Choose Tools⇨Options (Windows) or Firefox⇨Preferences (Macintosh) or Edit⇨Preferences (GNU/Linux) and click the General tab.**

   The General tab appears as shown in Figure 9-5. In the Location(s) input box is the address (or addresses) of the current page (or pages) that Firefox automatically loads when starting up.

3. **Choose one of the following:**

   • **Use Current Pages:** When you start Firefox, all the pages in the current browser window will appear in tabs (or a single window, if there is only one Web page in the current browser window).

   • **Use Bookmark:** A dialog box displaying your bookmarks appears, from which you can select a bookmark. (If you choose a folder, every address in that folder opens as a separate tab.)

   • **Use Blank Page.**

4. **Click OK.**

   Your home page or pages are now assigned. Feel free to change them as often as you want.

Getting rid of annoying pop-ups (and keeping the good pop-ups)

Some pop-up windows may be ads, whereas other pop-up windows may contain useful information. For this reason, Firefox gives you the flexibility to allow pop-up windows to appear from some sites, but not from others. Also, Firefox informs you with an icon (shaped like an exclamation point) in the bottom right of your window, as shown in Figure 9-6, when a Web site wants to send you a pop-up window. You can choose to allow it to do so or simply ignore the icon.

To block pop-ups, except for selected sites, follow these steps:

1. **Choose Tools⇨Options (Windows) or Firefox⇨Preferences (Macintosh) or Edit⇨Preferences (GNU/Linux) and click the Web Features button.**

2. **In the Options dialog box (Windows) or Preferences dialog box (GNU/Linux), be sure that the Block Popup Windows check box is selected.**

3. **If you want to allow pop-ups for some sites, do one of the following:**

   • Click the Allowed Sites button and in the Allowed Sites dialog box that appears, type the address of the site whose pop-ups you want to allow, click the Allow button, and click OK.

   • Click OK; then while you're surfing, if the Change Popup Blocking Settings For This Web Site button appears in the far right of the bottom bar of your browser, as shown in Figure 9-6, you can click on it and choose Allow Pop-ups for (*the name of the Web site*).

Figure 9-6:
The Change
Popup
Blocking
Settings for
This Web
Site button.

Change Pop-up Blocking Settings For This Web Site button

Installing and Using Search Plug-ins

Firefox comes with several search engines accessible right on the Navigation toolbar, as shown earlier in Figure 9-1. Click and hold down the disclosure triangle in the Search input box on the right of the Navigation toolbar, and a menu drops down with a list of search engines, such as Google, Yahoo!, Amazon.com, eBay, and more. Choose a search engine and type what you want to search for. Firefox responds with your search results.

Many search engines exist, and you can add them into your list by following these steps:

1. **Click the disclosure triangle in the Search input box on the Navigation toolbar, and choose Add Engines.**

Firefox loads a page at the Mozilla site listing eight more search engines, plus a Find Lots Of Other Search Engines link. The eight search engines are:

- **A9 Search:** Amazon's Web and shopping search.

- **AltaVista:** An Internet search engine similar to Google.

- **Ask Jeeves:** You ask questions and Jeeves responds.

- **CDDB:** Songs, albums, and artists search engine.

- **LEO:** Translates English to German.

- **IMDB:** The Internet Movie Database.

- **Merriam-Webster:** English dictionary search.

- **Wikipedia:** The fabulous, free encyclopedia that anyone can edit.

2. **Click on one of the search engine links.**

   A dialog box appears, asking whether you want to add the search engine link to your Search bar.

3. **Click OK.**

4. **Repeat steps 3-4 for as many search engines as you want to add.**

5. **If you want to find more search engines, click the Find Lots Of Other Search Engines link.**

   Under the heading Browse By Categories are the following links (and the number in each category, as of this writing).

- Arts (61)
     - Literature (26)
     - Music (55)
- Business and Economy (26)
- Classified (10)
- Computer (155)
     - File Sharing (19)
     - Mozilla (10)
     - Programming (38)
- General (283)
- Health (13)
- Kids and Teens (6)

- News (46)
     - Tech News (19)
- Recreation (8)
     - Games (28)
     - Travel (9)
- Reference (66)
     - Academic (64)
- Language dictionary (154)
- Shopping (154)
     - Auction (24)
     - Society (5)
     - Religion (21)
     - Weblogs (11)
- Undefined (27)

6. **Click on a link, click on the search engine that you want, and click OK from the dialog box that appears.**

    Each search engine that you click on gets added to your Search list when you click OK.

Turbo-searching in Firefox

Firefox's Find feature is so unique (to me anyway) that it made me laugh the first time I used it. It lets you know right away with an alert beep when what you are typing is not in the document. This feature lets you refine your search even before you finish typing it! And that saves you from a lot of frustration by making sure you'll be successful at finding what you want — at least, if it exists.

To use Firefox's Find feature, perform the following steps:

1. **Choose Edit⇨Find In This Page.**

    The Find toolbar appears at the bottom of the Firefox window, as shown in Figure 9-1.

2. **Type what you're searching for in the Find input box.**

    If you start typing a word and the input box turns red and an alert beep sounds, then you know right away that the word is not in the Web page. Press Backspace to delete letters until the box is white again, and try another word or words to search.

3. **Select one of the following search criteria, if you want.**

    • **Select Match Case** to match the uppercase and lowercase of the letters as well as the words themselves.

    • **Select Highlight** if you want every instance of the word highlighted and not just the first instance.

4. **Click Find Next to find the next instance of what you entered in the Find input box, or click Find Previous to find the previous instance.**

5. **To search another Web page with the same search criteria, open the Web page in a new tab. The Find toolbar remains at the bottom of the window. Click Find Next.**

    To close the Find toolbar, click the Close button on the left of the Find toolbar.

Reading RSS News Feeds with Live Bookmarks

Firefox lets you view current news headlines or other RSS feed headlines in your Bookmarks sidebar, which you can click on to load the page with the full article. These bookmarks are called "Live" because they change as the headlines change, in Yahoo News, for instance. And you follow only a few simple steps to create the live bookmarks that you want.

To create an RSS news feed, follow these steps:

1. **Go to a site from which you want to get an RSS feed, such as** news.yahoo.com **or** news.bbc.co.uk.

   If an RSS feed is available for the site, an orange Add Live Bookmark button appears at the bottom-right corner of your browser window, as shown in Figure 9-7.

Figure 9-7:
The Add Live Bookmark button.

Add Live Bookmark button

2. **Click the Add Live Bookmark button and choose Subscribe To RSS from the pop-up menu. Choose the folder where you want the news feed located (the Bookmarks Toolbar folder might be a good place). Click Add.**

   A folder is created in the Bookmarks Toolbar folder (or whatever folder you chose in this step). In the folder are the headlines from the Web page listed as bookmarks for you. Clicking on the bookmark takes you to the Web page of the link. The bookmarks get automatically updated as the original Web page gets updated.

RSS is an extremely powerful tool. You can search the Web not only for news, but practically anything. You can look for jobs, keep up to date on your favorite blogs, or find the latest bargains. Whatever your interests, probably several RSS feeds exist that you'll appreciate.

RSS feeds are all over the Internet, and you can find scores of them at `www.feedster.com`, `www.technorati.com`, or `www.syndic8.com`.

Adding and Using Extensions to Firefox

If you want more features than those provided by the core of Firefox, you can add them through extensions. Some popular extensions are:

- **Tabbrowser Preferences:** Automatically opens new pages from the URL input box or search engine into new tabs. Lets you put the tab bar at the bottom of the page and opens the Web page when you move the mouse over the tab.

- **Bandwidth Tester:** Reveals to you the bandwidth of your Internet connection.

- **ForecastFox:** Gets the weather forecast and displays it on a toolbar or status bar.

- **DictionarySearch:** Looks up words on an online dictionary.

To add an extension, do the following:

1. **Choose Tools⇨Extensions. In the Extensions window that appears, click the Get More Extensions link.**

   A new window opens to the Mozilla site Web page that contains a list and descriptions of the most popular and latest extensions.

2. **Click on the name of the extension that you want.**

   A new window appears.

3. **Click the Install Now button.**

   The extension will be operational after you quit and restart Firefox.

If the instructions above do not work, you may need to de-select the Allow Web Sites To Install Software check box, which is found in the Web Features tab of the Options dialog box (Windows) or Preferences dialog box (Macintosh and Linux). Choose Tools⇨Options (Windows) or Firefox⇨Preferences (Macintosh) or Edit⇨Preferences (Linux) to bring up the dialog box.

Extensions are constantly being created for Firefox, so you may want to do step 1 just to check out what's new or to update your extensions.

Chapter 10

Reading E-mail with Mozilla Thunderbird

In This Chapter

▶ Discovering why Thunderbird is probably the most secure mail client available

▶ Migrating mail using the wizard or using a simple manual procedure

▶ Managing junk mail intelligently

▶ Getting RSS feeds

▶ Using automatic spellchecking, the smart address book and more

*T*hunderbird is a great e-mail program that offers you much better security than programs like Microsoft Outlook. Because Thunderbird does not allow scripts to run automatically, attachments with worms or viruses cannot run in Thunderbird. Using Thunderbird can help stop worms and viruses from attacking your computer and spreading on the Internet.

Thunderbird provides an efficient and productive environment for your e-mail tasks with its latest features:

✔ **Advanced Security** to disallow viruses or worms to wreak havoc through your e-mail program.

✔ **Intelligent junk mail filter** to monitor what you decide is junk mail. Then, when it's ready, you let it do it for you!

✔ **Smart address book** to remember your friends and saves you time writing addresses for you.

✔ **Automatic migration** from Outlook Express, Outlook, Netscape 6 or 7, and Mozilla 1.x

✔ **Built-in RSS reader,** for easily reading headlines from weblogs and zillions of Web sites

  ✔ **Fully integrated newsgroup reader**

  ✔ **Multiple e-mail accounts**

  ✔ **Automatic spellchecking**

  ✔ **Customizable look and saved search folders**

  ✔ **Extensions** for including a dictionary and more

Mozilla Thunderbird's customizable interface lets you easily resize its various panes, as shown in Figure 10-1. This chapter introduces you to the best features of Mozilla Thunderbird.

Figure 10-1: Thunderbird has many unique features in addition to its advanced security.

Migrating Your Mail to Thunderbird

You can use Thunderbird's Import Wizard to migrate your mail from Outlook, Outlook Express, Mozilla, Netscape, or Eudora. Otherwise, you can use a manual procedure to migrate your mail. Thunderbird uses a standard mail format that's used by many other mail clients, so migrating mail either manually or with the Import Wizard is not complicated.

Migrating from Outlook, Outlook Express, Mozilla, or Netscape using the wizard

After you download and install Thunderbird, and start it in Windows for the first time, the Import Wizard appears, requesting that you choose the e-mail program that you want to import your settings, address book, and mail folders from: Outlook Express, Outlook, Netscape 6 or 7, or Mozilla 1.x. Choose your former e-mail program, or choose Don't Import Anything.

If you want to import your e-mail anytime after you first start your program, choose Tools ⇨ Import to bring up the Import Wizard.

If you're importing from Netscape 6 or Mozilla 1.x, importing when you first install the program is a good idea, because if you don't you'll need to do it manually. (This is not a problem with Outlook Express or Outlook. They can be imported at any time.)

If you get the message "Unable to import mailboxes, cannot create proxy object for destination mailboxes," open the e-mail program that you're trying to import mail from and rename your folders so that they do not contain any special characters, such as !, @, #, $, %, ^, &, *, and ( ). Then try importing again.

Migrating from Eudora or Netscape Communicator using the wizard

Choose Tools ⇨ Import to open the Import Wizard; click the application that you want to import mail from and click OK.

Migrating from other e-mail programs

Thunderbird reads files in standard Unix mailbox format (.mbx). To migrate your mail from other e-mail programs, follow these steps:

1. **Export your mail, in your original e-mail program, into .mbx format.**

2. **Quit your old e-mail program and change the name of the file by deleting its extension. For example, change myMail.mbx to myMail. Delete the period, too, and any special characters in its name, if it has any, such as !, @, #, $, %, ^, &, *, and ().**

3. **Close Thunderbird if it is running.**

4. Locate Thunderbird's Profile directory on the Desktop or in the Finder (Mac). See Table 10-1 for the most likely locations of the profile folder.

If your operating system is Windows 2000 or Windows XP, you need to enable Windows Explorer to see both hidden and system files in order to see the Documents and Settings folder.

5. Move the file in step 3 to the /Mail/Local Folders subdirectory of Thunderbird's Profile directory.

Now when you start Thunderbird, you can access your imported files.

Table 10-1	Location of Thunderbird Profile Directories	
Operating system	*Log In*	*Location*
Windows 95	No	C:\Windows\Application Data\Thunderbird\ Profiles\ *[random string]* .default\
Windows 95	Yes	C:\Windows\Profiles\ *[Log-in Name]*\ Application Data\Thunderbird\Profiles\ *[random string]* .default
Windows 98	No	C:\Windows\Application Data\Thunderbird\ Profiles\ *[random string]* .default\
Windows 98	Yes	C:\Windows\Profiles\ *[Log-in Name]*\ Application Data\Thunderbird\Profiles\ *[random string]* .default
Windows ME	No	C:\Windows\Application Data\Thunderbird\ Profiles\ *[random string]* .default\
Windows ME	Yes	C:\Windows\Profiles\ *[Log-in Name]*\ Application Data\Thunderbird\Profiles\ *[random string]* .default
Windows 2000	—	C:\Documents and Settings\ *[Log-in Name]*\ Application Data\Thunderbird\Profiles\ *[random string]* .default\
Windows XP	—	C:\Documents and Settings\ *[Log-in Name]*\ Application Data\Thunderbird\Profiles\ *[random string]* .default\
Windows NT	—	C:\WINNT\Profiles\ *[Log-in Name]*\ Application Data\Mozilla\Thunderbird\ Profiles\ *[random string]* .default\
Mac OS X	—	~/Library/Thunderbird/Profiles/ *[random string]* .default/
Linux	—	~/.thunderbird/ *[random string]* .default/

Creating Your E-mail Account

When you first run Thunderbird, you'll probably want to set up an e-mail account. You can set up many e-mail accounts, or just one — whatever suits you. Also, if you have an AOL mail account, you can access it with Thunderbird by using a simple setup procedure, which I describe in the next section.

Setting up one or multiple e-mail accounts

You may want to create a new e-mail account because you're just starting Thunderbird, or you may want to create an additional e-mail account in Thunderbird. To do either of these, perform the following steps:

1. **If you have not created any e-mail account, then select "Create a New Account" in the message pane of the Thunderbird window. If you have already created an account, select your top e-mail folder for your account (this is generally above the Inbox and has your e-mail address as a name), and choose "Create a New Account" in the message pane of the Thunderbird window. You can also choose Tools ⇨ Account Settings ⇨ Add Account.**

2. **In the New Account Setup dialog box of the Account Wizard, as shown in Figure 10-2, choose Email Account if it is not already selected, and click Next.**

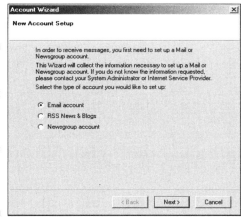

Figure 10-2:
The Account Wizard leads you through the process of creating new e-mail accounts.

3. **In the Identity dialog box, type your name and e-mail address and click Next.**

4. **In the Server Information, select either POP (for almost everything) or IMAP. Enter the names of your incoming and outgoing servers. If you**

want a single Inbox, Trash, and Drafts folder for multiple e-mail accounts, then click Use Global Inbox (otherwise, be sure it is not selected), and click Next.

If you're not sure of the names of your incoming and outgoing servers, then contact your Internet service provider to find out what they are.

5. **Type in your official incoming and outgoing e-mail address (usually these are the same thing!). This is the e-mail address that you got from your Internet service provider. Click Next.**

6. **In the Account Name dialog box, you can give your account a title, such as Personal or Work. Click Next.**

7. **Verify the information and click Back to change it or Finish to set up the e-mail account.**

Thunderbird gets your mail automatically after you click Finish.

8. **Repeat steps 1–7 for each e-mail account you want to add.**

Thunderbird automatically gets mail when it is opened or when you finish creating a new account. If you leave Thunderbird open, you need to click Get Mail whenever you want to check your mail.

Using Thunderbird to access AOL mail

You can use Thunderbird to access your AOL mail by creating a new account, as described in the preceding section. However, in step 4, choose IMAP and if you're in the U.S., type **imap.aol.com** for your incoming server. For your outgoing server, type **smtp.aol.com.**

To find out what the AOL e-mail server addresses are for other countries, go to `http://members.aol.com/adamkb/aol/mailfaq/imap/#foreign`.

You can't migrate your mail that's already at AOL without using a third-party commercial application.

Composing and Sending E-mail and Attachments

You can send mail to one e-mail address or many e-mail addresses. You can also send attachments. The basic steps of composing and sending an e-mail are as follows:

1. **Click the Write button, shown earlier in Figure 10-1.**

   The Compose window appears, as shown in Figure 10-3.

Figure 10-3: Thunderbird's Compose window.

2. **Type a subject in the Subject input box, and type your message.**

   (When you're done, you may want to run the Spellchecker on it, as described in the following section.)

   TIP

   Leave the e-mail address to the last, so you don't accidentally send the message before it's done.

3. **If you want to add attachments, click the Attach button, navigate through your files to select the file you want to attach, and click Open.**

   The attachment appears in the Attachment pane of the Compose window.

4. **To send your e-mail, type an e-mail address into the To input line, or click the Contacts button to scroll through your Address book and double-click on the name that you want to send to. If you want to send to more than one person, type an address into the next line, too. You can change the To: to Cc: (courtesy copy), Bcc: (blind courtesy copy — where the receivers cannot see the addresses of those on the Bcc: line), or others by pulling the down arrow and choosing from the menu. Click Send.**

Spellchecking

With Thunderbird you can easily make e-mails containing misspellings and typos a thing of the past. Thunderbird has a powerful spellchecker that you can start by clicking the ABC Spell button in the Compose window. It immediately checks your message for possible spelling mistakes and gives you suggestions to choose from for the correct spelling. You can choose to Replace, Replace All, Ignore, or Ignore all. You can also train your spellchecker to identify words that you commonly use but that are not in its lexicon by clicking the Add button.

Configuring Thunderbird Your Way

Thunderbird offers many ways to configure it. Thunderbird offers three views: Classic, Wide, and Vertical. To try out these views, choose View ⇨ Layout ⇨ *view of your choice*. My favorite is the Wide view, which truncates the folders list to allow more room for the message below.

You can also choose the columns that you want to see, such as Subject, Sender, Date, Read, Label, Priority, and more. You can do this by clicking the last box on the column headings, shown in Figure 10-1, and marking the items that you want to view as a column in the list.

Searching Your Mail

Thunderbird offers several ways of searching your messages. You can do any of the following:

- ✔ **Sort your e-mail by any of the column headings to locate it** by clicking any column heading.

- ✔ **Choose what columns to display** by clicking the rightmost button on the Column Headings bar and selecting the names of the columns.

- ✔ **Search your messages** with the Search Messages dialog box, shown in Figure 10-4, and, if you want, save them as copies in a new folder.

To search your messages, follow these steps:

1. **Choose Edit ⇨ Find ⇨ Search Messages.**

2. **Select either Subject, Sender, Body, Date, Priority, Status, To:, Cc:, To: or cc:, or Age in Days from the first drop-down list box. Choose either contains, doesn't contain, is, isn't, begins with, or ends with from the middle drop-down list box. Enter your criteria in the input box.**

3. **Click More to make the filter even more specific, and choose either Match All Of The Following or Match Any Of The Following.**

4. **Click Search.**

   The e-mails that match the search criteria are listed in the pane at the bottom of the dialog box.

5. **If you want to copy the e-mails into a Saved Search folder, click Save As Search Folder.**

6. **If you save the folder, name it in the dialog box that appears and click OK.**

To delete a Saved Search folder, just drag it to the Trash. To empty the Trash, select it, and choose File ⇨ Empty Trash.

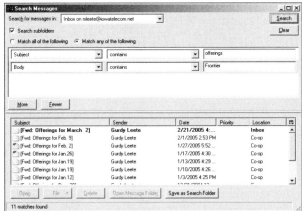

Figure 10-4: Thunderbird's message searching feature.

Teaching Thunderbird to Recognize and Filter Junk Mail

Junk mail is easy to get rid of in Thunderbird. You can adjust your settings so that when you click the junk mail column for any e-mail, the e-mail vanishes into the Junk folder. (The heading of the junk mail column has a circle with a slanted line in it.) But before you get rid of your junk mail in that way, be sure that Thunderbird is attentive to what you are doing and learning from you. Then Thunderbird can take over for you.

To set your junk mail controls, do the following:

1. **Choose Tools ⇨ Junk Mail Controls.**

   The Junk Mail Controls dialog box appears, as shown in Figure 10-5.

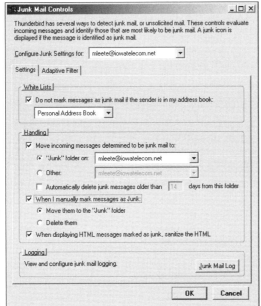

Figure 10-5:
Thunder-
bird's
junk mail
controls.

2. **Select the check boxes that you want to apply to your mail.**

3. **Click the Adaptive filter table and select the Enable Adaptive Junk Mail Detection option.**

4. **Click OK.**

Now Thunderbird will learn what you consider junk mail and be able to automatically send e-mails to your Junk folder. (Until it learns completely, you'll probably want to keep an eye on what's in your Junk folder.) It may take a few weeks for Thunderbird to learn, but when it does, it should be 99 percent accurate about what it sends to the Junk folder.

Using Message Filters

Normally, message filters sort your mail automatically and move it into folders. But you can also use message filters to assign different levels of priority to your messages, or label them as Important, Work, Personal, To Do, or Later. You can filter incoming messages as they arrive, or you can filter what's already in the Inbox. You can turn individual filters on or off whenever you want. Some reasons to filter include the following:

✔ If you belong to e-mail lists and get lots of messages from them.

✔ If you want to label messages about a topic or from a person as To Do, Work, Personal, Important, or Later, so that you can choose the same label from the View list, shown in Figure 10-1, and view only those marked e-mails.

✔ If you have someone who sends you a lot of e-mails, or you get lots of e-mails about a certain topic.

✔ If you want to separate your business e-mails from your home e-mails into folders.

✔ If you have many unsorted messages in your Inbox and you want to do some spring cleaning, without having to move them individually to folders.

✔ If you're using one account for more than one person, you may want to filter messages into different folders for different people.

✔ Automatically sort e-mail list messages into the folder for the appropriate e-mail list. (I get about 100 messages per day from just one of the OpenOffice.org e-mail lists. Filtering is a must!)

To filter your messages, do the following:

1. **Choose Tools ⇨ Message Filters.**

2. **In the Message Filters dialog box, click New.**

3. **In the Filter Rules dialog box, shown in Figure 10-6, type the name of the filter. (Any name will do.)**

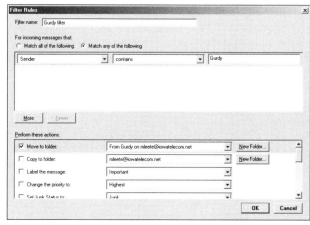

Figure 10-6:
Choose your filtering criteria and where to relocate filtered messages in the Filter Rules dialog box.

4. **Select either Subject, Sender, Body, Date, Priority, Status, To:, Cc:, To: or cc:, or Age in Days from the first drop-down list box. Choose either contains, doesn't contain, is, isn't, begins with, or ends with from the middle drop-down list box. Enter your criteria in the input box.**

5. **Click More to make the filter even more specific, and choose either Match All Of The Following or Match Any Of The Following.**

6. **Select none or more of the following:**

   Label the Message: Choose the label from the list box.

   Change the Priority to: Choose the new priority from the list box.

   Set Junk Status to: Choose Junk or Not Junk.

   Mark the Message As Read: Use this, for example, when forwarding messages you already read from another computer.

7. **Click OK.**

8. **In the Message Filters dialog box, you can deselect the Enabled check box of the filter if you don't want it to be currently active.**

9. **Click Run Now.**

   Now any messages currently in the Inbox are filtered as well as any new messages that arrive.

Using the Smart Address Book

Thunderbird adds a new card to your address book for every e-mail that you send. You may have noticed that it suggests e-mail addresses as you type an address into a new message. You can open your address book by clicking the Address Book button on the main toolbar, as shown in Figure 10-7. In the address book, you can do the following:

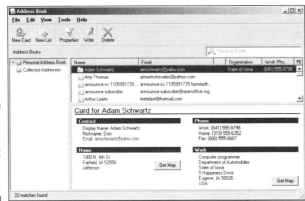

Figure 10-7:
Thunderbird's smart address book.

✔ **Add a new card** by clicking the Add Card button and filling out the information in the New Card dialog box.

✔ **Add a new address book** by choosing File ➪ New ➪ Address Book, filling out the name, and clicking OK.

✔ **Delete a card** by selecting it and clicking the Delete button.

✔ **Edit a card** by clicking the Properties button.

✔ **Open a new message** with the selected address in the Address book in the To: section of the new message by clicking the Write button.

Using Thunderbird's Built-in RSS Support

RSS is an acronym that used to stand for Rich Site Summary, but has changed in time to stand for Really Simple Syndication. With RSS you can receive the latest news about whatever you're interested in as e-mails in your News and Blogs folder. For example, I wanted the latest news about Mozilla Thunderbird, so I entered the Thunderbird RSS news feed URL in Thunderbird's RSS Subscriptions dialog box, and now whenever I get my mail, the latest news about Mozilla Thunderbird arrives as well.

To use the built-in RSS feed feature, you need the URL for the RSS feed. You can get URLs for RSS feeds from a variety of sources — here are four:

✔ **Syndic8:** `http://www.syndic8.com`

✔ **NewsIsFree Directory:** `http://www.newisfree.com/sources/bycat/`

✔ **RDF Ticker:** `http://www.anse.de/rdfticker/findchannels.php`

✔ **Yahoo! News:** `http://jeremy.zawodny.com/ynews-search-rss.php`. (Enter a search criteria in the input box and click Go; the URL for the RSS news feed link appears.)

Go to one of the preceding links, and copy the link of the URL for the RSS news feed that you want so you can use it in the following instructions.

To get e-mails using RSS, do the following:

1. **Select News & Blogs in the Folders pane. (If you have no News & Blogs folder, choose File ➪ New ➪ Account, select RSS News & Blogs, and click Next. Click Next again, and click Finish. Select the News & Blogs folder.)**

   The message pane changes to a list of links under three main headings: RSS News & Blogs, Accounts, and Advanced Features.

2. **Click Manage Subscriptions.**

3. In the RSS Subscriptions dialog box, click Add.

In the News Feed Properties dialog box, paste the URL that you generated from one of the RSS URL Generators listed earlier or from elsewhere, as shown in Figure 10-8.

Figure 10-8:
Type or
paste your
RSS feed
URL to start
your RSS
feed.

4. If you want to get an article summary in your e-mail instead of the article, select the check box.

5. Click OK on the News Feed Properties dialog box, and click OK in the RSS Subscriptions dialog box.

Your news feed starts automatically. You can read the articles or two-sentence summaries in a folder in the News & Blogs folder.

To delete an RSS feed, select News & Blogs in the Folders pane, click the Manage Subscriptions link, select the RSS feed in the RSS Subscriptions dialog box, and click Delete. Click OK.

Using Advanced Security Features

Thunderbird does not allow any scripts to run automatically in it. This stops many worms and viruses in their tracks. For additional security and privacy, however, you may want to disable the loading of remote images in your mail. This keeps any secret scripts embedded in some spam files from running when you open them.

To give yourself this added measure of security, choose Tools ➪ Options and click the Advanced button. Select Block Loading of Remote Images in Mail Messages, if it is not already selected, and click OK.

Anyone can make an e-mail look as if it were coming from your bank or credit card company or anyone (just as anyone can snail-mail you a forged letter that looks like it comes from your bank). Be suspicious of any e-mail asking for financial information, credit card numbers, passwords, social security numbers, or anything of that nature. If you're concerned, call the party who wants the information, using their known and listed number —not one from the e-mail!

Be suspicious of any links to Web sites in e-mails. Web sites can appear official but may not be. If you need to go to a Web site, then instead of using the link in the e-mail, use your Web browser to go to the official site. If you don't know the URL, find it at Google.com.

Extensions

Do you want a dictionary for use in Thunderbird? Would you like to listen to music without having to leave Thunderbird? Or how about a feature that lets you insert a custom signature by right-clicking wherever you want it and choosing it from a context menu? These are just a few of the extensions that are available at `https://addons.update.mozilla.org/extensions/?application=thunderbird`. When you find an extension that you want, download it and save it to your hard drive. Then in Thunderbird, choose Tools⇨Extensions and click the Install button on the Extensions dialog box. In the Select An Extension To Install dialog box, navigate to the downloaded extension and click Open, Your extension installs. You may need to quit and restart Thunderbird for the extension to take effect.

Chapter 11

Publishing Web Pages with OpenOffice.org Writer

. . . .

In This Chapter

▶ Publishing your Writer documents as Web pages

▶ Creating Web pages using tables

▶ Using hyperlinks

▶ Viewing your HTML

. . . .

*O*penOffice.org offers an HTML editor within the Writer application that you can use to create elaborate (or simple) Web sites or transform your existing Writer documents into Web pages or Web sites in various ways. In the Web Layout view, you can start from scratch by adding tables, frames, hyperlinks, and more. This chapter gives you the rundown on the various ways you can use Writer to create Web pages.

Getting Started

OpenOffice.org Writer offers four methods to create a Web page or turn existing Writer documents into single or multiple Web pages. The four methods are described in detail in the following sections and listed briefly as follows:

✔ **Create a new Web page,** using the Web Layout view. An example of a Web page created using the Web Layout view is shown in Figure 11-1.

✔ **Change your existing Writer document into a single Web page,** by saving your document as an HTML file.

✔ **Change your existing Writer document into multiple Web pages using heading styles as links,** by choosing File➪Send➪Create HTML Document.

✔ **Change multiple Writer documents into multiple Web pages and generate an index page with their filenames as links,** using the Web Page Wizard.

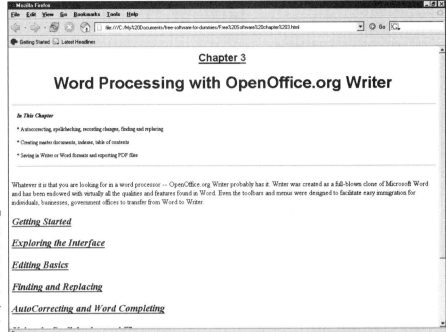

Figure 11-1:
A Web page
created
using the
OpenOffice.
org HTML
editor.

Creating a new Web page

To create a new blank Web page, in OpenOffice.org Writer, choose File⇨
New⇨HTML Document. A new document appears with the following
characteristics:

- ✔ Shrunken margins
- ✔ No automatic page breaking.
- ✔ The Apply Style input box on the Formatting toolbar contains styles
  optimized for Web pages.

After you save your document for the first time using the default file type of
.html, you can view your document on a Web browser.

When you save your document as an HTML document for the first time, save
it in its own folder. Doing so enables you to keep all the elements of your Web
page together with the HTML document.

Converting a Writer document into a Web page

You can view a Writer document using the Web page layout by choosing View⇨Web Layout. Your document does not get converted to an HTML document until you save it in HTML format.

To save an existing Writer document as a Web page, do the following:

1. **Open the Writer document and choose File⇨Save As.**

2. **In the Save As dialog box that appears, click the Create New Folder button and give your folder a name.**

   You want to create a new folder because any pictures get saved as separate files. You want to keep them together so you can upload them easily to your server. Even if your document doesn't have pictures, creating a new folder is a good idea.

3. **Double-click on the new folder name in the dialog box to open it.**

4. **Type a filename in the dialog box and choose HTML Document from the File Type drop-down list.**

5. **Click Save.**

   Your document saves with the .html extension and is now readable using your Web browser. Open your Web browser; if you're using Mozilla Firefox, choose File⇨Open File, navigate in the Open File dialog box to your file, and double-click on it. Your document opens into a Web browser, as shown in Figure 11-2.

Converting an existing Writer document into a Web site using styles as links

If a document contains styles, such as multiple Heading 1s, then you can convert the document to a Web site with the headings serving as links to separate Web pages. This gives your document an instant table of contents and in many cases makes it more accessible to the viewer.

1. **Choose File⇨Send⇨Create HTML Document.**

2. **In the Name and Path of the HTML Document dialog box, click the New Folder button and give your folder a name.**

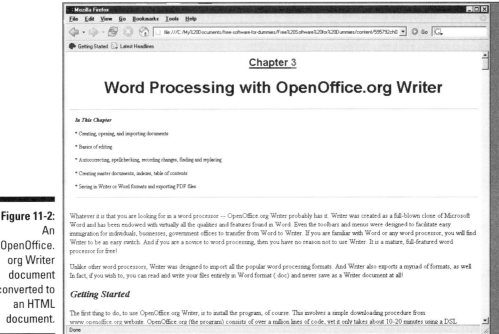

Figure 11-2:
An OpenOffice.org Writer document converted to an HTML document.

3. **Double-click on the new folder name in the dialog box to open it.**

4. **In the dialog box, type a filename for the Web page.**

5. **Choose a style from the Styles list box; for example, Heading 1.**

6. **Click Save.**

    Your HTML document appears with each occurrence of the style that you chose in step 4 as a link, as shown in Figure 11-3.

Test your links by opening the document in your Web browser. Your main Web page has the name that you chose earlier in step 3. The linked pages have numbers appended to that name.

Converting multiple documents from Writer to HTML using the Web Page Wizard

The Web Page Wizard allows you to convert lots of documents to HTML at once and automatically generates a page of links to these documents. For example, I used the Web Page Wizard to create HTML documents of every chapter in this book, as shown in Figure 11-4.

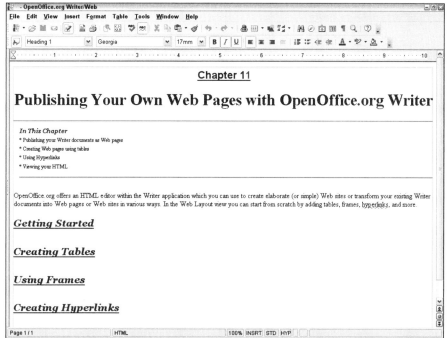

Figure 11-3:
A Writer document converted to an HTML document with links for each Heading 1 style.

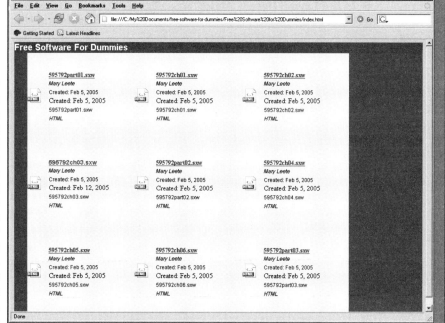

Figure 11-4:
The links page is generated by the Web Page Wizard to access multiple Writer documents as HTML documents in a browser.

To use the Web Page Wizard, do the following:

1. **Create a new folder where the files of the Web site can reside.**

   This can be anywhere on your computer.

2. **Choose File⇨Wizards⇨Web Page.**

   The Web Page Wizard dialog box appears.

   To run the Web Page Wizard, you need to have a Java Runtime Environment (JRE) installed. See Chapter 1 for more information on how to install a JRE.

3. **If you've used the Web Page Wizard before, then you can choose a setting in the list box; otherwise, choose Default and click Next.**

   A dialog box appears in which you select the documents that you want to publish as HTML.

4. **Click Add to bring up the Open dialog box and select a file that you want to convert into a Web site. Click Open. Add as many documents as you want and click Next. You can also type a Summary for each document that you add.**

   (The summaries will appear on the Web page that the wizard generates, beneath the links for each document.)

5. **In the Main Layout dialog box that appears, choose a layout for your new Web page and click Next.**

6. **In the Layout details dialog box, choose what you want to appear by each document link. Also choose the screen resolution that you want to optimize the layout for. Click Next.**

   If you're not sure what screen resolution to choose, click 800x600, if it is not already selected.

7. **Choose a Style for your table of contents. Choose from Water, Light Gray, Marine, Orange, and more.**

8. **Fill out some General Information, if desired, such as the Title, Description, Copyright Notice, and so on. Click Next.**

9. **You can click Preview to see your Web site in your browser. If you want to change anything, close or hide the browser and click in any of the steps on the left of the Web Page Wizard dialog box to redo any of the preceding steps. Then return to the last step by clicking "7. Preview."**

10. **In the Publish the new Web site section, you probably want to accept the default setting of To a Local Folder. Then click the button beside that input box.**

The Local Destination Directory dialog box appears.

11. Select the folder that you created in step 1.

12. Click Finish.

The Web Page Wizard converts all the documents that you specified in step 4 into HTML documents and saves them in two folders entitled "content" and "images" in your Web site folder, along with two more files: Style and Index.

To view your Web page with links to all the documents, open your browser and navigate to the folder containing your Web site. In the folder, double-click on the Index file to open it.

Creating Tables

Tables are a great way of organizing the look of your Web page. For example, you can have one row for your logo and title, another row with lots of cells to handle each menu item, and perhaps a column down the left side or right side — or both — for side menu bars. You can do all this using a table.

Adding a table

To create a table, choose Insert⇨Table, choose the number of columns and rows from the Insert Table dialog box, and click OK. Or you can click the table button on the Standard toolbar and drag across the pop-up grid to select the number of rows and columns that you want in your table. A table appears, along with the floating Table toolbar, as shown in Figure 11-5. (Don't worry about your Web site looking like a grid. You can modify it in lots of ways to make it look right.)

Table button

Table grid

Figure 11-5:
Create a
table using
the Table
pop-up grid
on the
Standard
toolbar.

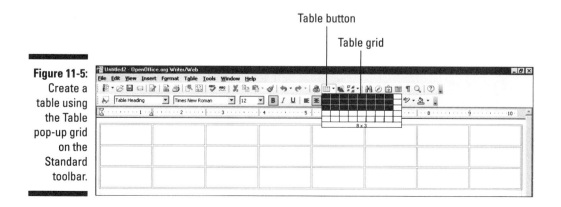

Don't worry about getting the number of rows and columns in your table exactly right; you can always split cells or merge cells later. I usually create one column for each button that I want to put on a top menu bar, and one row for each button that I want to put on a side menu bar.

Adding text into a table

After you create the table, you can add text into any cell of it by clicking in a cell and typing. Notice that the text in the top row of your table has a different style applied to it than the text in the rows below it. You can change the style by clicking in a word and selecting a style from the Apply Style drop-down box on the Formatting toolbar. In the Web Layout view, the styles in the Apply Styles box are those deemed suitable for HTML. You can choose other fonts, but there is no guarantee that your audience will have those fonts installed on their computers. For more information on applying styles, see Chapter 4.

When creating a Web page, viewing the Web page in a Web browser to see exactly what it will look like is always a good idea. In fact, you may want to view it in a several different Web browsers, such as Mozilla Firefox, Internet Explorer, and Safari, to make sure that what you're seeing in the Web Layout view is what your viewers will see in their browsers. You may need to make small adjustments. These adjustments are typical for any HTML editor.

Be sure to save your HTML document and reload the document in the Web browser to see your most recent changes.

Getting the right look for your table

You can do the following to start shaping your table the way you want it to look:

- **To merge cells together to create a single cell,** click and drag to select the cells that you want to merge and click the Merge Cells button on the Table toolbar. You can merge as many rows and columns as you want in one stroke.

- **To resize your cells,** click and drag a vertical border between two cells to make that column of cells wider or narrower. Click and drag a horizontal border between two cells to make that row shorter or taller. (You can also make a row taller by adding text. The row expands to fit the text.)

✔ **To split cells,** click in the cell that you want to split into more cells, click the Split Cells button on the Table toolbar, and choose the direction of the new border line(s) and number of splits in the Split Cell dialog box that appears. Then click OK. Your cell splits into the number of cells that you indicated.

✔ **To change the style of the border,** click and drag to select the cells that you want to give a new border style to, click the Borders button, and choose your border from the pop-up Border toolbar. You can choose the line style from the Line Style options and choose the Line Color from the Line Color options on the Table toolbar.

✔ **To add margins to each cell in your table,** click and drag to select the cells for which you want a margin, and click the Table Properties button on the Table toolbar. In the Borders tab, adjust the Spacing to Contents spin boxes to whatever margin you want, then click OK.

✔ **To delete your table,** click in a row and then click the Delete Row button on the Table toolbar repeatedly until all the rows are deleted.

Adding pictures

You can put pictures into your table or anywhere in your Web page by choosing Insert⇨From File. In the Insert Picture dialog box that appears, select the picture file that you want and click Open. You can resize your picture by dragging its handles. (Shift+drag resizes it while keeping its proportions intact.) To position it, click anywhere on the image (except the handles), and drag it.

For more information about anchoring your graphic and wrapping text around it, see Chapter 4. To use your picture as a hyperlink, see "Creating Hyperlinks" later in this chapter.

Creating Hyperlinks

A hyperlink is a handy feature that enables you to add a dynamic element to your Web page. Use hyperlinks to take your audience to other Web pages, other sections in your site or page, or even to get news or send e-mail.

Hyperlinks in Writer come in four flavors:

✔ **Internet hyperlinks:** These can be Web pages, FTP, or Telnet links.

✔ **Mail and news**

✔ **Hyperlinks within your Web page**

✔ **Hyperlinks to Web pages that are part of your Web site**

Internet hyperlinks

To create an Internet hyperlink, do the following:

1. **Using your Internet browser, locate the Web page that you want to link to, and copy the address.**

2. **In your Web page in OpenOffice.org Writer, select the text or picture that you want to use as your link.**

3. **Click the Hyperlink button on the Standard toolbar, or choose Insert⇨ Hyperlink.**

   The Hyperlink dialog box appears, as shown in Figure 11-6.

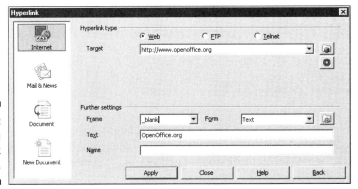

Figure 11-6: The Hyperlink dialog box.

4. **Click Internet from the buttons on the left of the dialog box, if it is not already selected, then select Web, FTP, or Telnet for the type of Internet link.** (Normally, you want to choose Web.)

5. **In the Target field, type in or paste the URL (such as** `http://www.infinityeverywhere.net/free`**) for the Internet Web page that you want to link to.**

6. **In the Further Settings section, if you want the Web page to open as a new page, choose _blank from the Frame list box. Otherwise, choose _self or don't do anything.** (Opening the new page in the current page is the default setting.)

7. **Be sure that Text is selected in the Form list box, whether your link is a text or a graphic.**

8. **Click Apply.**

9. **Click Close.**

Your link is now active.

Suppose you want to edit a hyperlink; however, if it's active, then every time you click on it, a new Web page opens. To solve this dilemma, you can deactivate the links in your document. To do that, click on the HYP field in the status bar at the bottom of your Writer window. HYP changes to SEL, which stands for Select. Now your links are no longer active. To activate them again, click SEL again so that it becomes HYP.

Mail hyperlinks

Mail hyperlinks open a blank e-mail that you can assign the address and subject to. This feature can be useful for that Contact Us link. To create a Mail hyperlink, do the following:

1. **Select the text or graphic that you want to use as your link.**

2. **Click the Hyperlink button on the Standard toolbar.**

3. **Click the Mail & News button and select E-mail.**

4. **Type the address for the e-mail recipient in the Receiver input box, and fill in the Subject dialog box.**

   You probably want to put your address in the Receiver input box, if you want to get the e-mails. And maybe title the e-mail "Customer Service Request" or something like it, so that you can recognize the e-mails immediately when you receive them.

5. **Click Apply, then Close.**

   Your link now opens a new e-mail document whenever it is active and clicked.

Linking to other documents or to other places in the same document

If you have a long Web page, you may want to link to sections in it. For example, if you're creating a FAQ (Frequently Asked Questions) page, you may want to use your questions as links to your answers. Or you may want to link to other Web pages that you created for your Web site. To do either of these, perform the following steps:

1. **Select the text or graphic that you want to use as your link.**

2. **Click the Hyperlink button on the Standard toolbar.**

3. **If you want to link to another document, click the New Document button. If you want to link in your document, click the Document button.**

4. **Do one of the following:**

    • If you're linking within your document, click the Target in Document button, and the Navigator window appears. Double-click the object in the Navigator that you want to link to. This can be a heading, table, graphic, frame, or whatever.

    • If you're linking to another document, choose your file type from the File Type list box. Then click the Select Path button and choose your file.

5. **Click Apply, then Close.**

Viewing Your HTML

To view your HTML, you can do one of the following:

✔ If you created your HTML document using File➪New➪HTML Document, then choose View➪HTML Source. Your document changes to the HTML code, as shown in Figure 11-7.

✔ If you created your HTML document using File➪Save As and then choosing HTML Document from the Save As Type list, you cannot view the HTML. To view the HTML, you need to select everything in your document, copy it, and create a new HTML Document using File➪New➪ HTML Document, then paste everything into the new document. Once you do that, you can use the instructions above to view the HTML Source.

Why would you ever want to view the HTML code? One common reason is that occasionally some browsers may view the same Web page in two different ways. This variation is not anyone's fault; it just reflects a variety of protocols in use on the Internet. This kind of problem can keep a Webmaster busy. To precisely adjust how a Web page looks on different browsers, a Web designer may need to tinker with the HTML code.

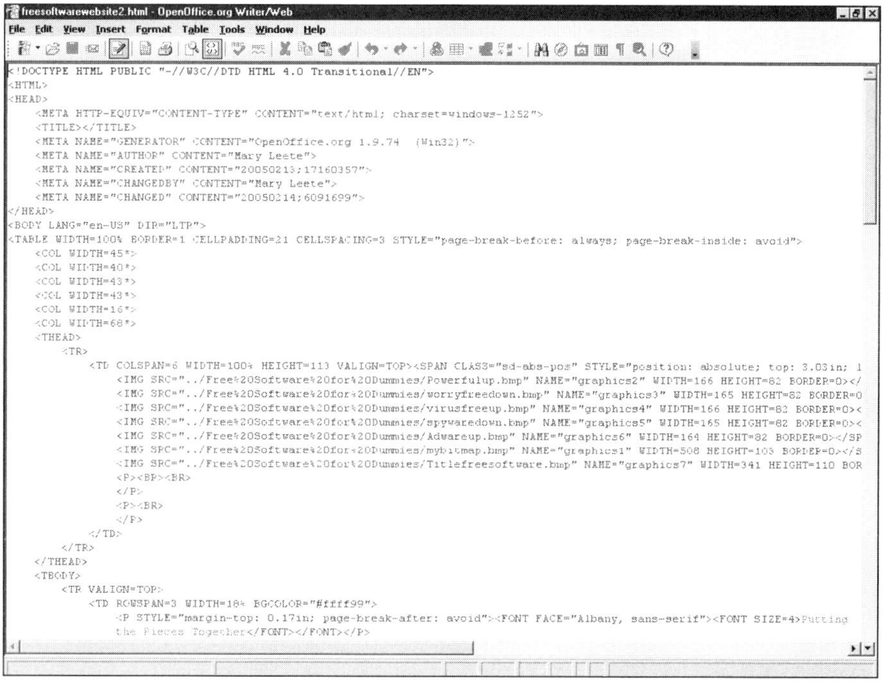

Figure 11-7:
The HTML
code for the
Web page
shown in
Figure 11-3.

Chapter 12

Enjoying Podcasts with iPodder

*i*Podder is an application that enables you to choose Internet audio programs you want to listen to and then downloads them to your computer via RSS feeds. Whenever you're ready, just click on the audio program you want to listen to, and the media player on your computer plays it. iPodder continues to periodically download the latest episodes of your programs automatically, so you always have the most recent audio files. You can also load audio files into an iPod (or other portable digital media player) to play them whenever and wherever you want. This chapter introduces you to iPodder and some of its cool features.

Exploring the Interface

For information on downloading and installing iPodder, see the section "iPodder: The Podcast Receiver" in Chapter 1.

iPodder, as shown in Figure 12-1, has a main menu and four or five tabs, depending on whether you have started downloading files or not. The tabs are as follows:

✔ **Downloads:** This tab lists the audio files that iPodder has downloaded. Click on one of them to play it on your computer's media player.

✔ **Subscriptions:** This tab lists what podcasts you're subscribed to. When you tell iPodder to get new feeds, it checks to see whether any new programs have come out for those programs that you subscribe to. If so, it then downloads them.

✔ **Podcast directory:** This tab has URLs for lots of podcasts that you can choose to subscribe to or not. It also has the URL input box where you can type in or paste any podcast URL you want to subscribe to. (You find podcast URLs on the Internet.)

✔ **Cleanup:** This tab allows you to delete files from the Downloads tab and from the actual folder on your computer where they are stored.

✔ **Log:** After you start downloading files, you'll also have a Log tab, which contains a log of what has been downloaded and when. It also informs you if it can no longer find a URL of a podcast, which is subject to change.

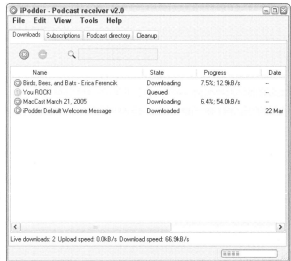

Figure 12-1:
The iPodder
interface.

Selecting Podcasts

The first thing you probably want to do with iPodder is to select podcasts. iPodder contains a directory of popular podcasts, but what you're looking for may or may not be in the directory. iPodder also lets you enter any URL of a podcast feed. To find URLs of RSS feeds, a good place to start looking is www. podcastalley.com. Thousands of podcasts in a wide variety exist on the Internet. You can find podcasts ranging from professional radio shows to a single individual discussing a topic.

To select the podcasts that you want iPodder to download, follow these steps:

1. **To select a podcast from either the Internet or the Podcast Directory, click the Podcast directory tab, shown in Figure 12-2.**

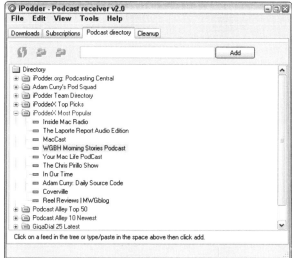

2. **Do one of the following:**

    • **If you want to choose a podcast from the Podcast directory,** click on any folder in the Directory (not on the + sign) to expand the folder. (Within each folder are names of podcasts you can subscribe to.) Select the podcast of your choice.

    • **If you want to choose a podcast from the Internet,** then browse the Internet and copy the URL of the podcast. In iPodder, paste the URL into the input box near the top of the Podcast directory tab.

3. **Click the Add button.**

    The Add a Feed dialog box appears.

4. **Click Save.**

    The Subscriptions tab appears with the new podcast highlighted; the episodes may be listed in the pane at the bottom of the window.

5. **Select the episodes you want to download.**

6. **Choose Tools⇨Check All to download your selected episodes.**

    The Check All command causes iPodder to also check for any new episodes for any other podcasts you may have subscribed to earlier.

Playing Audio Files

To play audio files, click the Downloads tab, shown in Figure 12-1, and click on the file that you want to play. The media player, either iTunes or Windows

Media Player, appears, playing your selection. (If it doesn't, you can set your preferences for it to do so.)

You can also play the audio files by double-clicking their icons in the folder that they are saved in on the hard drive.

Setting Preferences

iPodder offers several preferences that you can set by choosing File⇨ Preferences. The Preferences dialog box opens, in which you can set the following preferences:

- ✔ **Select Run a Check for New Podcasts When the Application is Started,** if you don't want to have to choose Tools ⇨ Check All to manually download new episodes of your podcasts. (Alternatively, you can choose Tools ⇨ Scheduler to tell iPodder what time you want it to download new episodes. This option is handy if you have a slow Internet connection and want to download in the middle of the night.)

- ✔ **Select Play Downloads Right After They're Downloaded,** if you want to do so, but if you're downloading automatically in the middle of the night, this option may cause your computer to act as a radio alarm clock.

- ✔ **If your hard disk is not gigantic, you may want to type a smaller number into the Stop Downloading If Hard Disc Reaches a Minimum of: input box.** Leaving at least 200 Mb free may be a good idea.

- ✔ **If you want your files to be downloaded onto the D drive instead of the C drive, or you want them in a directory other than the default directory,** create a folder on your hard drive (not using iPodder), return to iPodder, click the Browse button, and select that folder.

- ✔ **If files don't play when you click them in the Downloads tab, click the Player tab in the Preferences dialog box and choose a player.**

For your preferences to take effect, click the Save button.

Chapter 13

Making Free Phone Calls with Skype

Skype has over 29 million users and is gaining users at the rate of about 155,000 per day. Why? Here are some reasons:

✔ **It has superior sound quality to even your own telephone.**

✔ **It has a high success rate of connecting calls.**

✔ **It works even with your firewall operating, so your computer is not defenseless.** (You may have to adjust certain settings on the firewall, which I discuss later in this chapter.)

✔ **You can choose who you want to receive calls from.** Any unwanted calls are completely blocked.

✔ **Encrypted phone calls.** No one is listening in on your phone calls when you use Skype for computer-to-computer connections.

✔ **It's free!** However, you're not free to modify it. This software is proprietary, but you're free to use it, even for your business.

✔ **You can conference call with up to five contacts.**

✔ **You can use it as an instant messenger.**

✔ **It offers SkypeOut,** which you can use to call telephones and mobile phones all around the world for about 2 cents/minute.

✔ **It offers SkypeIn,** which you can use to get a telephone number assigned to you for about $4/month. You can receive calls with this number, plus get free VoiceMail from Skype.

✔ **It offers VoiceMail,** which you can use to receive messages for about $2/month.

Millions of Skype users around the world are very enthusiastic about Skype. One user reports that he gets strange looks when he talks into his laptop at airports and other public places, but he doesn't care. In this chapter we cover the ins and outs of using Skype.

What You Need to Get Started

Everyone who uses Skype needs the following:

✔ **Microphone.** A headset with a microphone is greatly preferred.

✔ **Internet connection,** either a dial-up with a minimum 33.6 Kbps modem, or cable, DSL, or other broadband connection

✔ **At least 128 MB RAM**

In addition, Skype requires the following:

✔ **For Windows:**

  • **Windows 2000 or XP**

  • **400 MHz processor or more**

  • **Sound card and speakers or earphones**

✔ **For Mac OS X:**

  • **Mac OS X version 10.3 or newer**

  • **G3, G4, G5, or better processor**

Setting Up

In most cases, setting up your Skype application involves three steps:

- ✔ **Downloading Skype.**
- ✔ **Installing Skype.**
- ✔ **Signing Up:** You need to request a Skype name to be able to make phone calls. This process is quick, easy, and free.

Downloading and installing Skype

To download Skype, go to www.skype.com and click on the "Download Skype Now. It's Free" button at the top of the page. The download may start immediately. If not, click on the Download Skype for (*your operating system here*) link. Save the file to your disk.

To install Skype on Mac OS X version 10.3 or higher, double-click on the downloaded .dmg file. Drag the Skype application to the Applications folder, or anywhere on the hard drive; you may also want to drag the icon to the Dock.

To install Skype on Windows, double-click on the downloaded file, SkypeSetup. Follow the instructions of the Installation Wizard.

Signing up

When you click Finish in the Installation Wizard, the Create a New Skype Account Wizard appears, as shown in Figure 13-1. This is where you sign up to use Skype. Here are the steps:

1. **In the Create Account dialog box, enter a name that you want to use; then enter a password twice. (Write down your password so you don't forget it!)**

   You won't be able to change your account name later. If you want a different name, you will need to create a new account.

Figure 13-1:
The Create
a New
Skype
Account
Wizard.

2. **If you want, check the Log this user on automatically check box, if you're at your own computer and not at a public computer or temporary computer. Enter your e-mail address.**

3. **Click Skype End User Agreement, if you want to read it, and select the check box indicating you've read and agreed to the terms.**

4. **Click Next.**

   Your Skype Personal Profile page appears, as shown in Figure 13-2.

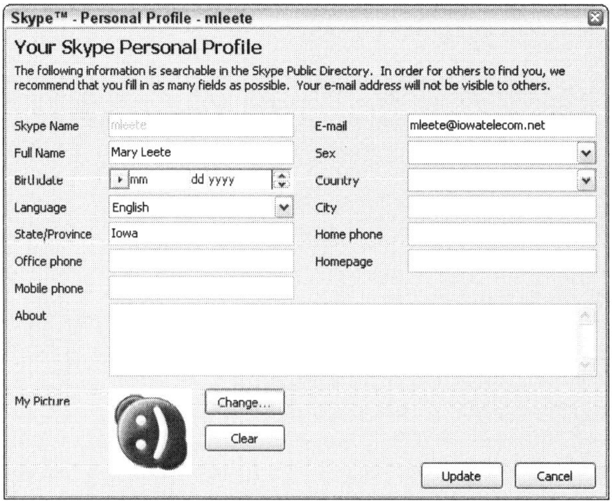

Figure 13-2:
Fill in your
Skype
Profile,
which can
be seen
(except for
the e-mail
address)
by any
Skype user.

5. **Fill out any information that you don't mind millions of people around the world reading. Click Update.**

   The Getting Started Wizard and the Skype window appear, as shown in Figure 13-3.

Figure 13-3: The Skype window and the Getting Started Wizard.

6. **Click the following buttons in the Getting Started Wizard to perform the following tasks:**

   • **Configure Privacy Options:** You may want to set these options immediately. Personally, I chose to allow calls and chats only from my Contacts, as shown in Figure 13-4.

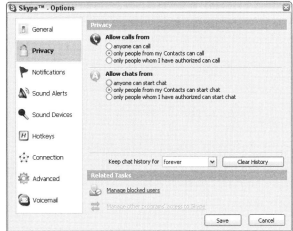

Figure 13-4: You can set privacy options using the Getting Started Wizard.

- **Import Contacts from My Computer:** Click this option if you want the Import Contacts Wizard to automatically check to see whether any of the people in your e-mail address book are using Skype and add them to your contact list.

- **Search for Other Skype Users:** Why not type your last name in the Look For box and see whether any long lost relatives of yours use Skype?

- **Edit My Profile:** Use this option if you want to change something in your profile that millions of people can see.

- **Make a Test Call:** Go ahead. Be brave. Is your microphone hooked up and are your speakers on? Skype has an automated Echo Test Service where you can test the volumes of your speakers and microphone. You probably really want to do this before you call anyone else. If you have any problem, see the section "Troubleshooting" at the end of this chapter.

For the best sound quality, Skype suggests that each person use headphones with attached microphones.

Don't have a microphone? For a quick fix, you can plug a pair of headphones into the microphone jack of your sound card and talk into them! (But don't let anyone see you!)

Adding Contacts

Skype provides an easy way for you to compile a list of your favorite Skype users. After you add Skype users to your list, all you need to do is double-click on their name to call them. Depending on the preferences that you set, the Skype users in your contact list may be able to see if you are online or not, and also may be the only people who are allowed to call you.

To add Skype users to your list of contacts, you can do the following:

1. **Choose Tools ⇨ Search for Skype Users.**

   The Search for Skype Users dialog box appears.

2. **In the Look For window, enter the name of the person you want to add to your contacts.**

   The list of search results appears in the dialog box.

3. **Double-click on the name of a Skype user if you want to open the user profile to make sure this person is the one you want.**

4. **Click the Add Contact button at the bottom of the list.**

5. **In the Authorization form that appears, choose one of the two options and click OK:**

   - Request authorization to see his/her status and allow this user to see when I am online

   - Request authorization to see his/her status, but do not allow this user to see when I am online

   An Authorization Request pop-up dialog box appears on your contact's computer, which, if he or she accepts, will allow you to see whether he or she is online.

   The contact is added to your contact list, as shown in Figure 13-5.

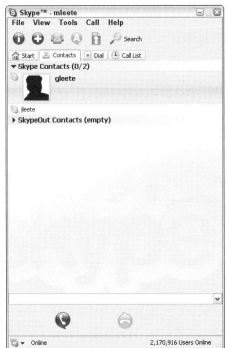

Figure 13-5:
The
Contacts
tab of the
Skype
window.

Making and Receiving Calls

Calling a friend with Skype is easy. Just double-click on the contact's Skype name in the Contacts tab of the Skype window. Or select the person's name and click the Call button at the bottom of the window. You hear the muted ringing sound, just as you would when making a call on a normal telephone. Then when you hear the person's voice, you just start your conversation.

When you are done talking, click the Hang up button at the bottom of the window.

When you're the person being called, you hear a loud ringing sound, like a telephone, and your Skype icon flashes. In the Skype window, click the Incoming Call tab and choose Answer the call or Reject the call. If you choose Answer the call, say "Hello" or "Joe's Pizza" or whatever you want.

During a call, you can do any of the following tasks by right-clicking in the main part of the Skype window and choosing the appropriate option:

- ✓ **Hold the Call**
- ✓ **Hang Up**
- ✓ **Mute the Microphone**
- ✓ **Start Chat**
- ✓ **Send File**
- ✓ **Send Contacts**

To hang up, either right-click and choose Hang Up, or click the Hang Up button at the bottom of the window.

Making Conference Calls

Conference calls are handy, and when you start using Skype regularly, you'll probably find yourself making lots of conference calls.

Follow these steps to make a conference call using Skype:

1. **Choose Tools ➪ Create Conference.**

   The Start a Skype Conference Call dialog box appears.

2. **If you want to enter a topic for your conference call, type it into the Conference Topic box.**

3. **While pressing the Control button, click on up to four contacts from the list on the left side of the dialog box. Click Add.**

   The contacts appear in the Conference Participants list box on the right.

4. **Click Start.**

   Wait for a few seconds for everyone to answer. The icons of the conference participants appear in a Conference tab.

To get the best-quality sound without delays for your conference call, you may want to have the person who starts the conference call be the person with the best Internet connection.

Using SkypeOut

SkypeOut lets you call real telephones practically anywhere in the world, either fixed or mobile, for a small charge (about 2 cents a minute.) Before you can use SkypeOut you need to put money into your account. You can use a credit card to do so, or you can pay through PayPal. You need to pay 10 Euros to start with, which is about $13 (USD).

SkypeOut does not carry the same encrypted phone service as the computer-to-computer connection. Also, SkypeOut does not support emergency calls. (You can't dial 911 and expect to get a response.)

Giving yourself credit

To pay in advance for SkypeOut, you can do the following:

1. **Click the Get SkypeOut and Call Your Offline Friends in the Start tab of the Skype window.**

   A page opens on the Skype Web site.

2. **Type in your password and press Return.**

3. **In the new Web page that appears, click Buy SkypeOut Credit.**

   You have to buy 10 Euros' worth, which is about $13 (USD).

4. **Click the Buy This button.**

5. **Fill out all the information and click the Save button at the bottom of the page.**

6. **Choose to pay either through Moneybookers or PayPal (BETA). (The people at Skype are constantly bringing you new products and services, and you may notice that some are in the Beta stage of development. You may or may not want to use a Beta version.) Click Continue.**

7. **Continue to enter all the requested information.**

   The Skype window shows a balance in your account; you can now use SkypeOut.

Calling with SkypeOut

After you have credit in your SkypeOut account, the rest is easy. To make a call using SkypeOut, follow these steps:

1. **In the Skype window, click the Dial tab.**

2. **Type the numbers that you want to dial in the input box near the bottom of the tab, as shown in Figure 13-6.**

3. **Click the Call button.**

   The telephone of the person you are calling starts ringing.

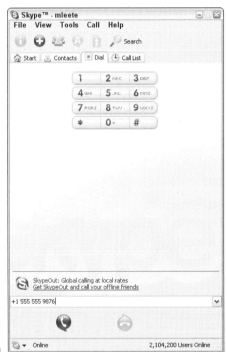

Figure 13-6:
Use
SkypeOut
to call
telephones
and mobile
phones.

Instant Messaging

You can use Skype as an instant messenger. You can chat with up to about 50 friends at the same time. To start a chat, select the contact name in the Contacts tab and click the Chat button on the Skype toolbar (the big A), or right-click on the name of your contact and choose Start Chat. The Skype window widens and becomes the Chat window. You type what you want to say, and then click the Send button when you want to send it. If you need to chat with more than one person at a time, click the Add More Users to This Chat button, select the contacts that you want to add, and click Add.

If you add offline users, the chat window pops up for them when they log on to Skype, and they can see what has taken place and participate.

If you're unable to chat with a friend, it may be because he or she is using an older version of Skype. You may want to suggest to your friend that he or she upgrade.

Troubleshooting

You probably won't have any trouble getting Skype to work, but if you do, you may have a problem with either your firewall or a problem with a delay. See if these sections are useful to you; if not, check out the next section, "Getting Help."

Setting up your firewall

Skype would like to have outgoing TCP connections available to it for all 65,535 ports. But if it can't have all of them, it will settle for one — port 443. Generally, you don't need to know this information; you just need to know how to configure the firewall, as I describe in the steps that follow.

Here are the steps for configuring the Windows XP SP2 Firewall:

1. **Choose Start ➪ Control Panel.**

   The Control Panel appears.

2. **Click the Windows Firewall button.**

   The Security Center window appears.

3. **At the bottom of the window, click Windows Firewall; in the Windows Firewall dialog box that appears, click the Exceptions tab.**

   A list of programs appears with check boxes.

4. **If Skype is in the list, be sure it has a check in the check box. If Skype is not in the list, click the Add Program button, select Skype from the list of programs, and click OK. Be sure to select the check box, if it is not already selected. Click OK.**

Dealing with an echo or delay

It could happen that when you use Skype, you may experience a delay from the time you speak into the mic until the person on the other end hears what you say. This can have a few possible causes:

✔ Your microphone is too close to your speakers. You may want to try changing to a headset.

✔ If you are using a modem, try quitting all Internet activity, such as your browser while using Skype.

✔ If you are using a router and having a problem, you may need to use a direct connection to the Internet instead.

✔ Be sure that both you and the person you are calling are both using the latest versions of Skype.

✔ If you use a realtek ac97 soundcard, you may want to download the latest driver.

Getting Help

Help is always close at hand with Skype. You can go to www.skype.com and click the Help tab. Then do one of the following:

✔ Type some key words into the Search Knowledgebase text box and click Search Knowledgebase.

✔ Click Forum and then click the Search The Forums button to search all of the 13 active forums simultaneously.

✔ Click the Users Guides link, if you think the answer to your problem may reside there.

✔ Click the Submit Support Request for an e-mail form and submit your question.

Part IV

Using Powerful, Free Multimedia Software

The 5th Wave   By Rich Tennant

"It's a horse racing software program. It analyzes my betting history and makes suggestions. Right now it's suggesting I try betting on football."

In this part . . .

We explore the world of free multimedia software designed to record sound, create drawings and clipart, manipulate digital images, design presentations, create 3D models and animations, and design diagrams. In Chapter 20, I describe how to use the fabulous sound recording and editing software called *Audacity*. Chapters 16 and 17 explore the GIMP, which performs basically the same tasks as Adobe Photoshop, and is extremely powerful and versatile. Chapter 14 covers OpenOffice.org Draw which is so easy to use that it can make an artist out of anyone. In Chapter 15, I describe step-by-step how to create a presentation using OpenOffice.org Impress. Chapter 19 explores the world of 3D art and animation, using the amazing Blender 3D software. And Chapter 18 is a little chapter describing Dia, the free software diagramming program.

Chapter 14

Creating Graphics with OpenOffice.Org Draw

For the task of creating clip art, OpenOffice.org Draw is a remarkable tool. You can create complex shapes simply and easily and modify those shapes by distorting them or pulling points. You can duplicate an object while rotating it, such as a petal to create a whole flower. You can make your lines and fills partially transparent, or create glows. You can create 3D objects and give them a realistic look using gradients. If you want to do flow-charts or organizational charts, Draw offers a whole set of diagram boxes and glue points to join the boxes together. A bonus is that Draw is fun and intuitive to use, as you will see as we cover its major features in this chapter.

Exploring the Interface

Draw offers floating toolbars, shown in Figure 14-1, which you can drag anywhere or close. This feature allows you to have your tools close to you when you want them and unseen when you don't want them. Using the floating toolbars keeps your Draw window highly functional yet uncluttered.

To open a floating toolbar, on either the Drawing, Standard, or Line and Filling toolbar, click on the disclosure triangle (the small triangle) to the right of the button for the toolbar that you want. The floating toolbar appears. Click and drag the toolbar so that it does not disappear when you click something else.

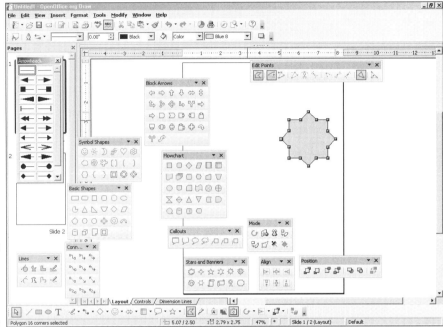

Figure 14-1:
Draw's floating toolbars.

Creating Your Own Clip Art

Draw offers an assortment of features for creating your own line drawings, logos, or other clip art for cutting and pasting into your documents. Tons of clip art is available on the Internet; however, usually it is available only for non-commercial uses. If you want to use clip art commercially, you probably need to either buy it or make it yourself. Using Draw, even a non-artist (like me) can create art (or something like it), as shown in Figure 14-2.

Adding shapes, lines, arrows, and text

When you create clip art, or any art, often you start with basic shapes, as shown in Figure 14-2. Draw offers lots of shapes. It has toolbars for creating Star Shapes, Symbol Shapes, Block Arrow Shapes, Flowcharting Shapes, and Basic Shapes. These toolbars are all available on the Drawing toolbar at the bottom of the Draw window. You can open a floating toolbar by clicking any of the small triangles next to the buttons for a specific toolbar (refer to Figure 14-1). Or you can choose View➪Toolbars and choose the toolbar that you want. The Drawing toolbar also has buttons for drawing lines and text, enabling you to do the following:

- ✔ **To draw shapes,** click the shape that you want, then click and drag in the Draw window. The shape appears in the size that you dragged.

- ✔ **To draw lines,** click on the Line button and then click and drag in the Draw window.

- ✔ **To draw arrows,** click on the Line button; then click and drag in the Draw window. Click the triangle next to the Arrow Style button on the Formatting toolbar, and click the arrow style you want for either end of the line.

- ✔ **To insert text,** click the Text button, and click in the Draw window. A text box appears. Type whatever you want; the text box expands to contain your typing.

- ✔ **To fill your shape with a color, gradient, hatching, bitmap, or to make the fill area transparent,** click on the shape, and choose either Color, Gradient, Hatching, Bitmap or Invisible from the Area Style/ Filling list box on the left. (Yes, there are two Area Style/Filling list boxes side-by-side on the Line and Filling Toolbar.) Then unless you chose Invisible, choose the specific color, gradient, hatching, or bitmap from the second Area Style/Filling list box to the right.

- ✔ **To change the size, color, or style of the lines of your line, arrow, or shape,** click on it. Choose your selections from the Line Style list box, the Line Width spin box, and the Line Color list box on the Formatting toolbar.

- ✔ **To resize a line, arrow, or shape,** click on it and pull the handles to make it larger or smaller. You can Shift+drag to keep the proportions the same.

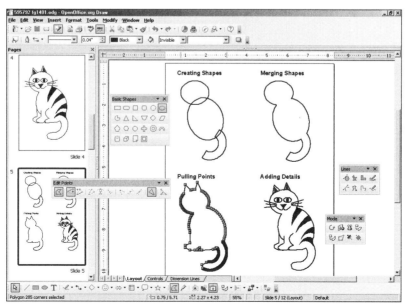

Figure 14-2:
Clip art created in Draw.

When creating clip art, having a model to refer to is always a good idea. This can be some clip art that you like but can't use because it's copyrighted. Don't worry. Your clip art will turn out different from the model.

Merging, intersecting, and subtracting shapes

If you're making clip art (refer to Figure 14-2), you need to merge your shapes. To merge your shapes, first select them all.

You can select objects in several ways:

- ✔ Click the Selection tool (the leftmost button on the Draw toolbar); then click (not on any object) and drag to include whatever objects you want selected in the dotted rectangular border that appears.
- ✔ Shift+click on objects to select more than one at a time.

When you select more than one shape, you can merge, intersect, or subtract the shapes. Choose Modify➪Shapes➪Merge (or Subtract or Intersect) to do the following:

- ✔ **Merging shapes** makes the shape into a single object with a single line bordering it, as shown in Figure 14-2.
- ✔ **Intersecting shapes** generates the shape that is the intersection of the two or more shapes selected.
- ✔ **Subtracting shapes** erases whatever is in the bottom shape and below the top shape. The top shape also disappears. Think of the top shape as the eraser.

Grouping shapes

Grouping shapes is useful for selecting a group of objects in a single click. Then if you want to move them, resize them, copy them, or more, you can just click on a grouped object as if it were a single shape, line, or text.

To group objects, select the objects that you want to group and choose Modify➪Group. To ungroup a grouped object, click on the grouped object and choose Modify➪Ungroup.

Creating polygons and curves

You can draw curves by using the Curve tool on the Lines toolbar. You have the choice of filled or unfilled curves, but you can always fill or unfill at a later time, so your choice is not so crucial. You also can draw curves with the Freeform Line tool on the Lines toolbar, but freeform lines may be less smooth and sometimes may give a less professional look. The kind of curve that you create with the curve tool is known as a Bézier curve.

To create a curve, do the following:

1. **Click the disclosure triangle next to the Curve button on the Drawing toolbar to open the Lines toolbar.**

2. **Drag the Lines toolbar away from the Drawing toolbar so that it doesn't disappear when you click anything else.**

3. **Click the Curve button.**

4. **Click at the point in the Drawing window where you want the curve to begin and drag a short way. Release the mouse button and move the mouse to the point where you want the curve to end, and then double-click.** (Don't worry about the arc of the curve, at first, just establish the two end point locations.)

   Either two handles or eight handles appear around your curve.

5. **If eight handles appear around your curve, click the Points button on the Drawing toolbar, if it is not already selected.**

   Six of the eight handles disappear. Only the two end point handles remain, and one is larger than the other.

6. **To adjust the arc of the curve, click the larger of the two handles.**

   A control line appears with a handle.

7. **Click and drag the handle on the control line to change the shape of the curve however you want it to look.**

8. **To change the size or position of the curve, click and drag either end-point of the curve.**

To create a curve with more than one arc in it, first see if the Edit Points toolbar is visible. If it is not visible, select the curve. If the Edit Points toolbar still does not appear, then click the Points button on the Draw toolbar. Then to add another arc in your curve, click the Insert Point button on the Edit Points toolbar and click and drag on the curve that you just created using the preceding procedure. A new handle appears that you can move (or click on, for the control line to appear).

Pulling points

Pulling points is the ability to drag handles on an image in a way that creates a new shape, and not just resize the image. This gives you the ability to create the image you want, as shown in Figure 14-2. You can either generate lines between two points that you pull, or you can generate curves with handles that allow you to specify exactly the curve for you.

To pull points, follow these steps:

1. **Click on the object to select it; then, if the Points button on the Drawing toolbar is not selected, click on it.**

2. **Do one of the following:**

   • **If the Edit Points toolbar appears,** as shown in Figure 14-2, then you can drag handles on the object one at a time to create a new shape for that object.

   • **If the Edit Points toolbar does not appear,** click it again (just in case it was already there and you made it disappear). If it still doesn't appear, you need to convert your object into a Curve or a Polygon by choosing Modify⇨Convert⇨Curve or Modify⇨Convert⇨Polygon. Then click the Points button again.

If you want curves between most of your handles, you can convert your shape to a curve. If you want straight lines between most of your handles, you can convert your shape to a polygon.

3. **Pull any of the handles to reshape your object.**

   If your object is a curve, a control line appears with two handles at each end to adjust the arc of the curve. No such control lines appear if your object is a polygon, since straight lines have no arc.

4. **If your object is a curve, drag the handles to adjust the arc of the curve. Or, if you want to modify any curve, click on a handle and adjust the handles on the control line that appears.**

5. **To get a precise look for your object, you can do any of the following, using the buttons on the Edit Points toolbar:**

   • **To insert a point,** click the Insert Point button, and click and drag on a line where you want to insert a point.

   • **To delete a point,** click on the point and press Delete or Backspace (depending on your keyboard).

- **To convert a polygon point to a curve,** click on the handle and click the Convert to Curve button.

- **To convert a curve to a polygon point,** click on the handle, and click the Convert to Curve button. (Yes, this is correct, in my version, at least.)

- **If you want your curve to appear symmetrically on both sides of your handle,** select the handle and click the Symmetric Transition button.

- **If you have more handles than you need in your object,** select the object and click the Eliminate Points button.

To turn off Edit Points mode, click the Points button on the Drawing toolbar.

Distorting, rotating, and flipping

Draw's distortion tools reside on the Mode toolbar, as shown in Figure 14-1. Draw offers three main distortion tools:

- ✔ **Distort:** Allows you to distort an object as if it were on a transparent piece of paper and you are folding or expanding a corner of that paper to distort the image.

- ✔ **Set In Circle (Perspective):** Allows you, for example, to make a petal shape out of an oval with a single click and drag.

- ✔ **Set In Circle (Slant):** Distorts in a circular way. For example, the stripes on the cat in Figure 14-2 were triangles distorted with Set In Circle (Slant).

To use the distortion tools, follow these steps:

1. **Open the Mode floating toolbar by clicking the disclosure triangle next to the Effects button on the Drawing toolbar, shown in Figure 14-1.**

2. **Drag the Mode toolbar from the Drawing toolbar, so that it stays visible.**

3. **Select the shape that you want to distort and click the Distort, Set In Circle (Perspective), or Set In Circle (Slant) button.**

4. **Click and drag the corner points or side points to create the effect you want.**

To use the rotation tool, select the object that you want to rotate by clicking on it. Click the Rotate button on either the Drawing toolbar or the Mode floating toolbar, which appears when you click the disclosure triangle beside the

Effects button on the Drawing toolbar. The handles of the object turn red, and if you click and drag a corner point, the object rotates. Notice that the angle of rotation appears on the status bar.

If you try to rotate an object and it doesn't work, you may be in Edit Points mode. Click the Points button on the Drawing toolbar to exit Edit Points mode; then click the Rotate button and try again.

To flip an object, select it and choose Modify⇨Flip⇨Horizontal or Modify⇨Flip⇨Vertical.

Aligning and arranging

If you have lots of shapes, text, or imported graphics that you want to align so that they make nice neat columns or rows, or both, you can select the objects in a single row or column and click the disclosure triangle on the Alignment button of the Drawing toolbar to open the Align toolbar, shown in Figure 14-1. Then click the appropriate button: Left, Centered, Right, Bottom, Center, or Top.

When you put one object on top of another, unless the top object is transparent or smaller than the object below it, the object below is not seen. OpenOffice.org Draw stacks objects in the order of when they are created or imported into the Draw window. You can change this stacking by selecting an object and clicking the disclosure triangle beside the Arrange button on the Drawing toolbar to open the Position toolbar, shown in Figure 14-1. Then click the appropriate button: Bring To Front, Bring Forward, Send Backward, Send To Back.

Duplicating and Cross-fading

Draw's duplicating and cross-fading features allow you to create multiple copies of an image in several ways. The Duplication tool creates copies that you can specify to rotate, enlarge or shrink, or change colors gradually. The flower in Figure 14-3 was created with the help of the Duplication tool. The Cross-fading tool changes the shape of one object through a series of copies into the shape of a second object. It also changes the color and position.

Cross-fading is simpler than duplicating. To cross-fade, select two objects that you want to cross-fade together; then choose Edit⇨Cross-fading. In the Cross-fading dialog box that appears, choose the number of increments, and click OK.

Figure 14-3:
The
Duplicate
dialog box
contains the
settings
used to
duplicate
the image of
the double
petal in the
upper-left
slide to
create the
image,
which was
copied and
pasted into
the slide
below it.

To use the Duplication tool to create an image, such as the flower in Figure 14-3, do the following:

1. **Select the object that you want to duplicate and choose Edit⇨Duplicate.**

   (The image that was rotated to produce the flower in Figure 14-3 is in the upper left-hand corner preview of slide 6. It is an airplane propeller-type shape.)

   The Duplicate dialog box appears, as shown in Figure 14-3.

2. **In the dialog box use the spin boxes to fill in the following five bits of information:**

   Number of copies

   Angle: Angle of rotation at which you want copies to appear.

   X-axis and Y-axis: If you want the copies to move from the center, specify how far and what direction.

   Enlargement Width and Height: How much you want the size of your copies to grow or shrink.

   Colors: Starting color and ending color.

3. **Click OK.**

Your duplication occurs. The settings in Figure 14-3 created the image in the lower left-hand slide of Figure 14-3. To finish creating the flower image on the right, I copied and pasted the image in slide 9 and shrank it to give the flower a center. Then I made the stem and leaves by subtracting and intersecting oval shapes, respectively.

Adding Transparency and Glows

OpenOffice.org Draw offers any level of transparency that you want for an object, and you can make your transparency increase gradually to achieve a glowing or other interesting effect. You can specify where you want the transparency gradient to start and end as well as its shape and angle.

A few easy ways to add or delete transparency to your object are as follows:

- ✔ **To choose a percentage of transparency,** select the object and choose Format⇨Area. Click on the Transparency tab, choose Transparency, and select the percentage of transparency from the spin box.

- ✔ **To gradually make your object transparent,** select the object and choose the Transparency button on the Mode toolbar. (To view the Mode toolbar, you can choose View⇨Toolbars⇨Mode.) Two boxes appear on the object. Click and drag the black box where you want the transparency to start to fade, and click and drag the white box to whatever edge you want to become transparent.

- ✔ **To delete any transparency,** select the object, choose Format⇨Area, click the Transparency tab, and choose No Transparency.

Don't forget to make your lines invisible to get the maximum effect for your transparency. To make your lines invisible, choose Invisible from the Line Style list box on the Line and Filling toolbar.

The gradient created by the Transparency button is a Linear gradient, which means it fades out in a linear shape. Alternatively, you can choose a Radial gradient, which fades out in a circular shape (or another gradient shape, such as Square, Ellipsoid, Quadratic, or Axial). You can choose to have your gradient be at an angle and can precisely control the starting and stopping transparency amounts.

To create your own custom-made transparency gradient (or glow), do the following:

1. **Select the object that you want to apply the transparency gradient to.**

   For example, you could choose a circle for a Radial gradient that you could use behind a picture of someone's head. In Figure 14-4, I chose an elongated star to contain the glow.

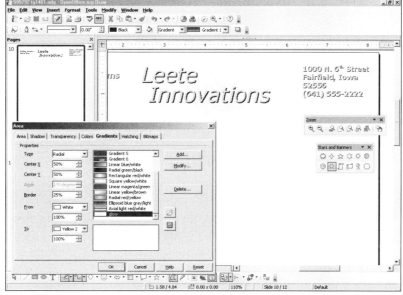

Figure 14-4: A glow in a letterhead can add visual interest to your stationery.

2. **Choose Format⇨Area, and select the Transparency tab.**

   The Transparency tab of the Area dialog box appears, as shown in Figure 14-4.

3. **Select Gradient and choose the type of gradient you want: Linear, Axial, Radial, Ellipsoid, Quadratic, or Square.**

   The preview pane changes to reflect the type of gradient you chose.

4. **Fill in the following spin boxes:**

   • **Center X and Center Y:** To make the center of your gradient be off center in the object.

   • **Angle:** To angle your gradient (this has no effect on a Radial gradient).

   • **Border:** To specify how much area around the edges you do not want to include in the gradient.

   • **Start Value and End Value:** The starting and ending percentage of transparency.

5. **Click OK.**

The transparency gradient is applied to your object. You may have to tweak it a few times to get it just the way you want it.

Adding Gradients

OpenOffice.org Draw offers several ready-made gradients. You can apply one of these gradients by selecting your object, choosing Gradient from the Apply Style/Filling list box on the Line and Filling toolbar, and then choosing the gradient that you want from the list box beside it. If the list box does not have the gradient that you were looking for, you can create your own gradient.

To create your own gradient, do the following:

1. **Choose Format⇨Area and select the Gradients tab.**

2. **Choose Add and give your gradient a name in the Name dialog box and click OK.**

3. **Fill in the following from the spin boxes in the dialog box: Type, CenterX, CenterY, Angle, Border, From and To.** (For more information about these fields, see step 4 in the preceding section.)

4. **Click OK.**

The name that you chose in step 2 is added to the list of gradients in the Area Style/Filling list box on the Line and Filling toolbar. You can select any object and choose the gradient from the Area Style/Filling list box to apply it.

The Line and Filling toolbar disappears when a bitmap is selected. To view the Line and Filling toolbar, first see if a bitmap is selected and, if so, click anywhere in the Drawing window (except on another bitmap) to de-select it.

Creating 3D

OpenOffice.org Draw offers you the ability to create 3D objects, such as the snowman in Figure 14-5. You can apply textures and lighting, and rotate your art in 3D. You can use Draw's collection of 3D objects, such as spheres and cubes, or you can make your own 3D rotation object, as shown in the two slides on the left in Figure 14-5. You can draw any curve or even a letter or number, such as 3, and Draw can create a 3D version of it. And, of course, you can extrude letters to make them 3D, such as for a 3D logo, but you may find in the long run that some nice shadows will do just as well. OpenOffice.org Draw generates shadows according to your specifications — big, small, colorful, or whatever.

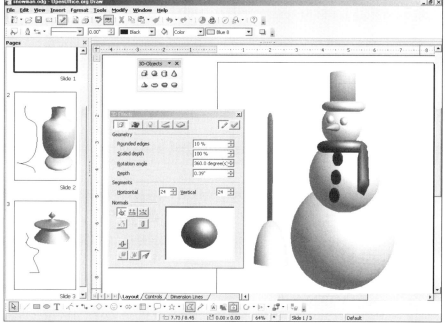

Figure 14-5:
A snowman
created
using
Draw's
3D tools
and the
Materials
tab of the 3D
dialog box.

Adding shadows

Shadows are not really 3D, but they give a 3D look and are incredibly easy to add. You can add shadows to text or objects. To add shadows to text, select the text by double-clicking in the text box, clicking and dragging the mouse over the text, and then clicking the Shadow button on the Formatting toolbar that appears. Your text now has a shadow.

Text shadows are gray and do not appear well with black type, so before you create a shadow for your text, be sure to change the color of your text.

To add shadows to an object, follow these steps:

1. **Click on the object and click the Shadow button on the Line and Filling toolbar.**

2. **If you want a bigger shadow or smaller shadow, or to position it differently or give it a different color, choose Format⇨Area and click on the Shadow tab.**

3. **Select the Use Shadow check box and fill in the position and the Distance, Color, and Transparency spin boxes. Click OK.**

Using the 3D Objects toolbar

Draw offers a 3D Objects toolbar with ready-made 3D shapes, such as a cube, cone, sphere, and more. To view the 3D toolbar, choose View➪Toolbars➪3D Objects. To use the 3D Objects toolbar, click a button and drag in the Draw window. The snowman in Figure 14-5 was made entirely using the 3D Objects toolbar.

To rotate the object in 3D, select the object and click the Rotate tool on the Effects toolbar. The handles turn red, and you can rotate the object in three dimensions by clicking and dragging the handles.

Creating 3D rotation objects

If the objects on the 3D Objects toolbar are not exactly what you're looking for, Draw has a feature for rotating whatever line or curve you draw and creating a 3D object out of it. For example, the two curves in Figure 14-5 were used to generate the 3D rotation objects beside them. To create 3D rotation objects, create a curve — it can have as many arcs in it as you want or can include straight lines; then choose Modify➪Convert➪To 3D Rotation Object. Voilà! A digital lathe.

Adding textures and modifying lighting

To add textures to your 3D object, click to select the object; then right-click and choose 3D Effects from the pop-up menu. Click the Material button, as shown in Figure 14-5 (fifth button from the left at the top), and choose either Metal, Gold, Chrome, Plastic, or Wood from the Favorites drop-down list. Click the green check mark.

To change the color of your 3D object, click on it and choose Color and the color you want from the Area Style/Filling list boxes on the Line and Filling toolbar.

To modify the lighting of your 3D object, click to select the object and right-click. Choose 3D Effects from the pop-up menu. Click the Illumination button and click and drag the light source in the diagram at the bottom of the window. You can move the light anywhere around the object in the diagram. Then click the green check mark. The new position of your light source changes the lighting of your 3D object.

Chapter 15

Making Presentations with OpenOffice.Org Impress

*Y*ou can use Impress to create presentations by creating slides and then filling them with information, pictures, charts, spreadsheets, diagrams, animations — whatever you need for your presentation. With Impress, you can assign animations for the transitions between your slides, and you can give those transitions ready-made sound effects to go along with them. Or you can import your own sound effects. You can create a slide show that automatically advances the slides, according to individual timings that you set, or you can advance the slides with a mouse click or choose the next slide using the Navigator. All these features are the topics of this chapter.

Impress is designed to be similar to PowerPoint and imports and exports PowerPoint presentations. It is also easy to learn and use. Because it's part of the OpenOffice.org program, if you know Writer, Calc, Draw, or other OpenOffice.org modules, you already know the basics of Impress, such as how to add pictures, how to choose font size and font type, and more.

Getting Started

You can get started using Impress either by creating a new presentation or by importing or opening an existing presentation. Normally, when you start Impress, the Presentation Wizard opens.

Creating a new presentation

To create a new presentation, follow these steps:

1. **Do one of the following to start the Presentation Wizard:**

   • **If you're not already running OpenOffice.org,** choose Start⇨ Programs⇨OpenOffice.org 2.0⇨OpenOffice.org 2.0 Impress.

   • **If you're already running OpenOffice.org,** choose File⇨ Wizards⇨Presentation, or choose File⇨New⇨Presentation.

   The Presentation Wizard dialog box appears, as shown in Figure 15-1.

2. **Choose Empty Presentation.**

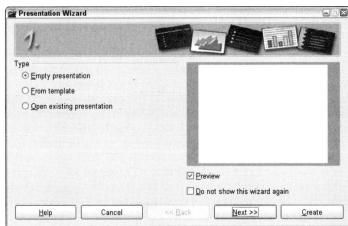

Figure 15-1: Choose to start a new presentation, open an existing presentation, or use a template, using the Presentation Wizard.

If you want to choose Open existing presentation, follow the instructions found later in the chapter in the "Opening an existing presentation or importing a PowerPoint presentation" section.

3. **Click Next.**

   The second dialog box of the Presentation Wizard appears, shown in Figure 15-2, in which you can choose a design for your slide.

Figure 15-2:
Choose a
background
and output
medium for
your slide
using
the Pre-
sentation
Wizard.

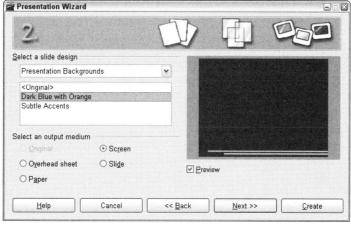

4. **Select a slide design, if you want.** You can choose from Presentation
   Backgrounds or Presentation. (Both categories offer only backgrounds —
   they are just categorized differently.)

   Be sure the Preview box is checked so you can see the background you
   select in the Preview pane.

   The parameters you choose in the Presentation Wizard can be modified
   for individual slides in Impress, or you can change your slide show completely. The wizard just provides a starting point, but you can easily
   change everything later.

5. **Choose the output medium:**

   - **Screen:** Use this option to show your presentation in the computer
     screen. This is the default.

   - **Overhead sheet:** This sizes your presentation for overhead
     projectors.

   - **Slide:** This option is for creating a slide show with real slides.
     (Impress uses the term *slide* for the pages of any type of presenta-
     tion, not just presentations to be exported as real slides.)

   - **Paper:** After you complete the wizard, you can choose Format⇨
     Page and choose the size of paper that you want your presentation
     to fit.

6. **Click Next.**

   The third dialog box of the Presentation Wizard appears, as shown in
   Figure 15-3.

Figure 15-3:
In this
dialog box
of the Pre-
sentation
Wizard,
you may
choose the
transition
effects you
want, and
whether
you want
your slide
show to be
automated.

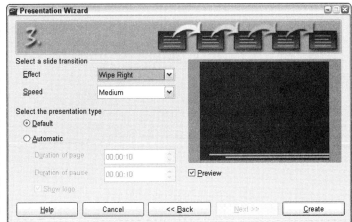

7. **Assign the following:**

   - **Effect:** Choose the transition effect from the drop-down list of over fifty effects.

   - **Speed:** Choose Slow, Medium, or Fast from the Speed list to assign the speed of the transition effect.

   - **Select the Presentation type:** Choose Automatic if you want your slides to appear automatically one after the other after a specific interval of time. The Duration of page option refers to the seconds, minutes, or hours for how long each page should remain on the screen. Choose the Duration of pause for the time interval between presentations, if any. (If you want the OpenOffice.org logo to display between presentations, go ahead and select the Show logo option.)

8. **Click Create.**

   Impress opens with the background and settings that you chose in the Presentation Wizard, as shown in Figure 15-4.

By default, Impress opens a new presentation using the Presentation Wizard. If you want to skip the wizard for each subsequent presentation, choose Tools⇨Options, expand the OpenOffice.org Impress menu on the left, and deselect the Start with Wizard check box. Then click OK.

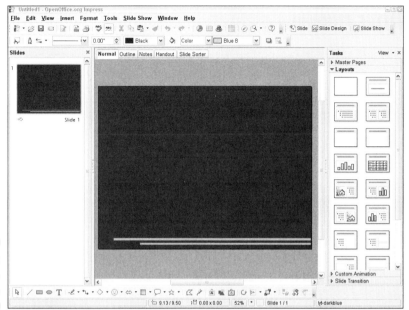

Figure 15-4:
OpenOffice.
org Impress.

Opening an existing presentation or importing a PowerPoint presentation

Opening a PowerPoint presentation is as simple as opening an Impress presentation. You can open either an Impress or PowerPoint presentation in three ways:

- ✔ **If you're already in OpenOffice.org Impress or OpenOffice.org Writer, or any of the OpenOffice.org modules,** choose File⇨Open, select the PowerPoint (or Impress file), and click Open. The file opens into OpenOffice.org Impress. (PowerPoint and Impress documents open exactly the same.)

- ✔ **If you're starting OpenOffice.org Impress and the Presentation Wizard appears,** then choose Open existing presentation. If the presentation appears in the list box, choose it and click Create. Otherwise, choose <Other Position> and click Create. The Open dialog box appears, where you select your file and then click Open.

- ✔ **Double-click on the Impress file in its folder.** Depending on how you install OpenOffice.org, PowerPoint presentations may also open in Impress when you double-click on them.

Defining a Master Slide

The master slide is the model for all the slides in a presentation. It defines the styles, the background, the transition effect, speed, and more. You can change the background, styles, or transition effects of any slide, and your change will override the master slide. Or you can change the master slide and the changes will apply to all slides.

Presentations can be as individual as you are. There is no need to confine yourself to the few backgrounds that Impress offers. So, unless you want to use one of Impress's default backgrounds, then the first thing you may want to do when you start a presentation is to define your master slide, beginning with the background.

Assigning your own background for the master slide

Because OpenOffice.org has very few backgrounds to choose from (and even if they had many), you may want to create your own or download one from the Internet.

Defining a new background has three major steps to it:

- ✔ **Finding or creating the background that you want for your presentation.**

    - **To download backgrounds from the Internet,** you may want to check out www.ellenfinkelstein.com, www.brainybetty.com/backgrounds.htm, or www.websiteestates.com/ppoint.html. Needless to say, the Internet is loaded with free PowerPoint backgrounds that you can use for your presentations, as long as they are designated as free for commercial use or public domain.

    - **To create a background in Draw,** choose File➪New➪Drawing to start Draw, and then choose Format➪Page. In the Page tab, choose Screen from the Format list, select the Landscape Orientation button, and click OK.

- ✔ **Importing the background into OpenOffice.org Impress's bitmap list.** See the instructions in the following section "Importing backgrounds." You can import lots of backgrounds into the bitmap list, if you want.

- ✔ **Applying the background to the master slide. See the instructions in the later section, "Adding a background to the master slide."**

Importing backgrounds

To import a background, follow these steps:

1. **Do one of the following:**

   • **If you created your own background in OpenOffice.org Draw,** then in Draw, export the background by choosing Edit⇨Select All, then File⇨Export. Choose a folder and a file format (usually JPEG is good), type a filename, and click Save.

   • **If you want to download a background from the Internet,** see Chapter 9 for more information.

2. **In Impress, choose Format⇨Area and click the Bitmaps tab.**

3. **Click the Import button and select the file that you downloaded or exported from OpenOffice.org Draw. Click Open.**

   The Name dialog box appears, allowing you to give the background a descriptive name other than the default name of the file.

4. **Give your background a name or accept the filename as the default name and click OK.**

   Your background is now added to the bitmap list.

To have your new backgrounds show up as options in the wizard, and in the Master Pages pane of the Tasks pane, you may need to save the JPEG file in the following folder: Program Files/OpenOffice.org 2.0/share/template/en-US(*or other language folder here*)/presnt.

Adding a background to the master slide

To insert your new background into each slide, you need to edit the master slide, by doing the following:

1. **Choose View⇨Master⇨Slide Master.**

   The Master Slide view appears, as shown in Figure 15-5.

2. **Choose Format⇨Page and click the Background tab. Select Bitmap and choose your background from the list of bitmaps. Deselect the Tile check box, if it is selected.** (Doing so automatically selects the AutoFit check box.)

3. **Click OK.**

   The background that you imported in the previous section is now the background for your master slide.

4. **Adjust your text boxes in the master document to fit properly within your new background** by clicking and dragging them to adjust their location or by resizing them by clicking and dragging their handles.

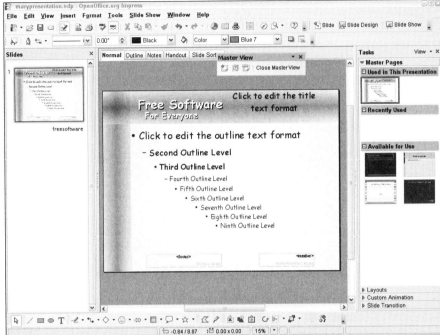

Figure 15-5:
Modifying
the master
slide using
the Master
Slide view.

Assigning styles to the master slide

Impress automatically assigns a style with a specific type size, font, and indentation for each outline level in the master slide. This gives your presentation appealing consistency. To change any of the styles, be sure you are in Master Slide view, as shown in Figure 15-5. (Choose View➪Master➪Slide Master), if you're not already in Master Slide view. Modifying any of the font types, font sizes, or indentations automatically changes the style for that outline level in the Stylist. (Remember the Stylist from Chapter 4?) For example, if you select all the text in the Master Slide view and assign a new font by choosing a font from the Font drop-down list box on the Formatting toolbar, all the text in your presentation changes automatically to that new font.

When you select text in the master slide, the Formatting toolbar appears automatically.

Creating Slides

After you have your master slide, you can go ahead and add more slides. Choose View➪Master➪Slide Master to deselect the Master Slide view or click the Close Master View button on the Line and Filling toolbar or floating toolbar.

Inserting slides

If the Layouts pane is not visible in the Tasks pane on the right side of the Impress window, click the Layouts disclosure triangle to reveal the layouts. If the Tasks pane is not visible, choose View⇨Tasks Pane, or click the Show/Hide Tasks Pane button, shown earlier in Figure 15-4.

To insert slides, choose Insert⇨Slide and click the type of layout that you want for your slide in the Layouts section. The layouts include:

- **Text frames.** This layout quickly and easily gives the presentation a uniform appearance, saving you from having to spend time and effort creating your own text frames. To add text, click in the text frame.

- **Picture frames.** To add pictures, click on any layout with a picture and double-click in the picture frame in the slide. The Insert Picture dialog box appears. Select your file and click Open. The picture conforms to the size of the frame without affecting its proportions. For more about pictures, see the section "Inserting and Linking Pictures" in Chapter 4.

- **Spreadsheet.** You can add a spreadsheet by clicking the Title, Spreadsheet layout and then double-clicking in the spreadsheet area in the slide to view the spreadsheet, using the handles to resize it, and right-clicking on it to format the cells, add rows, and other tasks. To exit Spreadsheet mode, click outside the spreadsheet.

- **Charts.** You can add a chart by clicking the Title, Chart layout; the Title, Text, Chart layout; or the Title, Chart, Text layout and double-clicking the chart area in the slide to view the chart and then right-clicking on the chart to define the chart. To exit Chart mode, click outside the chart. For more about charts, see the later section "Creating charts."

- **Blank.** Use this layout for complete flexibility, at the cost of non-uniformity. Click the Blank slide in the Layouts pane and then either insert a picture by clicking the From File button on the Drawing toolbar, or insert a text box by clicking the Text button on the Drawing toolbar and double-clicking to add text. Then you can resize your picture or text box by clicking on it and dragging its handles, or relocate the picture or text box by clicking the Select tool on the Drawing toolbar and clicking and dragging it.

If a dialog box appears warning you that "This action deletes the list of actions that can not be undone," you probably want to select the Do not show this warning again check box and click Yes.

Modifying and ordering slides

To modify any slide, click on the slide in the Slides pane, and modify it in the main Impress window.

Impress gives you the ability to define whatever order you want for your slides in your slide show. Your slides don't have to be ordered properly in the Slide pane or the Slide Sorter, but doing so is generally a good idea, not only to keep your slides more organized, but also because they need to be ordered if you want to export them. To order your slides you can do either of the following:

- ✔ Click and drag your slides to new locations in the Slide pane of the Impress window. If the Slide pane is not visible, then choose View⇨Slide pane, or click the Show/Hide Slide Pane button, shown earlier in Figure 15-4.

- ✔ Click the Slide Sorter button, and then click and drag the slides into the order in which you want them to appear.

When using the Slide Sorter tab, you may want to hide the Slide and Tasks panes to give you more room to view the slides. To do so, choose View⇨ Slide Pane and View⇨Tasks Pane, or click the Show/Hide Tasks Pane button and the Show/Hide Slide Pane button, shown in Figure 15-4.

Adding notes

You can add notes to your slides by choosing the Notes tab, or choosing View⇨Notes Page. Then just click in the text box to add notes. Notes are not viewed during the presentation, but you can include them when exporting to HTML.

Creating charts

Often, you may want to have charts in your slide show. Charts are easy to create. You can customize your chart with your data, titles, and a legend, as well as choose the type of chart. Impress offers several kinds of charts:

Pie charts	Stock charts
Bar charts	Net charts
Stacked charts	3D charts

To create a chart, follow these steps:

1. **Choose Insert⇨Slide and click the Title, Chart layout in the Layouts pane.**

   If the Layouts pane is not visible, click the Layouts disclosure triangle in the Tasks pane, as shown in Figure 15-4. If the Tasks pane is not visible, choose View⇨Tasks Pane, or click the Show/Hide Tasks Pane button, as shown in Figure 15-4.

2. **Double-click in the Chart area.**

   A bar chart appears.

3. **If you want a different type of chart, right-click in the chart and choose Chart type, choose the type of chart from the Chart Type dialog box, and click OK.**

   The new chart type appears. For example, the pie chart appears, as shown in Figure 15-6.

4. **Double-click on the Main title and enter your title.**

5. **To enter data, right-click in the chart and choose Chart Data.**

   The chart data spreadsheet appears, as shown in Figure 15-6.

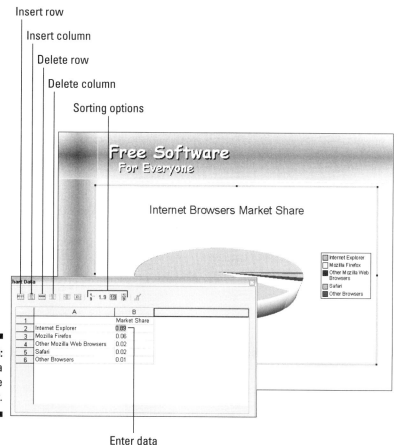

Insert row

Insert column

Delete row

Delete column

Sorting options

Figure 15-6:
Enter data
to customize
the chart.

Enter data

6. **Do any of the following:**

   To enter data into a cell, click in the cell and type.

   To delete a column or row, click in the column or row and click the Delete Column or Delete Row button, shown in Figure 15-6.

   To insert a column or row, click in the column or row and click the Insert Column or Insert Row button, as shown in Figure 15-6.

7. **Click the Apply to Chart button, shown in Figure 15-6.**

   Your chart appears with the correct values and correct names in the legend.

Click outside the chart to exit chart editing mode.

Adding Transition Effects and Sound Effects

Impress offers over 50 wipes that you can apply in any of three speeds: Slow, Medium, and Fast. It also offers over thirty sound effects to go with the transitions. You can assign a transition and sound effect globally, so that every slide uses the same one, or you can assign different transition effects for individual slides. To apply a slide transition, first click the disclosure triangle to reveal the Slide Transition pane of the Tasks pane, as shown in Figure 15-7.

In the Slide Transition pane, you can do the following:

✓ **To view and apply a transition to the current slide,** choose a transition from the transition list. The transition appears on the slide.

✓ **To choose the speed of the transition,** select the speed from the Speed list.

✓ **To hear and apply a sound to the transition for the current slide,** choose the sound from the Sound list.

✓ **To apply a transition to all the slides,** choose it from the transition list and click Apply to All Slides.

✓ **To set the Slide Show setting to advance the current slide when the mouse is clicked,** choose On Mouse Click. To advance each slide when the mouse is clicked on it, choose On Mouse Click and then click Apply to All Slides.

✓ **To automatically advance the current slide after a certain period of time,** click the Automatically After button and fill in the number of seconds in the spin box for the slide to appear on the screen.

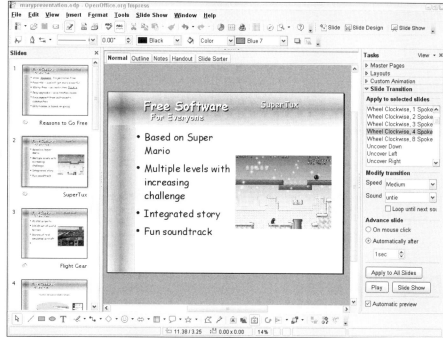

Figure 15-7:
In the Slide
Transition
pane on
the far right,
you can
assign the
transition
effect for
your slide
or slides.

Presenting a Slide Show

You may want to present your slides by clicking the mouse, or you may want your slides to play automatically. You can play your slides in the order that they appear in the Impress window, or in another order — or even several orders, depending on your audience. You may want to establish the order ahead of time, or be flexible while you give your presentation and choose the order as you go from the Navigator.

You can set your individual slides or all the slides as a whole to proceed automatically or when you click on the slide. See the preceding section for details.

Showing slides

To play your slides sequentially in the order they appear in Impress, click on the first slide that you want to start with, and then choose Slide Show➪ Slide Show or press F5. Click on any slide or press the spacebar to proceed to the next slide, unless the slide is set to advance automatically. To end the slide show, press Esc.

If your slide show does not proceed as you expect — for example, if it does not proceed automatically or if it proceeds automatically and was supposed to proceed manually —check to be sure that the Slide Show settings are not overriding your other settings. To check the Slide Show settings, choose Slide Show➪Slide Show Settings and deselect the Change Slides Manually check box, or deselect Auto. Then click OK.

Saving a custom slide order

To create a custom order for slides, choose Slide Show➪Custom Slide Show (not Custom Animation). In the Custom Slide Show dialog box that appears, click New; then choose the slides one by one in the Existing Slides list. Click the arrow button pointing to the Selected Slides list, as shown in Figure 15-8. When the list is complete and in the order that you want, type a name into the Name input box and click OK.

Figure 15-8:
Create a custom order for your slides and save it as a custom slide show.

Define Custom Slide Show	
Name Free Software Presentation 20 minutes	OK
Existing slides	Selected slides
Mozilla Thunderbird	Mozilla Firefox
Mozilla Firefox	Mozilla Thunderbird
OpenOffice.org Writer	The Gimp
OpenOffice.org Calc	OpenOffice.org Writer
OpenOffice.org Impress	OpenOffice.org Calc
The Gimp	OpenOffice.org Impress
Audacity	
Gaim	
Skype	

To play a custom slide show, choose Slide Show➪Custom Slide Show and select the Use Custom Slide Show check box. Choose the name of the slide show that you created earlier, and click Start.

Presenting with the Navigator

If you want complete flexibility in your slide show, try using the Navigator, shown in Figure 15-9. The Navigator lists the names of each slide, and to advance to any of them, you just need to double-click on the name of the slide. You may want to name your slides before using this method. To name your slides, right-click on a slide in the Slide pane, choose Rename, and type a name.

To set up your slide show to use the Navigator to advance your slides, choose Slide Show➪Slide Show Settings, and select the Navigator Visible check box. (Also, you may want to select Window, so that the Navigator won't cover any of your slide.) Click OK.

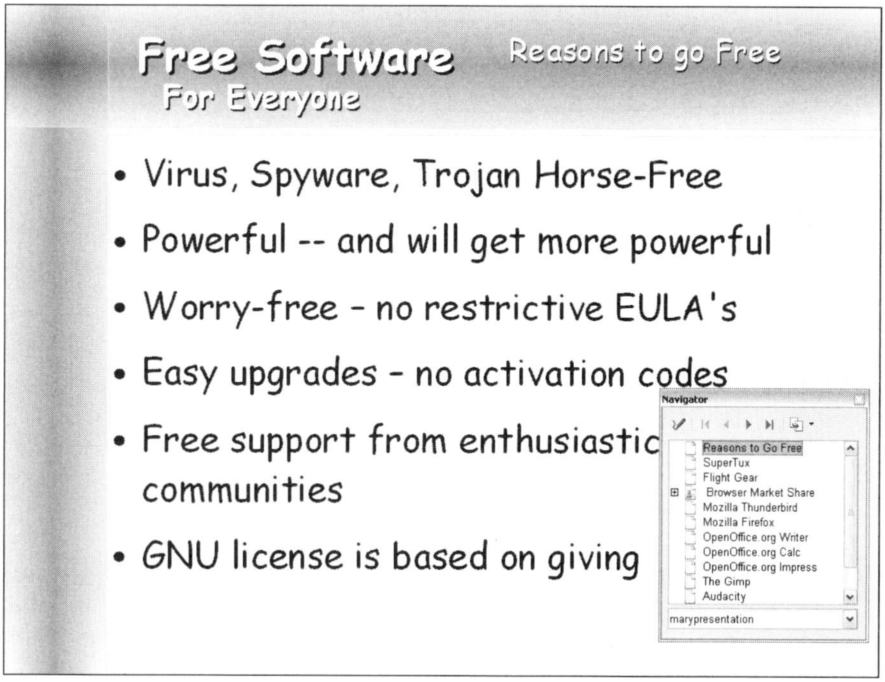

Free Software Reasons to go Free
For Everyone

- Virus, Spyware, Trojan Horse-Free
- Powerful -- and will get more powerful
- Worry-free - no restrictive EULA's
- Easy upgrades - no activation codes
- Free support from enthusiastic communities
- GNU license is based on giving

Figure 15-9:
For complete flexibility in your slide show, you can use the Navigator.

To open the Navigator, click the Navigator button on the Standard toolbar or choose Edit⇨Navigator.

You may want to position the Navigator over either the Slide pane or the Tasks pane, and then hide the other pane, either by clicking on its Hide button, as shown in Figure 15-4, or choosing View⇨Tasks Pane, or View⇨Slide Pane.

To start a slide show choose Slide Show⇨Slide Show or press F5. Now you can double-click on a slide to advance to it. You can also use the buttons on the Navigator: First Slide, Last Slide, Next Slide, and Previous Slide. Press Esc to end the presentation.

Saving or Exporting a Slide Show

You can save your file as an Impress or PowerPoint file, or you can export the entire presentation as a Flash movie, as a set of Web pages, or as a PDF document. Or you can export individual slides in any one of numerous file formats.

Saving in Impress format or PowerPoint format

To save your presentation in PowerPoint format, you probably first want to remove any sound effects that you may have added for your slide transitions. Sound does not convert properly to PowerPoint. Then you can choose File➪ Save As. In the Save As dialog box that appears, choose Microsoft PowerPoint 97/2000/XP (.ppt) from the Save As Type list. Type a filename, double-click on the folder that you want your file to reside in, and click Save.

To save your presentation in Impress format, do all the aforementioned steps, except choose OpenDocument Presentation (.odp) from the Save As Type list, which is the default.

Exporting to SWF

You can export your presentation as a Flash file in .swf format so that it can be viewed in a Web browser that has the free Flash player installed, as many Web browsers do. To export your file, perform these steps:

1. **Choose File➪Export.**

2. **In the File Format list of the Export dialog box, scroll up and choose Macromedia Flash (SWF) [.swf].**

3. **Type a name in the File Name input box.**

4. **Open the folder that you want the file to reside in and click Save.**

Exporting to HTML

Impress can automatically create a separate Web page for each slide of your presentation with links to the next and previous slides, as well as a link to the Overview page for the presentation, which contains links to every page. This way you can have your presentation up and running on the Internet in no time!

To export your presentation to HTML, follow these steps:

1. **Remove any sound effects you may have because Web browsers may view these sound effects suspiciously.**

   You can get rid of sound by clicking the Slide Transition disclosure triangle to open the Slide Transition pane in the Tasks pane, choosing <No Sound> from the Sound list, and clicking Apply to All Slides.

2. **Be sure your slides are arranged in the order that you want them to appear in the HTML document.**

   To rearrange your slide order, click and drag the slides in the Slides pane of the Impress window to the order that you want them to appear. (You can also click the Slide Sorter tab in the Impress window and click and drag your slides to the order you want in the Slide Sorter tab.)

3. **Choose File⇨Export.**

   The Export dialog box appears.

4. **Enter a filename and choose HTML Document from the File Type list. (It's the first option, but you need to scroll up to see it.)**

5. **Click Save.**

   The HTML Export Wizard appears, as shown in Figure 15-10.

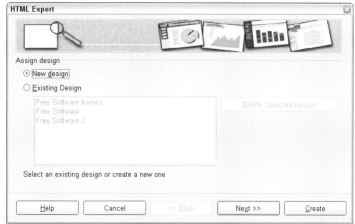

Figure 15-10: The HTML Export Wizard.

6. **If you have saved the presentation as HTML previously, the name of an existing design may appear in the list box below the Existing Design button, which you can choose if you want. Otherwise, click Next.**

7. **You can choose from the following options for advancing your slide show in your HTML page:**

   • **Standard HTML format:** Use this option to create Web pages linked with buttons to proceed through the pages. You can select or deselect the Create title page check box or Show notes check box, depending on whether you want the notes to be published beneath your slide, or whether you want a title page with links to each slide.

- **Standard HTML with frames:** This option creates links to every page and places them as a frame beside the frame containing the slide show, as shown in Figure 15-11. You probably want to deselect the Create title page check box, because all the links to every slide are on every Web page anyway. You can deselect the Show notes check box if you don't want your notes to be published beneath your slide.

- **Automatic:** Select this option if you want your slide show to automatically advance. Choose As Stated in Document to advance with the timings that you set in the document, or choose Automatic to override the timings that you set in the document, and assign a single timing to be used for all the slides with the Slide View Time control.

- **Webcast:** Choose this option if you're doing a telephone presentation with everyone watching your slides on the Internet. You can set the slides' advance rate so that everyone's slides will advance simultaneously. You can export your Webcast either in Perl or ASP, depending on the requirements of your server. Unless you're familiar with Webcasting, if you're planning to do a Webcast, you may want to get someone experienced to help you. (Maybe my next book should be *Webcasting For Dummies!*)

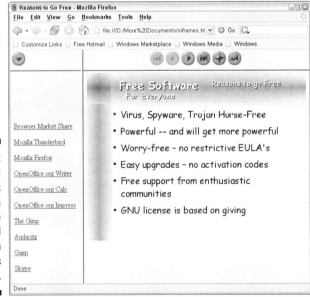

Figure 15-11:
An exported Impress presentation using the Standard HTML with Frames option.

8. **Click Next.**

   The HTML Wizard's page appears, where you can define the resolution of your HTML Web pages and the graphics within them.

9. **Deselect Export Sounds When Slide Advances, because the sounds may not work on some browsers (however, you can test this option to check whether the sounds work). Choose the Monitor Resolution: 640x480, 800x600, or 1024x768. Also choose the format that you want to save your graphics as, and click Next.**

   Most people currently have 800x600 or better for their monitor resolution, so you may want to choose this option. Also, you probably want to choose JPG for your graphics and maybe about 75% Quality. If your Web pages take too long to load, you can export the presentation again and reduce the length of time it takes to load.

10. **Fill in the Title page information if you plan to have a title page, and click Next.**

11. **Choose your buttons, or select the Text only check box, and click either Next or Create.**

   A Name HTML Design dialog box appears with an input box for you to type in a name for your HTML Wizard settings.

12. **If you want, type in a name to save your settings and click Save. Otherwise, click Do Not Save.**

   If you type a name, then if you redo your slide show, you can export it again, but in Step 6 you can choose the name that you entered and click Create instead of Next.

Your slide show saves as an HTML document. To view your slide show, open Mozilla Firefox, choose File⇨Open File. Select your file and click Open. (See Chapter 9 for more details.)

Chapter 16

Digital Imaging with the GIMP

· ·

In This Chapter

▶ Cropping images

▶ Cutting, copying, pasting, flipping, rotating, and scaling all or part of an image

▶ Layering images

▶ Adding colors, gradients, glows, and patterns

▶ Changing brightness, contrast, saturation, color balance, and more

▶ Saving an image in any of over 30 file formats

· ·

GIMP, which stands for GNU Image Manipulation Program, has all the major features of Adobe Photoshop but is available for free under the GNU General Public License. With the GIMP, you can create or open images and manipulate them by cutting, pasting, enlarging, shrinking, flipping, cropping, and much more. You can adjust the color balance, saturation, brightness, and so on to make your colors more vibrant and an image more appealing. The GIMP offers many filters for a multitude of effects, which are explored in Chapter 17. You can layer your images with the GIMP to compose new and extraordinary creations. The GIMP also has a drawing and painting program, plus you can create animations with each frame as a new layer and export them as animations. And that's just the beginning!

Touring the Interface

The GIMP has an unusual interface because it does not have one major window that fills the screen. Instead, the GIMP has three major floating windows, as shown in Figure 16-1, that you can resize and move around your desktop as you like. They are

▸ **Main Toolbox:** This box contains the buttons and controls for the image manipulation tools. When you open the GIMP, the Main Toolbox by default is the only window that appears. When you click on a tool, the options for that tool appear in the pane beneath the tools.

Main toolbox

Layers window

Image window

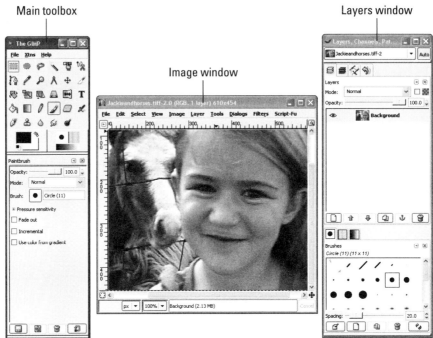

Figure 16-1:
The GIMP.

You can undock the Tool Options pane from the bottom of the Main Toolbox, but I wouldn't recommend doing so, because redocking it may not be easy to do, and having too many windows open gives a confused and cluttered feel to your desktop.

✔ **Image window:** This window, of course, contains your image. To view an Image window, choose File➪New or File➪Open from the menu on the Main Toolbox. You can have as many image windows open as your computer has the memory for. (See the following section for instructions on creating and opening images.)

✔ **Layers window:** This window allows you to add new layers, choose which layer you want to make active, hide and lock layers, or apply transparency to any layer. If you want to use pieces of images to create other images — for example to copy and paste someone's face into another picture — then you probably want to use a separate layer for each image in your picture. To view the Layers window, from the Main Toolbox, choose File➪Dialogs➪Layers.

Opening an Image File into the Image Window

To open an image, choose File➪Open and select the filename in the Open Image dialog box. The GIMP can open more than 30 types of image files, including Photoshop files.

Creating a New Image Window

You may want to cut and paste an image from another application into the GIMP, or you may want to create a new image using the painting and drawing tools. In either case, choose File➪New. The New Image dialog box appears. In it, you can set the following options:

✔ **From Template:** Choose from standard resolutions, including standard screen sizes, paper sizes, banner sizes, CD covers, and NTSC, or PAL.

✔ **Image Size:** The size is shown in pixels as the default, although you can choose other units of measurement from the Unit of Measurement list box, as shown in Figure 16-2. If you choose a unit of measurement other than pixels, you may want to also select a resolution in the Advanced Options, since resolution is measured in pixels and not inches or other units of measurement.

If an image resides in the clipboard, you may find that the image size in the Create a New Image dialog box is automatically set for that image, but this is not always the case.

✔ **Portrait or Landscape:** Click either the Portrait button or the Landscape button, as shown in Figure 16-2 to exchange the width and the height, if you want. Landscape makes the width larger and Portrait makes the height larger.

✔ **Advanced Options:** Click Advanced Options to reveal more options, as shown in Figure 16-2.

• **X resolution and Y resolution:** These options are set automatically if you choose a template or if you choose your image size in Pixels or if an image is copied into the clipboard. You may want to set the resolution, for example, if you set your image size in inches and you want to print your image at a high resolution, such as 600 dpi (dots per inch) or even higher. You can set the resolution for the values that you want. The Image Size (in pixels) changes to reflect the higher resolution. (Pixels are generally square for computer graphics work, so you'll probably want the X and Y values to be the same, otherwise the proportions of your image may be affected.)

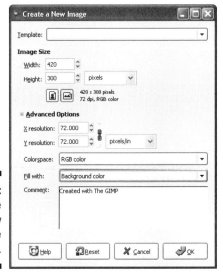

Figure 16-2:
The Create
a New
Image
dialog box.

• **Colorspace:** Choose RGB for color or Grayscale for black and white. (RGB stands for Red Green Blue, which when combined in various proportions can create all the colors of the rainbow.)

• **Fill with:** Notice that in the Main Toolbox are two squares near the bottom of the upper pane. These are the foreground and background colors. For this option, choose Foreground if you want the new image to be filled with the foreground color. Or you can choose Background, White, even Transparent if you want a transparent background.

• **Image Comment:** Add a comment about the image, if you want. This will be embedded in the file but won't be visible when the image is viewed.

Click OK and a new Image window appears. If you want to paste an image that you copied from another application, choose Edit⇨Paste.

You can also use the GIMP to generate screenshots, by choosing File⇨ Acquire⇨Screenshot in the Main Toolbox. Then choose whether you want just a single window or the whole screen and how many seconds' delay you want before the screenshot occurs.

Pasting an Image into a New Image Window

Another way to create a new image is to paste an image into a new Image window by choosing Edit⇨Paste As New. A new Image window appears with the copied image.

Cropping and Resizing Pictures

One handy use for the GIMP is cropping or resizing pictures. You may have a great photo that has a minor flaw on one side or the other. Using the GIMP, you can crop out what you don't want, or resize the photo. Resizing a picture appears to crop it, but the image outside the borders is not lost and can be reclaimed.

To crop or resize an image, follow these steps:

1. **Click the Crop or Resize an Image button in the Main toolbox.**

2. **Click and drag the image so that the border that appears surrounds the area that you want to crop.**

   A border appears with handles, and the Crop & Resize dialog box appears, as shown in Figure 16-3.

3. **You can adjust the border by doing any of the following:**

   • **Enter new values into the spin boxes in the Crop & Resize dialog box.** New values in the Origin X and Origin Y boxes reposition the cropping borders. New values in the Width and Height boxes change the size of the border. A new value in the Aspect Ratio box changes the proportion of the width to the height.

   • **Click and drag the handles of the border.**

   If you want to keep the cropped image in the same proportions as the original image, then select the Keep Aspect Ratio check box on the Options pane of the Main toolbox.

4. **Choose one of the following:**

   • **To crop the picture,** click the Crop button or click inside the border in the Image window.

   • **To resize the picture,** click the Resize button.

   The cropped image appears in the Image window. If you want, you can resize the Image window by clicking and dragging the lower right-hand corner, so that it better fits your image.

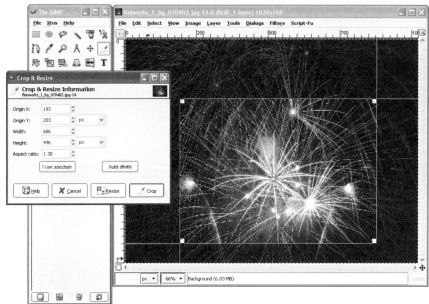

Figure 16-3:
Cropping an
image with
the GIMP.

Alternatively, you can select the area that you want to crop first. (See the instructions in the following section for selecting areas.) Then click the Crop or Resize an Image button, click anywhere in the image, select the From Selection button in the Crop & Resize dialog box, and click either the Crop or Resize button. The selected area is cropped or resized.

Selecting Areas of an Image

The first six buttons in the top row of the Main Toolbox are the selection buttons, as shown in Figure 16-4. Obviously, the GIMP gives you many ways to select items, and that's a good thing. You may want to select items for just some of the following reasons:

- ✔ To cut out part of an image from the rest of the image
- ✔ To fill in part of an image with a different color or gradient
- ✔ To apply an effect to part of the image, to blur, or to sharpen part of the image, for example
- ✔ To apply a color filter on part of the image; for example, to brighten or add contrast to part of the image
- ✔ To flip, resize, or otherwise manipulate part of the image

You can also select the entire image by choosing Edit⇨Select All.

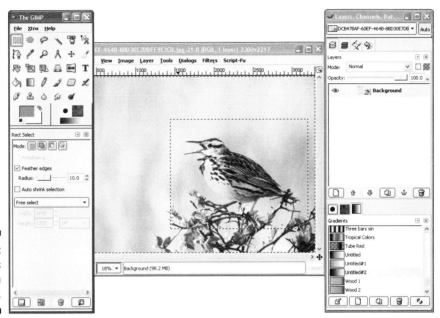

Figure 16-4:
The GIMP's
selection
tools.

Rectangular or elliptical areas

To select rectangular or elliptical areas, click the Select Rectangular Regions button or the Select Elliptical Regions button, shown in Figure 16-4; then click and drag in the image in an area that is not already selected. A dotted marquee appears, indicating the selected area. (To cancel the selection, choose Edit⇨Undo from the Image Window menu.)

If you choose Edit⇨Cut, the selected area is cut from the image.

If you click and drag in an area that is already selected, you will find that you are dragging the selected area around to new positions.

TIP

You can adjust the position of your selection by using the arrow keys.

The Rectangular and Elliptical selection tools also offer options, which appear in the pane below the tools. For example, the Select Rectangular Regions tool options are as shown in Figure 16-4. Using these options, you can do any of the following:

✓ **Click the Replace the Current Selection button** to nullify a previous selection and redo it.

✓ **Click the Add to the Current Selection button** to continue selecting rectangular regions without losing the previous selections. (You can also Shift+click and drag to select multiple rectangular regions.)

✔ **Click the Subtract from the Current Selection button** to deselect the area that you choose from the current selection.

✔ **Click the Intersect with the Current Selection button** to select only the area contained within the intersection of your new current selection that you click and drag and the previous selection.

✔ **Select the Feather Edges check box** if you want to round the corners of your rectangle. You define how much to round them in the Radius box.

✔ **Choose one of the following:**

  • **Free Select** if you want to click and drag to create the selection rectangle of the size desired. This option is the default.

  • **Fixed Size** if you want a selection rectangle of a specific size. You use the spin boxes to choose the size; when you click and drag in the Image window, the selection rectangle appears the size that you indicated. You can then use the arrow keys to adjust the location of the selection.

  • **Fixed Aspect Ratio** to choose a rectangle of the proportions that you specify in the Width and Height spin boxes.

Hand-drawn selection areas

If you want to extract a person's head, for example, to place it into another photo, you may want to hand draw the selection area.

To hand draw a selection, click the Select Hand-drawn Regions button, also known as the Lasso tool, and click and drag in the image around whatever you want to select. A dotted line appears as a border. If your selection does not end where it began, when you release the mouse, the GIMP will enclose your selection with a straight line from the ending point to the beginning point.

You don't have to be exact on the edges, because if you click and drag anywhere outside the image, the GIMP makes the selection by using the border of the image from the spot that you leave the image to the spot where you re-enter the image.

As with the Rectangular and Elliptical selection tools, you can choose the Add to Current Selection mode, Subtract from Current Selection mode, or Intersect with the Current Selection mode. You can also select the Feather Edges check box to smooth your hand-drawn line, and choose the amount of smoothing from the Radius slider or spin box.

To get good results using the Select Hand-Drawn Regions tool, you may want to zoom in. You can use the zoom drop-down menu from the bottom of the Image window to increase your zoom. Or you can click the Zoom tool in the Main Toolbox, then choose either Zoom in or Zoom out from the Options pane and click in the Image window. Each time you click, the zoom increases or decreases by an amount you can adjust using the Threshold slider in the Main Toolbox's Options pane.

Selecting by color

To improve the look of a photograph, you may want to increase the saturation of a certain color to make it more vibrant. (This is just one example of a million reasons why you may want to select by color.) To do that, you may want to select the shade of color in either a contiguous area of that color or in all the areas of that color in the image.

- ✔ **To select all the areas in the image of a color,** click the Select Regions By Color button in the Main Toolbox and click in the image on the color that you want to select. You can adjust the Threshold in the Options pane to include or exclude shades that are similar to what you clicked on.

- ✔ **To select only contiguous areas of the same color,** click the Select Contiguous Regions button, also known as the Fuzzy Select button, and click in the Image window. The GIMP selects all contiguous areas of that color. You can set the Threshold in the Options pane to increase or decrease the selection.

Selecting with the Scissors tool

Using the GIMP's Select Shapes from Image tool, also known as the Scissors tool, you can create a selection by detecting the edges of what you want to select. This tool is best used with selections of high-contrast areas. To use the Scissors tool, follow these steps:

1. **Click the Scissors tool.**

2. **Click on the border of an area that you want to select. Move the mouse and click on another spot on the border.**

   The GIMP fills in the selection line in-between by following a high-contrast edge.

3. **Continue to click on the border until you completely enclose the selection by clicking on the first point.**

4. **Pull any points (by clicking and dragging) to adjust the selection.**

5. **Click inside the bordered area to complete the selection.**

Cutting, Copying, Scaling, Rotating, and Flipping a Selection

After you have something selected, you can do lots of things with it. For example, an effective way to crop an image without using the Crop tool is to select the area that you want to crop and choose Edit➪Cut or Edit➪Copy and then paste the image into a new Image window. (See the earlier instructions for creating a new Image window.)

Scaling a selection

Another option you have is to scale the selection. In Figure 16-5, the galaxy was selected and then scaled to a larger size. To scale part or all of your image, do the following:

1. **Select the part of the image that you want to scale. If you want to scale your entire image, don't select anything (unless your image has more than one layer — then click on the layer that you want to scale in the Layer window).**

2. **Click the Scale the Layer or Selection button in the Main Toolbox.**

3. **Click in the Image window.**

   A solid border with handles appears around the selected area or around the entire layer, and the Scale dialog box appears, as shown in Figure 16-5.

4. **Do one of the following:**

   • **Enter different values in the Scale dialog box.**

   • **Pull the handles to resize the image.**

   Control+dragging constrains the height, or you can click the Keep Height button in the Options pane of the Main Toolbox.

   Alt+dragging (for some systems this may be Shift+Alt+dragging) constrains the Width. Or you can click the Keep Width button in the Options pane of the Main Toolbox.

   The entire image, layer, or selected area scales as you pull the handles.

5. **Apply any of the following options** in the Options pane of the Main Toolbox:

   • **The Transform Layer, Transform Selection, and Transform Path buttons** allow you to scale the selected part of the layer, the selection marquee, or a selected path, respectively. You probably want the Transform Layer button.

Rotate button

Scale button

Flip button

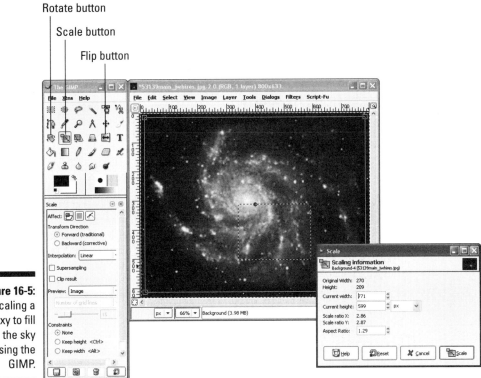

Figure 16-5:
Scaling a
galaxy to fill
the sky
using the
GIMP.

- **Transform Direction:** You probably want to always make sure that Forward is always selected in this area, unless you want the frustrating experience of dragging your border larger and having your image shrink when you click Scale.

- **Choose a method of interpolation:** Choose None (Fastest), Linear, or Cubic (Best) to specify how you want the GIMP to apply color to the extra pixels that are created by increasing the scale.

- **Supersampling:** Choose this option if you want even better picture quality, at the cost of increased time to render and increased file size.

- **Select a Preview:** Whatever you select (Outline, Grid, Image, Image+Grid) is what you see enlarged or shrunk until you click the Scale button. If you choose Image, the Image enlarges as you pull the handles or adjust the values in the Scale dialog box. If you choose Image+Grid, a grid appears over the image and they both enlarge or shrink. If you choose Outline or Grid, just the border or the grid that appears changes in scale until you click the Scale button in the Scale dialog box to complete your scaling effect.

• **Constraints:** See Step 4 for a description of constraining an image.

6. **Click Scale in the Scale dialog box to apply the scale effect, click Cancel to cancel the effect, or click Reset to perform the scale again.**

Rotating an image

The procedure for rotating an image is very similar to that for scaling an image. You can rotate an entire layer (which is the entire image if you only have one layer), or you can rotate a selected area of the image. (For more about layers, see the later section "Working with Layers.")

To rotate your image, first select the area that you want to rotate (unless you want to rotate the entire layer). If you want to rotate the entire layer and you have more than one layer, then click to select the layer that you want to rotate in the Layer window. Click the Rotate the Layer or Selection button in the Main Toolbox and click and drag in the Image window to rotate the entire layer or selected area. You can also adjust the values in the Rotate dialog box that appears Then click Rotate in the Rotate dialog box to apply the rotation.

Flipping an image

To flip your image, select the part of it that you want to flip, unless you want to flip the entire layer. If you want to flip the entire layer and you have more than one layer, click to select the layer that you want to flip in the Layer window. Click the Flip the Layer or Selection button, choose Horizontal or Vertical from the options in the Main Toolbox's Options pane, and click in the selected area in the Image window, or anywhere in the Image window if nothing is selected. The selected area or layer flips.

Working with Layers

Layers give you the flexibility to make changes in one layer without affecting anything in another layer. This feature gives you the power to easily move, scale, adjust colors, or manipulate in a million other ways parts of your image while keeping the rest of the image unchanged. For example, I used layers to add cartoon drawings to a photograph, as shown in Figure 16-6. Unless you're just cropping or improving the color of single images, you will probably find layers to be indispensable while using the GIMP.

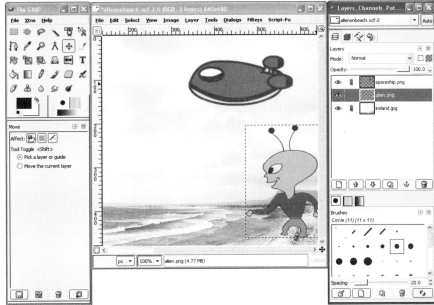

Figure 16-6:
Using layers
gives you
the flexibility
to move
parts of
images
around,
scale them,
and more.

Fundamentals of Layering

Here are some basic rules regarding the use of layers:

- ✔ **Layers are viewed in the order that they appear in the Layers window** with the topmost layer covering the next layer down and so on. (For example, if the topmost layer is opaque and fills the window, you won't see any layers below it.)

- ✔ **To change the order of the layers,** click and drag the layer names or layer previews in the Layers window.

- ✔ **If a layer is larger than the Image window, you only see the part that is visible in the Image window,** but the rest of the layer still exists and you can select it and move it around to see the entire layer, if you want.

- ✔ **The Background layer has no transparency by default.** You can add transparency to it by adding an Alpha Channel. Just right-click (Windows and GNU/Linux) or Control+click (Macintosh) and choose Add Alpha Channel.

- ✔ **Floating layers are pasted areas that you can incorporate into the layer below by clicking the Anchor button. You can also right-click (Windows and GNU/Linux) or Control+click (Macintosh) on the layer in the Layers window and choose New Layer to give the pasted area a new layer to reside on.**

Public domain photos

The photo in Figure 16-6 is a photo taken in Ireland and posted as a public domain photo at `http://pdphoto.org/`. The Internet has lots of Web sites that have public domain images available for download. You can use public domain photos for whatever purpose you want — unless they contain faces of people, in which case you need to get permission from the person or their estate. Also, if the image contains company logos or other copyrighted material, you may need to get permission for using the image as well.

Even though a Web site has public domain images available, it's important to make sure that the actual photo that you want to use is public domain. For example, not all photos at PDPhoto are public domain, so you need to read the terms for each photo.

Other good places for public domain photos are listed in "Free Photos and Graphics" in Chapter 24.

✔ **To lock a layer, so that it cannot be modified in any way unless you unlock it,** click in the space beside the layer preview in the Layers window, as shown in Figure 16-6.

✔ **To hide a layer (or if the layer is already hidden, then to show a layer)**, click on the eye on the same row as the layer that you want to hide or show.

✔ **To add transparency to an entire layer,** click on the layer in the Layers window and choose the Opacity level by moving the Opacity slider or using the Opacity spin box. An opacity of 100% means no transparency.

✔ **To add transparency to part of a layer,** use the Color to Alpha filter described in Chapter 17.

✔ **To delete a layer,** right-click (Windows and GNU/Linux) or Control+click (Macintosh) on a layer in the Layers window and choose Delete Layer. Or select the layer and click the Delete Layer button in the Layers window or choose Layer⇨Delete Layer.

✔ **To merge all layers,** choose Image⇨Flatten Image.

Creating layers

You can create layers in two main ways:

✔ **To create a new layer,** click the New Layer button in the Layers window, shown in Figure 16-6. Then fill in the name, width, and height of the new layer and choose what color you want to fill the layer with (Foreground, Background, or White) or choose Transparency for a transparent background. Click OK.

✔ **To open a file as a layer,** choose File⇨Open As Layer from the Image window. Select the file that you want to open from the Open Image As Layer dialog box and click Open. The image appears in a new layer in the Layers window.

If your newly opened file is not visible in the Image window, click on its name and drag it to the topmost level in the Layers window.

Working with Colors, Patterns, and Gradients

The GIMP allows you to apply any of over 16 million colors and offers you a wide array of gradients, including glows, which are gradients that fade to transparency. You can also create your own gradients. The GIMP also offers lots of patterns to paint or fill with.

In addition to colors, patterns, and gradients, the GIMP provides color tools such as Brightness-Contrast, Color Balance, Levels, and Curves, described later in this chapter. The GIMP also offers a large assortment of color filters, which are described in detail in Chapter 17.

Adding colors

You can add a solid color to any selected area just by dragging either the Foreground color or Background color in the Main Toolbox into a selected area in the Image window. (If nothing is selected, then the color fills the Image window.) To assign the Foreground or Background color, double-click on one of the Foreground and Background Color squares in the Main Toolbox and in the Change Foreground Color (or Change Background Color) dialog box that appears, click the hue you want on the rainbow bar; then click in the large square to choose how much black and white you want mixed with the hue. The color you chose appears in the Current box. Click OK.

Adding gradients and patterns

You can also drag the active pattern or the active gradient from the Main Toolbox to the selected area in an Image window or to the entire Image window. (To apply the active gradient, drag it from the Main Toolbox and then drag in the Image window to set he direction of the gradient.)

To change the active pattern or active gradient, choose the Patterns tab or the Gradients tab at the bottom of the Layers window and select your pattern or gradient from the options.

Applying a gradient using the Blend tool

The Blend tool allows you to define the size of the gradient that you want to add. This feature is especially wonderful when you're using gradients with transparencies — in other words, to add glows, as shown in Figure 16-7. The moon and the glow behind the moon are added to the skyline of San Diego.

To use the Fill a Color Gradient (or Blend) tool, do the following:

1. **Click the Gradients tab in the Layers window and choose a gradient as the active gradient.**

2. **Click the Fill with a Color Gradient button in the Main Toolbox.**

3. **Choose the shape of the gradient from the Shape drop-down list in the Options pane. (In Figure 16-7, I chose Radial so that it would appear in the same shape as the moon.)**

4. **You may want to create a new layer for the gradient by clicking the New Layer button. Then click and drag where you want the gradient to start and end. (A radial gradient will begin from the center and spread outward.)**

   Your gradient appears. Now, if the purpose of the gradient is to create a glowing effect, you can place the layer that you want to appear as if it were glowing, such as the moon in Figure 16-7, on a layer on top of the gradient.

Figure 16-7:
The glow of the moon is added with the GIMP's Blend tool.

Creating a new gradient

If the gradient that you want is not available, you can create it by following these steps:

1. **Choose two of the colors for your gradient as the Foreground and Background colors in the Main Toolbox.**

2. **Click the Gradients tab at the bottom of the Layers window, right-click (Windows and GNU/Linux) or Control+click (Macintosh) on any gradient name, and choose New Gradient.**

   The Gradient Editor dialog box appears.

3. **Right-click (Windows and GNU/Linux) or Control+click (Macintosh) the leftmost triangle on the bar below the gradient and choose Load Left Color From⇨FG Color (or BG Color).**

4. **Right-click the rightmost triangle and choose Load Right Color From⇨BG Color (or FG Color).**

5. **Drag the white triangle in the middle of the bar below the gradient to refine the gradient.**

6. **Close the Gradient Editor dialog box by clicking the Close box in the upper right-hand corner.**

7. **Double-click on the name next to your new gradient (which is probably Untitled) and give your gradient a name.**

Using color tools

Adjusting the color can subtly or even drastically improve the quality of your digital photo. The GIMP offers both color tools and color filters, so if you don't find what you're looking for in the following list, check out the color filters in the next chapter. To apply the color tools, in the Image window choose Tools⇨Color Tools and choose any of the following:

✔ **Color Balance:** This tool increases or decreases the Red, Green, and Blue values of your image. These values also correspond to Cyan, Magenta, and Yellow because with this tool when you increase Yellow, Blue decreases, and vice versa. When you increase Cyan, Red decreases and vice versa. (The same relationship is also true for Magenta and Green.)

When applying any color tools or filters, be sure that the layer that you want to apply the effect to is selected in the Layers window.

✔ **Brightness-Contrast:** You can use this tool to change the brightness and contrast of an image. For example, the photo in Figure 16-8 was taken in the shade, so I increased both its brightness and contrast before increasing its color saturation.

✔ **Hue-Saturation:** As shown in Figure 16-8, use this tool to adjust the saturation (which is how free from black and white the color is). You can also adjust the hue and lightness of the image.

✔ **Colorize:** This tool changes an image into a single color, as if it were black and white and seen through colored glass.

✔ **Levels:** This tool displays a histogram that shows from dark to light how many pixels have each value of darkness. If you move the black triangle to the right, the dark parts of your image get darker. If you move the white triangle to the left, the light areas of your image get lighter. If you move the gray triangle in the middle, you can make the midtones of your image darker or lighter if you move the triangle right or left, respectively.

✔ **Curves:** You can pull the curve (by clicking and dragging) to adjust the way that the colors appear in the image. And you can click on the curve to add points that you can drag to create new arcs in the curve. As you drag the curve, the color changes in the image. You can create some wild effects using Curves.

✔ **Posterize:** Posterize gives the image a fun look by reducing the number of colors in the image, as shown in Figure 16-9.

Figure 16-8:
The Brightness-Contrast color tool was applied to correct for the darkness of the shadow, and then the Hue-Saturation filter was used.

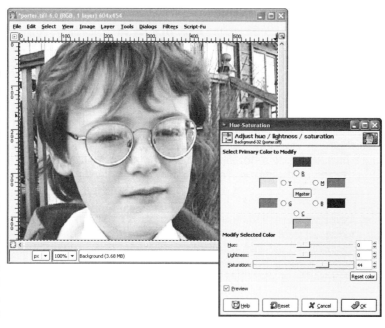

Why red, green, and blue?

Every pixel in an image has a color value to it. This color value is assigned in terms of 256 levels of red, 256 levels of green, and 256 levels of blue. When you blend any of the levels of red, green, and blue together, you get a different color. For example, the color turquoise has the approximate values of Red 17, Green 185, and Blue 172; White is 255 Red, 255 Green, 255 Blue; black is 0 Red, 0 Green, and 0 Blue. Using this system for generating colors, your computer can create 256x256x256=16,777,216 unique colors.

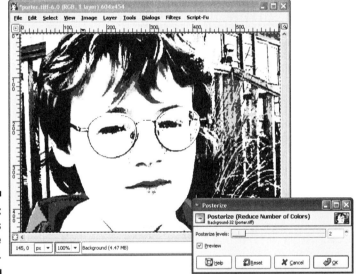

Figure 16-9: The GIMP's Posterize color tool.

Saving an Image

In the GIMP you can save an image in more than 30 different formats. When you choose File⇨Save from the main menu in the Image window, your image automatically saves in the file type that you opened it in. For example, if you open a TIFF file, apply filters, and then choose File⇨Save in the Image window, the GIMP saves your file as a TIFF file. If your file is a new file, then when you type the name, you need to choose a file format from the Save Image dialog box, as described next.

You may want to change the file format of your image for a variety of reasons, some of the most common of which are as follows:

✔ To reduce the file size for an image by, for example, using the JPEG format, which compresses images more than some other formats.

✔ To use the native GIMP file format (.xcf) in order to save the layers in your images and other attributes that may be lost in other file formats

✔ To change the file format into a format readable by programs used by other people

To save your image with a different file format, or to save a new image, follow these steps:

1. **Choose File⇨Save As from the Image window main menu.**

   The Save Image dialog box appears, as shown in Figure 16-10.

2. **Type a name for your file, or change the default name, if you want.**

3. **Click the Select File Type button and choose a file type from the File Type list.**

   If you want the native GIMP file type, choose XCF. The file type that you choose is appended to the end of the name.

4. **Click Save.**

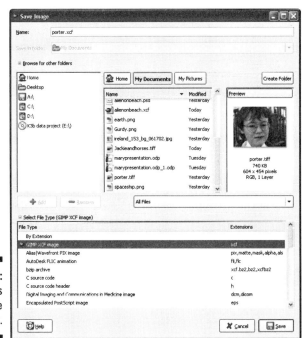

Figure 16-10:
The GIMP's
Save Image
dialog box.

Chapter 17

Drawing and Filtering Images in the GIMP

*T*he GIMP has a wide variety of filters that enable you to enhance photos and other images in a multitude of ways. For example, you can use the Light Effects filter to add up to six separate lights to an image. You can sharpen an image with the Sharpen filter, or make it even sharper with Unsharp mask, or add interesting color effects with the Retinex filter, all of which can enhance the appeal of a photo. Or you can make a photo look like a painting, a cartoon, or a line drawing.

The GIMP also offers paintbrush, pencil, and airbrush tools with fifty different types of brushes, including calligraphy brushes and a sparks brush. And you can set them for any level of transparency. The Airbrush tool colors an area more the longer it stays in one place. You can even eliminate blemishes or unwanted areas of an image using the Clone tool. In this chapter, we explore both the filters and the tools that the GIMP has to offer.

Using the GIMP's Drawing Tools

The GIMP has several handy drawing tools that you can use to draw neat stuff from scratch or to enhance photos, including the Paintbrush, Pencil, Airbrush, Clone tool, and Eraser. (In case you're wondering, you can draw with the Eraser, especially on a dark background, which disappears as you erase.)

The Paintbrush, Pencil, and Airbrush tools

The three main drawing tools in the GIMP are the Paintbrush, the Pencil, and the Airbrush. Each of them offers a slightly different effect:

- **Paintbrush:** Use this tool when you want a fuzzier look for artwork.

- **Pencil:** Use this to draw with a sharp edge.

- **Airbrush:** Use the Airbrush when you want the color to spray on more the longer you hold this tool in one place, just as a real airbrush puts more paint in an area the longer you hold it there.

To use any of these tools, click on the Paintbrush, Pencil, or Airbrush button in the Main Toolbox and then click and drag in the Image window to draw. You can adjust the Paintbrush, Pencil, and Airbrush by selecting from the following options in the Options pane in the Main Toolbox:

- **Choose from about fifty brush sizes and shapes from the Brush option by clicking on the brush preview next to the word Brush.** Some of the brushes are very traditional, such as the brushes that can be used for calligraphy. You can use some brushes to add special effects to images, such as the Sparks brush, shown in Figure 17-1.

Paintbrush tool

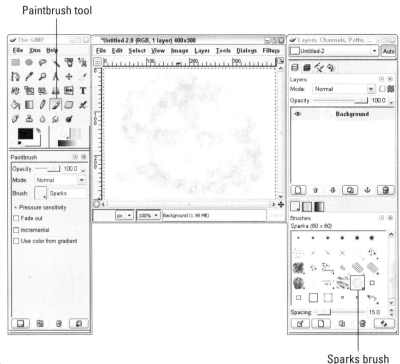

Figure 17-1:
You can choose the Sparks brush to add sparks to your artwork.

Sparks brush

✔ **Choose whether you want to paint or draw using the Foreground color or the active gradient.** To use the active gradient, select the Use Color from Gradient check box.

  • **To change the Foreground color,** double-click on the Foreground Color square in the Main Toolbox and choose the color from the dialog box that appears.

  • **To change the active gradient,** click the Gradients tab at the bottom of the Layers window and click on the gradient of your choice.

✔ **To add transparency to your strokes,** adjust the Opacity slider.

✔ **Make your strokes into a gradient** by selecting the Fade Out check box and assigning a length for the fade out in the Length value box which appears.

✔ **If you selected the Airbrush you can define the rate of flow of the color, and the pressure of the color,** using the value boxes or adjusting the sliders in the Options pane.

The Eraser tool

Normal erasing is just one of the tasks that the Eraser tool can perform. You can also use it to erase selectively to create images such as the pattern in Figure 17-2. To use the Eraser tool, do the following:

1. **Add a dark color into your Image window, so that you have something to erase.**

2. **Click the Eraser tool and choose options in the Options pane.**

  • **Transparency:** Adjust the Opacity slider. (In Figure 17-2, the lighter shades had 100% Opacity, and the middle shade was 50% Opacity.)

  • **Brush:** Choose any of the brushes available for the Paintbrush and Pencil tools. For Figure 17-2, I chose the Vine brush.

  • **Fade Out:** Select this check box for a gradient effect, and set the Length in the value box.

  • **Hard Edge:** Choose this option to erase the edges completely.

  • **Anti-erase:** Choose this option to undo an erasure of a layer with an Alpha Channel.

3. **Click and drag in the Image window.**

   The areas that you click and drag become transparent according to how much opacity you assigned.

Eraser tool

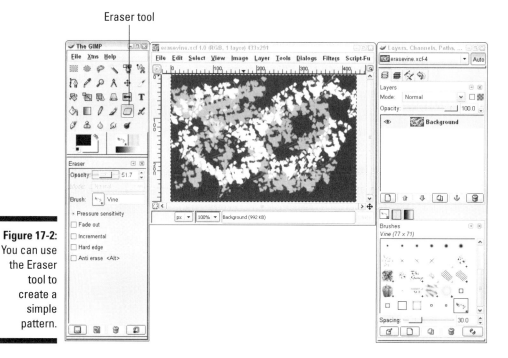

Figure 17-2:
You can use
the Eraser
tool to
create a
simple
pattern.

Retouching photos with the Clone tool

The Clone tool, which looks like a rubber stamp in the Main Toolbox, has two major uses:

- **Drawing patterns:** You can use the Clone tool to draw the active pattern. You can assign a Brush type to it, just as if it were the Paintbrush or Pencil.

- **Ridding photos of unsightly spots, pimples or blemishes, and to retouch it in other ways.** For example, in Figure 17-3, the fence in front of the horse was removed with the Clone tool.

Drawing patterns with the Clone tool

If you click the Clone tool and choose Pattern Source from the Options pane, you can use the Clone tool to draw the active pattern. Just click and drag in the Image window; the active pattern appears as you move your mouse. You can change the brush shape by clicking on the brush preview next to the word Brush in the Options pane, and you can change the active pattern by clicking the Patterns tab at the bottom of the Layers window and clicking on the pattern of your choice.

Clone tool

Figure 17-3:
You can use
the GIMP's
Clone tool to
remove
parts of your
image, such
as the wire
fence in
front of the
horse.

Ridding photos of unsightly spots, pimples and blemishes

You can use the Clone tool to copy a part of your image that is the size and
shape of the Brush that you choose in the Options pane of the Main Toolbox
and then stamp that part of the image over another part of the image to hide
a blemish or imperfection. For example, if you have a few telephone wires
framed by the sky in your otherwise perfect landscape image, you can copy a
part of the sky and stamp it over the wires. (Of course, you need to be very
selective about where you copy from, so that the stamped image blends well
in its new location.)

To use the Clone tool to retouch your photos, follow these steps:

1. **Click on the tool in the Main Toolbox.**

2. **Be sure that Image Source is selected in the Options pane. You can
   also choose the Brush and Opacity amount.**

   The Clone options are similar to the options available for the Paintbrush
   and Pencil tools described earlier.

3. **Control+click in the Image window where you want the Clone tool to
   copy a small part of the image from.**

4. **Click (or click and drag) on the spot (or in the area) that you want to replace with the part of the image that you chose in Step 3.**

   An *x* appears in your image, showing you the spot where you Control+clicked the image.

5. **Repeat Steps 3 and 4 until the area that you want to hide is completely covered.**

Adding, formatting, editing, and repositioning text

To add text to your image, do the following:

1. **Click the Add Text to the Image button.**

2. **Choose the Font size, Font type, Color, Line spacing, and Justification from the Options pane.**

3. **Click in the image where you want your text to be and type your text into the Text Editor dialog box that appears.**

   Your text simultaneously appears in the image and in the dialog box as you type.

4. **Click Close.**

   A new layer appears containing the text box, and named as the first words in your text box.

To adjust the position of your text, click the Move Layers and Selections button in the Main Toolbox and click and drag the text where you want it to reside. (It may take a few tries to select the text and not the layer below the text. You need to click on a letter and not the gaps between letters to drag the text.)

To edit text, click the Add Text to Image button in the Main Toolbox, select the layer containing your text, then click on the text box. The Text Editor dialog box appears with your text in it, ready for you to edit.

Using Filters

The GIMP offers many filters that you can apply to all or parts of an image. Different filters are better suited to different images; sometimes you just need to try them to figure out which best suits your needs. When you use the filters, you can adjust the settings in the filter's dialog box and view the image in the Preview box.

You can apply filters to either entire layers or selected areas. To apply a filter, select either the layer or the area, and choose the filter from the Filters menu options. The filters are divided into several categories, including:

- Color filters
- Blur filters
- Noise filters
- Edge-detect filters
- Enhance filters
- Generic filters
- Glass Effects filters

- Light Effects filters
- Distortion filters
- Artistic filters
- Mapping filters
- Render filters
- Combine filters

If you want to apply a filter to an entire image with lots of layers, then you can choose Image⇨Flatten Image to combine all the layers into a single layer. You may want to choose Image⇨Duplicate before you flatten the image, in order to preserve a copy of the image with the layers intact.

Color filters

The GIMP's Color filters can change the colors of an image in various ways, or change parts of an image from color to transparency. Figure 17-4 shows several color effects on the same photo (a public domain image from www. pdphoto.org). You may want to use filters for the following reasons:

- **To restrict your colors in your image to a particular gradient of colors of your choice,** choose the gradient that you want from the Gradients list on the Layers window. For example, I chose Golden for the image in Figure 17-4. Choose Filters⇨Colors⇨Map ⇨Gradient Map, and the image appears golden, or with the colors in whatever gradient you chose. You can also use a gradient that fades to transparent, such as the FG To Transparent gradient.

- **To vary the range of the colors used in your image,** you can choose Filters⇨Colors⇨Map⇨Color Range Mapping. In the dialog box that appears, in the Source Color Range section, choose the From and To colors; in the Destination color range also choose the From and To colors, then click OK. For example, in Figure 17-4, I chose black and white for the Source color range, so that all the colors were included in the range. I chose Blue and white for the Destination color range. This took all the black out of the image and made it blue instead.

Figure 17-4:
Here are
some of the
GIMP's
Color filters.
(You can
see these
images in
color at
www.
infinity
every
where.
net/free.)

✔ **To make a particular color transparent,** such as white, choose Filters⇨ Colors⇨Color To Alpha. Then choose the color that you want to change to transparent by clicking on the From color and choosing the color from the Color To Alpha Color Picker dialog box. Click OK. Whatever color you choose becomes transparent wherever it exists and to whatever degree it exists in the image. For example, in the central image in Figure 17-4, I chose white.

✔ **To convert your image to black and white and maybe one color, if you want,** choose Filters⇨Colors⇨Colorify. Then you can click on one of the colors and see the preview of the image. You can also choose a custom color by clicking in the Custom Color box and choosing a color from the Colorify Custom Color dialog box. Then click OK. The image in Figure 17-4 is black and white plus yellow.

✔ **You can use the Decompose filter to change your image to grayscale, or to extract an Alpha channel,** which you can add to another image to add the same level of transparency to that image. Choose Filters⇨ Colors⇨Decompose; in the Decompose dialog box that appears, choose RGB (to change to grayscale) or Alpha to extract the Alpha Channel.

✔ **To see previews of Hue, Saturation, and Value variations for the Shadows, Midtones, and Highlights of an image,** use the Filter pack Simulation. Choose Filters⇨Colors⇨Filter Pack and then, in the dialog box that appears, you can view its twelve preview windows by selecting either the Shadows, Midtones or Highlights and either Hue, Saturation, and Value (which adds up to 108 possible previews.) To apply the filter, you can select a preview window, and click OK.

✔ **To bring out the details of an image in a strange, or perhaps appealing way,** use the Retinex Color filter, as shown in Figure 17-4. It may even add extra color to your image. I used this filter on several images and it never failed to make extraordinary improvements. You may want to try this filter on all of your photos. Choose Filters➪Colors➪Retinex to access it.

✔ **To invert the luminosity of your image, use Value Invert,** shown in Figure 17-4. Bright areas appear dark and dark areas appear bright. Choose Filters➪Colors➪Value Invert to use this filter.

✔ **To convert the colors in your image into two colors, which you select in the Foreground and Background colors in the Main Toolbox,** choose Filters➪Colors➪Map➪Adjust FG-BG (see the second image in Figure 17-4). The foreground color was white and the background was turquoise.

✔ **To exchange one color in your image with another color,** choose Filters➪Colors➪Map➪Color Exchange. Adjust the scroll bars of the preview to see the part of the picture that you want and middle-click (or Control+click) on the color that you want as the From Color. Click on the To Color box, select a color from the Color Exchange dialog box, and click OK.

✔ **To give an image an alien look,** try the Alien Map filter. Choose Filters➪Colors➪Map➪Alien Map. You can adjust the sliders for the different colors and see the preview in the preview window.

✔ **To use the Channel Mixer to adjust all three channels of colors** (Red, Green, and Blue) to get the ideal color definition for an image, choose Filters➪Colors➪Channel Mixer. Then adjust the Red, Green, and Blue sliders for the best effect, as shown in Figure 17-5. You can also select the Monochrome check box to see how adjusting the colors affects the black-and-white image.

Blur filters

Blur filters are handy for many reasons. Here are just three of the main reasons that you may want to use them:

✔ **If you're cutting and pasting images together, you can select areas around their edges and use the blur filters to blend the edges together,** so they don't look like paper doll cutouts. The Gaussian blur serves this purpose well by giving gives the image a nice soft blur.

✔ **If an image contains a foreground and a background, you can blur the background a little bit, which in some cases can give some depth to the scene.** You probably want to use the Gaussian blur for this as well.

✔ **You can use motion blur to imply motion with the streaks that it leaves.**

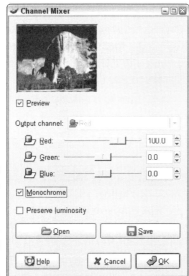

Figure 17-5:
Use the Channel Mixer to adjust colors.

Noise filters

Noise filters add little speckles to an image. They can give a sandy look to images. Some of them can also make an image appear as if it is under water or under glass. You may also want to use the noise filters to blend images together seamlessly. The Noise filters are as follows:

✔ **Hurl:** This filter adds randomly colored speckles to your image.

✔ **Pick:** You may want to use this filter for an underwater look. You need to use it repeatedly to create a noticeable effect.

✔ **Scatter HSV:** This filter scatters areas of hue, saturation, and luminosity. (The speckles appear bright and colorful.)

✔ **Scatter RGB:** Use this filter to scatter dots of whatever colors you define.

✔ **Spread:** This filter gives a nice through-old-glass look.

Edge-detect filters

The Edge-detect filters can turn an image into a line drawing. For example, the image in Figure 17-6 was created from a photograph using an edge-detect filter on an image which I first changed into a black and white image using Filters➪Colors➪Colorify. The GIMP offers several edge-detect filters. You just have to try them to find the one that works best for your image. Most of the filters produce white lines on dark backgrounds, so if you want to invert the filtered image, choose Filters➪Colors➪Value Invert.

Figure 17-6: The GIMP's Edge-detection filter can create a line drawing from a photo.

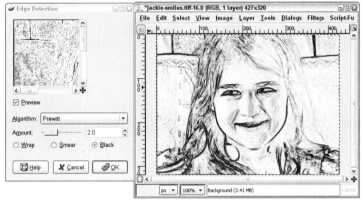

Enhance filters

The GIMP offers six Enhance filters that can improve the look of an image in various ways. My personal favorite is the Unsharp filter — give it a try.

- ✔ **If your image is marred by dust or scratches, or by the moiré pattern you may get when you scan an image from a magazine,** you may want to try the Despeckle filter to get rid of these problems, as shown in Figure 17-7.

- ✔ **If you want to make your image look sharper,** try the Sharpen filter, or better yet, the Unsharp Mask filter.

- ✔ **If you want an image to look like it is a reflection in still water,** or on a piece of slightly mottled paper, use the Destripe filter. You can also use this filter to remove stripes created by poor quality scans.

- ✔ **If you want to enhance the edges in your image**, you can use the NL Filter and select the Edge enhancement option.

- ✔ **If an image has jagged edges caused by fast-moving images in the video,** use the Deinterlace filter. This filter takes out every other line of the image and replaces it with a copy of either the line above or the line below.

Generic filters

The GIMP offers three Generic filters:

- **Convolution Matrix:** You can use this very flexible filter to create your own filters.

- **Dilate:** This filter makes the dark areas of the image bigger.

- **Erode:** This filter makes the light areas of the image bigger.

Glass Effects filters

The GIMP's Glass effects filters give the impression of looking at an image through either a lens or glass tile.

- **Apply Lens:** This filter magnifies the center of the image in an oval-shaped area; for example, framing a face. The edges of the oval can be set to your background color like a frame, as shown in Figure 17-8, or you can keep the background of the original image.

- **Glass Tile:** This filter gives the impression of looking at an image through cut glass, as shown in Figure 17-8. The lines in the glass can be set at various sizes, which you can preview in the Preview window.

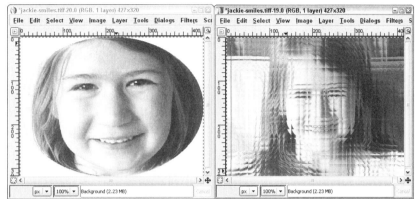

Figure 17-8:
The GIMP's
Apply Lens
filter and the
Glass Tile
filter.

Light Effects filters

The GIMP has a powerful Lighting Effects filter that you can customize for your images. You can also use the FlareFX, GFlare, and SuperNova filters to add different kinds of flares to an image. Or use Sparkle to add sparkles wherever areas of brightness appear in your image. You can finely adjust Sparkles to fit your image.

With Lighting Effects you can add up to six different spotlights to an image, and you can angle each one as you see fit. You can increase or decrease the intensity of the light and add color to the light, as well. A Lighting Effect filter was added to a photo taken in Yosemite National Park (another public domain image from www.pdphoto.org), as shown in Figure 17-9, to add a sunrise behind a mountain (which probably faces north or south). The figure required no cropping or layers to achieve this effect.

To use the Lighting Effects filter, do the following:

1. **Choose Filter⟳Light Effects⟳Lighting Effects.**

   The Lighting Effects dialog box appears.

2. **Click the Light tab and from the Type drop-down list box, choose one of the following:**

   • **Directional:** In the Preview window you can click and drag the blue dot, which represents a directional light. You can angle the light by dragging it, and you can increase or decrease its intensity by using the Intensity box.

Figure 17-9:
A sunrise is
added
bchind this
mountain
using the
GIMP's
Lighting
Effects filter.

> • **Point:** You can change the light's intensity by using the Intensity box. (A single point light generally needs a lot of intensity.)

> • **None:** This option deletes the light source.

The lighting effect appears in the Preview window, as shown in Figure 17-10.

Figure 17-10:
You can add
up to six
directional
or point
lights to an
image, angle
each light,
and adjust
its intensity
and color as
you like.

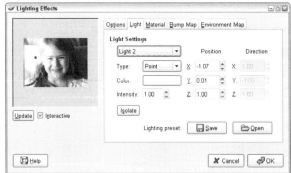

3. **Choose another light and repeat Step 2 for up to six light sources.**

4. **Choose the Material tab,** if you want to try different Material properties, which include Glowing, Bright, Shiny, or Polished. Or click Metallic for a metallic look for your reflecting light (however, unless your image is something that is made of metal, you may want to leave these controls alone).

5. **Click OK.**

Distorts filters

The GIMP has lots of distortion filters for you to choose from. In many cases, these filters have dialog boxes with many options to play around with. They also have preview windows in which you can see the effect of the filter for any part of your image by using the scroll bars. You can also, of course, apply these filters to a selection by selecting an area of an image and then choosing the filter. The Distorts filters distort an image in various ways as described in the following list and as shown in Figures 17-11 and 17-12:

- **Blinds:** Adds either vertical or horizontal stripes, varying in amount and size according to the options you choose.

- **Curve Bend:** Curves an image according to the curve that you pull in the Curve Bend dialog box.

- **Emboss:** Creates an embossed look for the image.

- **iWarp:** Let's you warp your image into a gooey mess by dragging your mouse around the preview image, which is loads of fun.

- **Mosaic:** Gives a mosaic-look to the image. You can adjust the size of the tiles.

- **Newsprint:** Makes fun of improperly calibrated four-color presses that don't quite print as they should.

- **Page Curl:** Adds a page curl in a layer above the image.

- **Polar Coords:** Distorts an image in a circular way.

- **Ripple:** Adds a ripple to an image with the amplitude that you assign.

- **Shift:** Shifts rows or columns of pixels randomly within the amount you specify, which results in an image that perhaps looks like you are viewing it through water.

Figure 17-11: Here are some of the GIMP's Distorts filters. (These can be viewed in color and in a larger size at www. infinity every where. net/free.)

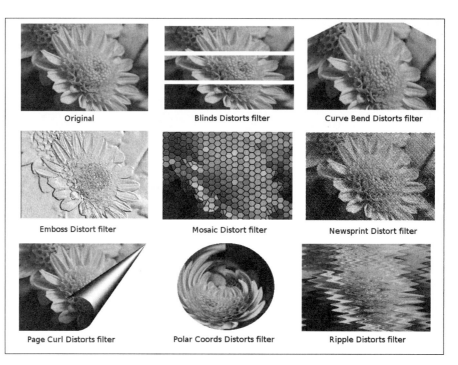

Original   Blinds Distorts filter   Curve Bend Distorts filter

Emboss Distort filter   Mosaic Distort filter   Newsprint Distort filter

Page Curl Distorts filter   Polar Coords Distorts filter   Ripple Distorts filter

Shift Distorts filter   Video Distorts filter   Waves Distorts filter

Whirl and Pinch Distorts filter   Wind Distorts filter

Figure 17-12: More of the GIMP's Distorts filters.

When using the Value Propagate Distorts filter, selecting a Lower Threshold higher than the Upper Threshold may cause the GIMP to crash.

✔ **Video:** Adds lines or other patterns to your image to give it a video look.

✔ **Waves:** Makes an image appear as if it were a reflection in water, with waves propagating from its center.

✔ **Whirl and Pinch:** This filter is a fun filter. It causes an image to look as if you took a spoon and stirred it around.

✔ **Wind:** Gives the image a directional motion effect.

Artistic filters

The GIMP offers seven artistic filters, each of which have settings that you can adjust, and preview windows where you can see a preview of the effect. The GIMPressionist filter is an especially versatile filter with loads of features in the eight tabs in its dialog box. The filters are as follows:

✔ **Apply Canvas:** Makes the image appear as if it were on canvas.

✔ **Cartoon:** Gives a cartoonish look to the image, as shown in the image of the moon in Figure 17-13.

✔ **Cubism:** Turns the image into one that resembles paintings in the Cubist style, as shown in Figure 17-13.

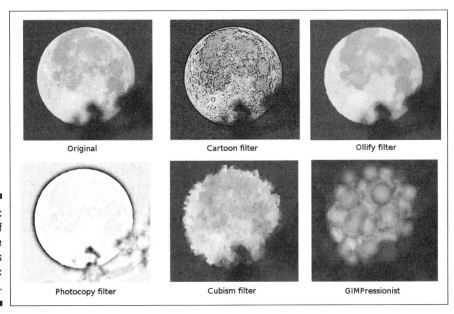

Figure 17-13:
Examples of some of the GIMP's Artistic filters.

Original · Cartoon filter · Ollify filter

Photocopy filter · Cubism filter · GIMPressionist

✔ **GIMPressionist:** This versatile filter offers more than 50 unusual brushes to choose from, ten different kinds of paper, as well as tabs for Orientation, Size, Placement, Color, and General settings. It also offers about 25 preset settings that you can try out. An example of GIMPressionist is shown in Figure 17-13. I used the Grad02 brush on the image of the moon.

✔ **Ollify:** Makes the photo appear more like a painting, as shown in Figure 17-13.

✔ **Photocopy:** Gives the image a blurry line drawing effect, as shown in Figure 17-13.

✔ **Softglow:** As the name implies, this filter gives a soft glow to the image, as shown in Figure 17-14.

Figure 17-14:
The GIMP's
Softglow
Artistic
filter.

Map filters

The GIMP's Map filters generally map the image in various ways, such as creating a bump map, or mapping the image around a 3D cylinder. As with the other filters, the GIMP offers adjustable options and often has preview windows in which you may view the filter's effect before rendering the entire image. The Map filters are as follows:

✔ **Bump Map:** This requires two images: a bump map and an image to apply the bump map to. In Figure 17-15, the sky pattern was used as a bump map to create the bump-mapped image beside it. Any image can be used as a bump map, and any image can have a bump map applied to it.

✔ **Displace:** This filter takes parts of the image and moves them to other parts, like a modern artist might do. It creates interesting landscapes, as shown in Figure 17-15, and looks strange for portraits.

✔ **Fractal Trace:** This filter stretches and repeats the image in a fractal way, as shown in Figure 17-15.

✔ **Illusion:** This filter repeats parts of the image and swirls them around the center, as shown in Figure 17-15.

Make Seamless filter   Illusion filter   Small Tiles filter

Paper Tile filter   Map Object filter   Fractal Trace filter

Bump Map filter   Bump map used for Bump Map filter   Displace filter

Figure 17-15:
The GIMP's
Map filters.

✔ **Make Seamless:** This filter takes the center of the image and repeats blended versions of it around the edges, as shown in Figure 17-15. Thus, if you then tile the image, the tiles will be seamless.

✔ **Map Object:** Use this filter to map an image onto a 3D plane, cube, sphere, or cylinder. In Figure 17-15, the image is mapped onto a cylinder.

✔ **Paper Tile:** Personally, I've never heard of tile made of paper, but I guess anything can exist. Anyway, it gives a nice effect, as shown in Figure 17-15.

✔ **Small Tiles:** This duplicates the image onto the same canvas as many times as you indicate in the dialog box.

✔ **Tile:** If you set the width and height to a new size larger than the current size, the GIMP tiles the image to fill the new size.

✔ **Van Gogh:** This filter is named after the painter Vincent Van Gogh and can give you a variety of impressionistic and post-impressionistic effects, as shown in Figure 17-16. The photograph of the coast of Ireland, that is also in Figure 16-6, has the Van Gogh filter applied to it. If you want to check out this photo in color, go to www.infinityeverywhere.net/free.

✔ **Warp:** This filter also changes the look of the image from a photograph to more of an impressionistic painting. You may like this filter even better than Van Gogh.

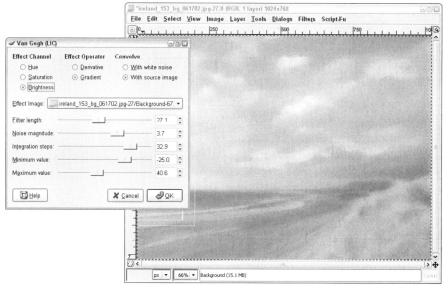

Figure 17-16:
The GIMP's
Van Gogh
filter.

Render filters

The Render filters offer a selection of interesting and sometimes colorful patterns that require no image to generate them. They include the following:

✔ **Clouds**

- **Plasma:** Causes a mass of color to fill the screen.
- **Solid Noise:** Causes mottled black and white cloudiness to fill the screen.

✔ **Nature**

- **Flame:** Causes a flame-like drawing. I used it to produce the effects in the image in the upper left-hand corner of Figure 17-17.
- **IFS Fractal:** This is a triangular shape with lots of triangles inside it. You can adjust it to create other images. (However, it's difficult to control.)

✔ **Pattern**

- **Checkerboard:** You can select how big the squares are.

- **CML Explorer:** This filter is flexible; it explores the artistic nature of about ten different mathematic functions which you can choose from.

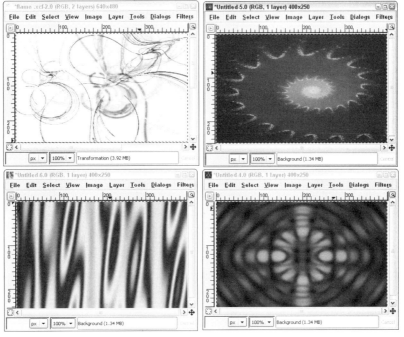

Figure 17-17:
The GIMP's Render filters can generate an enormous variety of interesting images that you can use however you want.

- **Diffraction Patterns:** This filter has a multitude of settings. An example of this filter is the symmetrical image shown on the bottom right corner in Figure 17-17.

- **Grid:** Creates a grid according to the size you specify.

- **Jigsaw:** Creates a jigsaw pattern

- **Maze:** Creates a maze-like pattern.

- **Obist:** Offers lots of colorful gradients and patterns.

- **Sinus:** Sort of resembles shiny oil floating on water, but prettier, as shown in the bottom left corner of Figure 17-17. It is very adjustable, as well.

- ✔ **Fractal Explorer:** The Fractal tab offers 26 different fractal shapes, including the Nautilus, as shown in the image in the upper right in Figure 17-17. You can choose the colors in the Color tab. This filter is highly adaptable with three tabs and many controls.

- ✔ **Gfig:** Enables you to add geometric shapes to your image.

- ✔ **Sphere Designer:** Enables you to design a 3D sphere.

Chapter 18

Drawing Diagrams with Dia

* *

* *

Dia is a free software package designed to create several kinds of diagrams, including flowcharts, networking diagrams, electrical circuits,
and UML. (UML, which stands for Unified Modeling Language, has become
quite popular in recent years and is used to model application structure,
behavior, and architecture, as well as business processes and data struc-
tures.) Dia has an intuitive interface and is easy to learn. It takes only about
five minutes to understand the basics and get started creating useful diagrams, which I find exciting and empowering. Dia also has the ability to convert your flowchart into programming code. In this chapter, we cover the
basics of getting started using Dia.

Dia is similar to the Visio program, which is a decidedly non-free Microsoft
program that runs on Windows. Dia runs on Windows or GNU/Linux operating systems.

Exploring the Interface

When you start Dia, two windows appear: the Canvas and the Toolbox. The
Canvas is the window in which you create your diagram, and the Toolbox
contains all the tools and objects you use to create your diagram. The windows, as they initially appear, are generally quite small. The first task you
may want to do is resize the Toolbox by dragging the edges so that it fills one-
third or one-fourth of the screen. Then resize the Canvas, if you want, to fill
the remaining screen, as shown in Figure 18-1. Dia gives you lots of flexibility
to resize and reshape your Toolbox and Canvases as needed.

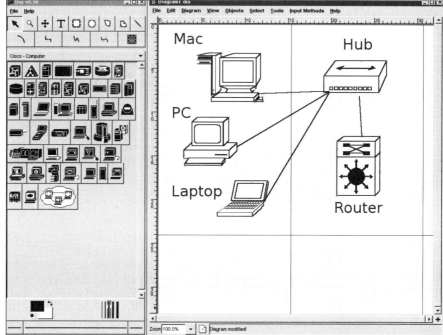

Figure 18-1:
A simple
networking
diagram
created
using Dia.

Diagramming Flowcharts, Networks, Electrical Circuits, UML, and More

To create a diagram, start by selecting the appropriate object category from the drop-down Object Category list in the Toolbox. For network diagrams, for example, choose either Cisco-Computer, Cisco-Hub, Cisco-Router, Cisco-Network, Cisco-Misc, or Network. For flowcharts, electrical circuits, or UML, choose flowchart, circuit, or UML, respectively. Or if you want to make a small map, choose Map, Isometric. The buttons in the pane below the Object Category list box change to reflect your selection, (refer to Figure 18-1).

Adding objects to your Canvas

To insert an object into the Canvas, click an object button in the Toolbox — either a button in the pane below the Object category or a button near the top of the Toolbox, such as a line, arrow, shape, arc, zigzag, and so on — and click in the Canvas. The object appears. (You can also drag the object from the Toolbox to the Canvas.)

Resizing and repositioning your object

Your object appears with eight adjuster dots. Click and drag any adjuster dot to resize your object. If you want to keep the proportions the same, such as for a shape, Shift+click and drag any of the corner adjuster dots.

If your object is a flowcharting or other object designed to contain text, then don't drag the adjuster dots to resize your object. Just type your text; your object resizes automatically to contain it (see Figure 18-2).

To position your object, click and drag anywhere in the object, except on an adjuster dot, and drag your object.

Dia allows you to connect objects to other objects when you resize and position them. For example, you can connect a line to two flowchart objects or any objects in your Canvas. Simply click on an adjuster dot of a line and drag to an adjuster dot of an another object. A red border appears around the object to show that the connection is established. Do the same with the adjuster dot at the other end of your line to connect it to another object. Now, when you move a connected object, such as a flowchart object, the line also moves to remain attached to both objects. This connection feature and automatic resizing ability makes flowcharting quite easy using Dia.

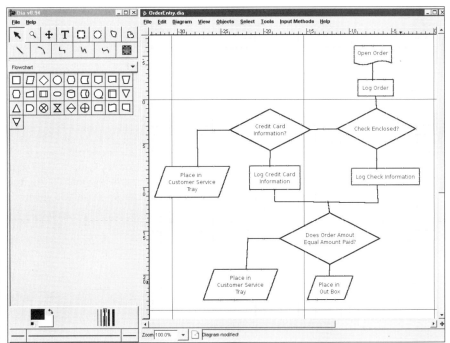

Figure 18-2:
A simple flowchart using Dia.

Deleting an object

Deleting an object is not completely intuitive. To delete your object, click on it to select it; then press the Delete key (not the key that you use to backspace text) on your keyboard. You can also choose Edit➪Delete.

Modifying objects in your Canvas

You can also manipulate the shape, color, or other properties of an object by clicking it in your Canvas to select it, right-clicking, and then choosing a modification from the pop-up menu or choosing Properties to see the Properties dialog box for the object.

In the Properties dialog box, you can click any of the buttons or use the spin boxes to set properties such as Line Width, Line Color, Fill Color, Line Style, and more.

Modifying objects in your Toolbox

You can double-click a button in the Toolbox to view its default settings in a dialog box. You can change these settings so that anytime you insert that object into the Canvas, it reflects the new settings. For example, you can double-click the Text button to change the Font type and Font size settings for your text.

Changing your line or arrow style

You can change the line or arrow style of the line in your Canvas by using the Properties dialog box as described in the preceding section. You can also change the line style in the Toolbox, so that every time you drag a line into the Canvas, it is the type of line or arrow that you want. To change your line or arrow style in the Toolbox, click the Arrow Style button in the bottom-right corner of the Toolbox. A pop-up menu with 33 icons appears. Click the arrow style (or line) that you want. Now every time you click the Line button near the top of the Toolbox and click in the Canvas, your new arrow style or line will appear.

Adding color and inverting your foreground and background colors

You can assign a foreground and background color to the objects in your Canvas by double-clicking either the black or white box at the bottom of the Toolbox, shown in Figure 18-1, and assigning the color you want in the dialog box that appears. Now when you insert objects, their colors appear as you assigned.

To invert foreground and background colors, click the double arrow near the two boxes, also shown in Figure 18-1.

The foreground color may be your lines, and the background color may be your fills, depending on the category of your objects.

Opening, saving, and exporting a Canvas

You can have as many Canvas windows open as you want. To open a new Canvas, choose File➪New Diagram.

To save your document, choose File➪Save and navigate through the Save Diagram dialog box to open the folder in which you want to save your file. (To open a folder, double-click it in the Folders list box. To move up one level, double-click the "..\".) Type the name of the file in the Selection box along with the file extension .dia and click OK.

To export your diagram, choose File➪Export and open the folder into which you want to export your file. Choose one of 16 exporting categories: .cgm, .dia, .shape, .dxf, .eps, .png, .plt, .hpgl, .jpg, .svg, .mp, .tex, .wmf, .wpg, .fig, and .code. Type the name of the file along with the file extension in the Selection input box, and click OK.

Chapter 19

Creating 3D Animations with Blender

*B*lender is an amazingly powerful free software package for 3D modeling, animation, rendering, visual effects, compositing, creation of interactive 3D for games and architectural walk-throughs, and more.

This chapter offers a taste of the experience of using Blender. You can't just play with Blender and figure it out unless maybe you're a certified super-genius. For example, pressing one key in Blender can send you into a whole different mode of operation where nothing works as it did before. But Blender has the power to generate such rich, aesthetically wonderful 3D creations that even a novice using this program with patience and the right guidance can produce interesting work.

Understanding the Blender Interface

The Blender interface is abstruse to the newcomer, but I'll try to make it clear to you in this section, so hang in there. Blender is jam-packed with power and if you're interested in 3D, you can do fantastic things with it. This section contains some of the basics of the interface to get you started quickly.

When you start up Blender, you see a screen like the one in Figure 19-1. (If your window looks different, see the Tip below). It is divided into three main sections called windows, which are really panes of a single Blender window. However, for the sake of compatibility with what you may read on the Blender Web site or hear from other Blender users, in this chapter, I will call them windows even though they're only panes.

The windows are as follows:

✓ **Info window:** The gray bar at the top is the Info window. It contains the main menu. It can also be expanded to show other controls. (However, you don't need to do that in this chapter.)

✓ **3D window:** Below the Info window is a pane called the 3D window. This is a view into your 3D world. You build or place 3D objects in this window and move them around or otherwise transform them and view them from any distance or angle. By default the following objects appear in this window, as shown in Figure 19-1:

  • **Grid lines:** These disappear when you render the image. You use them in modeling to help you align objects and put them where you want them.

  • **Camera:** The black triangle or pyramid.

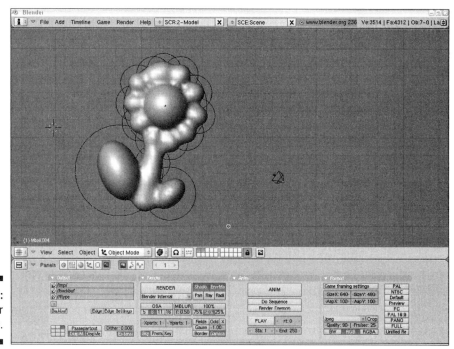

Figure 19-1:
The Blender
interface.

- **Lamp:** The yellow circle with the dot in the middle.

- **Standard plane:** A pink square around an object indicates that the object is selected.

- **3D cursor:** The crosshairs connected by the red and white circle, which by default is in the center of the screen. As explained later in "Creating an object," you use this cursor to specify where to place new objects or where the center of rotation or scaling is.

✔ **Buttons window:** Below the 3D window is a pane called the Buttons window. The top row of the Buttons window contains six buttons for six categories of tasks, including adding materials to objects and rendering the scene. When you click one of these buttons, almost everything else in the Buttons window changes to give you a new category of controls. This chapter focuses just on the controls that appear when you click the Shading button or the Scene button.

Some screens start out divided into more than one section, representing different 3D views. If that's the case, just drag the horizontal dividing line in the 3D window until it's almost off the screen; then drag the vertical dividing line in the 3D window until its almost off the screen. That way, you have a window resembling Figure 19-1 — not an elegant solution, but hey, it works.

Each Blender window has an important horizontal bar with its main controls, called a header. In the default screen that appears when you start Blender, the header for the 3D window is at the bottom of the 3D window, as shown in Figure 19-1. The header for the Buttons window is at the top of the Buttons window. The header for the Info window is the only part of the Info window showing. (Sorry, I didn't write this program; I just explain how things are.)

Creating a 3D World

Creating a 3D world starts with adding a single 3D object. You can then manipulate the object by scaling it; rotating it; assigning it color, lighting, and texture; or editing its geometry. Then you can add more 3D objects and combine them until you have a 3D world. Blender offers two kinds of ready-made 3D objects to choose from:

✔ **Mesh objects:** These are the typical 3D objects, as follows:

- Plane

- Cube

- Circle

- UVsphere

- Icosphere

- Cylinder
- Tube
- Cone

✔ **Meta objects:** These objects are like gooey clay that stick together and are great for doing claymation. They are my favorite 3D objects. Meta objects include:
  - Meta Ball
  - Meta Tube
  - Meta Plane
  - Meta Ellipsoid
  - Meta Cube

(You can also add 2D curves and surfaces and build your own 3D objects from them, but doing so is much more complicated.)

After you add a shape, you can manipulate it in the ways mentioned earlier.

Then you may want to add another shape and do the same and put the shapes together. By adding more and more shapes and editing, scaling, and moving them, you can build up your 3D world.

But probably the first thing you want to do when you create a 3D object is to get rid of the default cube created when Blender starts. To do that, you have first to select the cube.

Selecting and deselecting objects

Selecting objects is something you do quite frequently when working with Blender. To select an object, follow these steps:

1. **See whether Object mode is selected in the 3D Window header Mode indicator list, shown in Figure 19-1. If not, press Tab to switch from Edit mode to Object mode.**

2. **With the cursor in the 3D window, press B (which stands for Border Select).**

3. **Click and drag over part of the border around the object or borders around the objects that you want to select.**

   The border (or borders) around the object or objects turns pink, indicating that they are selected.

To deselect everything on your screen, you can do the following:

1. **Be sure you're in Object mode; if not, press Tab to switch from Edit mode to Object mode.**

2. **With the cursor in the 3D window, press A (which stands for Select/ Deselect All).**

   Whatever is selected becomes deselected. If nothing is selected, however, it selects everything. Tricky, huh? If that happens, press A again.

Deleting an object

To delete an object after you have selected it, and you're sure you're in Object mode, with the cursor in the 3D window, press X. A pop-up menu appears with two choices: OK? or Erase Selected. Choose Erase Selected and click. The selected object disappears.

Creating an object

To add a single 3D object, follow these steps:

1. **If you're in Edit mode, press Tab to switch to Object mode.**

2. **Be sure no other object is selected. If anything is selected, then with the cursor in the 3D window, press A to deselect all objects.**

   Objects appear surrounded by pink when selected.

3. **Click the spot in the 3D window where you want to place your object.**

   The 3D cursor moves to where you clicked.

4. **Choose either Add⇨Meta, and either Meta Ball, Meta Tube, Meta Plane, Meta Ellipsoid, or Meta Cube. Or choose Add⇨Mesh and select a type of Mesh object.**

   The 3D object appears in the 3D window at the position of the 3D cursor. (For example, in Figure 19-1, I started the center of the flower using a Meta Ball.)

At the time you create an object, you probably want to assign it a material, as well. Otherwise, if your object is joined with another object, it can be sometimes problematic to select just the single object. See the section below, Adding Color, Textures, and Lighting Effects. Even if you are not sure of the exact color, lighting, or texture, you can always edit that later.

Viewing a 3D object as a solid or otherwise

You can view the object that appears either as Textured, Shaded, Solid, Wireframe, or a Bounding Box. You can try out all the options and see which you like the best. I prefer to view it as Solid, as shown in Figure 19-1. To choose the type of shading view for your object, click the Viewport Shading button on the 3D window header, shown in Figure 19-1, and choose an option from the pop-up menu that appears.

Moving a 3D object

To move a 3D object, follow these steps:

1. **Be sure you're in Object mode. Press Tab if you're not in Object mode to switch from Edit mode to Object mode. (Sometimes you may need to click in the 3D window and then press Tab.)**

2. **Select the object** by positioning the cursor in the 3D window and pressing A to deselect all if anything else was selected. Position the cursor in the 3D window (anywhere), press B (for Border Select), and click and drag over at least part of the object to select it.

   A pink border surrounds the object, or the object turns pink, depending on what Viewport Shading you have chosen.

3. **Position the cursor anywhere in the 3D window and press G (which stands for Grab) and move the mouse.**

4. **If you want to move in a single axis only, you can do the following; otherwise, skip this step.** (Moving on a single axis is not the only way to move in 3D space.)

   • Press G and then press X to restrict the move to the X axis.

   • Press G and then press Y to restrict the move to the Y axis.

   • Press G and the press Z to restrict the move to the Z axis.

5. **Click to complete the move.**

Never try to move a selected object moving the arrow keys. You may not notice it, but the arrow keys increment the frame numbers of your animation, which could cause you some confusion if you increment them unknowingly.

To drag in 3D space, you may want to become familiar with the later section "Viewing objects in a 3D world." If you change your 3D view, you can move the object easily within the view that you chose.

When a meta object intersects with another meta object, they appear to mold together like clay.

Scaling a 3D object

When you add an object, such as a Meta Ball, you may want to scale it. For example, in Figure 19-1, the petals of the flower are made of Meat Balls, er, Meta Balls. They are just scaled differently from the sphere in the center of the flower. To scale your 3D object, follow these steps:

1. **If the 3D window header is not visible, click in the 3D window.**

2. **Be sure you're in Object mode. If you're not, position the cursor in the 3D window and press Tab to switch from Edit mode to Object mode.**

3. **Select the object that you want to scale, if it is not already selected. (Be sure nothing is selected except the object.)**

4. **Position your mouse in the 3D window and press S (which cleverly stands for Scale).**

5. **Move the cursor either farther from the center of the object or closer to the center of the object. Moving closer shrinks the size of the object; moving farther expands the size of the object.**

6. **Click to complete the scaling.**

Rotating a 3D object

Rotating 3D objects is often a vital step in creating a 3D world. You may not need to rotate a sphere, but the leaves on the 3D flower in Figure 19-1 are Meta Ellipsoids that were rotated to the correct angle. To rotate an object, follow these steps:

1. **If the 3D window header is not visible, click in the 3D window.**

2. **Check to see whether you're in Object mode; if you're in Edit mode, position the cursor anywhere in the 3D window and press Tab to switch from Edit mode to Object mode.**

3. **Be sure nothing is selected except the object.** Press A to deselect all the objects if anything other than what you want is selected. Press B (which stands for Border Select) and drag over part of the 3D object to select it.

4. **Position the cursor anywhere in the 3D window and press R (which cleverly stands for Rotate).**

    You can also restrict the rotation to a single axis — X, Y, or Z, if you press R and then press X, or Y or Z.

5. **Move the cursor to indicate the angle of rotation.** If you want to rotate on a different axis, middle-click the mouse and drag until you get the angle you want. (Mac users with a one-button mouse can Alt+Ctrl+Shift+click and drag.)

6. **Click to complete the rotation.**

Viewing objects in a 3D world

Blender offers several ways to help you visualize your 3D world. You can use the mouse to drag your view around in 3D space by middle-clicking. Or you can choose a view, such as Top, Side, Front, and Camera. You can split your screen into as many parts as you want and have a different view in each.

Dragging around the 3D view

My favorite part of Blender is its ability to move the view around in 3D space. It operates very intuitively, although sometimes it can also drive you nuts. First make sure nothing is selected. If something is selected, press A to deselect all objects. Then you can do the following:

✔ **To change your 3D view interactively,** middle-click the mouse and drag in the 3D window. The view changes the perspective of the image. You may need to practice a bit to get used to this. But hang in there. Figure 19-2 is an example of another view created by middle-clicking and dragging. (Mac users with a one-button mouse can Alt+Ctrl+Shift+click.)

✔ **To zoom in,** press + on the numeric keypad.

✔ **To zoom out,** press – on the numeric keypad.

✔ **To pan,** middle-click+Shift+drag in the 3D window.

Choosing Top, Side, Front, or Camera view

You can also assign different views to your 3D window, such as Top, Side, Front, and Camera. In the 3D window header (which is at the bottom of the 3D window), choose View⇨Top (or Side, Front, or Camera). Your view changes accordingly.

Splitting your screen into more than one view

When you start creating animations, it is useful to have a Camera view and at least one other view — either Top, Side, or Front, as shown in Figure 19-3. (Two windows, in the opinion of this humble beginner, is as much as I can handle.) Too many windows can be distracting. To see two views at once, you can split the screen.

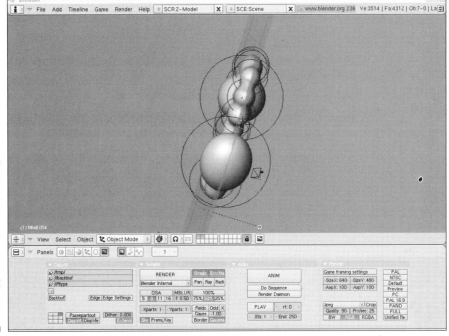

Figure 19-2:
Middle-click and drag in the 3D window to view objects from different perspectives.

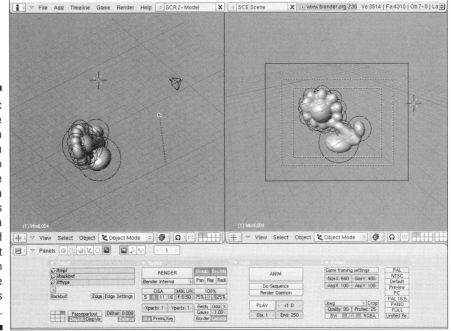

Figure 19-3:
Splitting the screen gives you the ability to see the Camera view, as well as a second view that you can change around as you like.

Splitting the screen has to be done with care, otherwise you'll split the Buttons window instead — although it's easy to join it back together if you do. To split the screen, you can do the following:

1. **Move the cursor on the border between the 3D window header and the Buttons window header.**

   The cursor changes to a double-arrow.

2. **Move the double-arrow so that most of it is in the 3D window header without changing back to an arrow. Right-click and choose Split area.**

   A vertical line appears through the 3D window, which moves as you move the mouse (without clicking the mouse).

3. **Move the line to where you want the split to be and click.**

   The line splits the window into two windows. Each 3D window has its own 3D window header.

Now you have two windows that you can set the views, by choosing View⇨ Camera in one window and View⇨Top (or Side or Front) in the other window.

To resize the 3D windows, click and drag the vertical or horizontal line separating them.

To join windows back together, place your cursor on the line where they are split, and when the cursor becomes a double-arrow, right-click the mouse and choose Join Areas.

Sometimes when joining windows, the 3D Window Header disappears. This is probably a bug. You may need to restart Blender to get the 3D Window Header back. (If you have problems with this, just drag the dividers to the edge of your screen when you want a single view, and drag them back when you want multiple view.)

Positioning the camera

To render colors and textures to get a good idea of what they look like in a higher resolution image, you'll want to position the camera. Rendering takes place in the Camera view, so getting a good shot with the camera is important. You have the choice of moving the camera around to see the object, or you can move the object to be better seen in the camera. If you have many objects, you'll probably want to do the former. If you have only a single object or a few objects, you may want to do the latter.

You can select, move, and rotate the camera, just as you may select, move, and rotate any object.

Adding color, textures, and lighting effects to a 3D object

Blender allows you to add colors, textures, and transparency to your objects. You can choose from some ready-made textures, such as marble and wood, or you can import your own images as textures that you can apply onto objects. You can also add lighting effects, such as adding highlights to an object or making an object appear as if it's glowing from within.

The combination of all the settings for color, textures, lighting effects, and transparency for a single object is what Blender saves as a *material*. Each time you create a new material, Blender saves it as well. This way, you can choose a previously created material to apply to new objects whenever you add an object, or you can create a new material. Whenever you edit an existing material, the changes you make appear in all objects that the material is applied to.

Adding color, transparency, and lighting effects

To add color, transparency, and lighting effects to an object, do the following:

1. **In the 3D window, select only the object that you want to apply the colors and lighting effects to.**

   This is sometimes easier said than done. If the object you want to select is small and near something large, you may need to select everything except the object and move it away from the object, so that you can select the object. This is why it is a good idea to assign materials to your objects as you create them.

2. **Click the Shading button on the Buttons window header (or press F5), and then click the Materials button on the Buttons window header,** as shown in Figure 19-4.

3. **Do one of the following:**

   • **If the Buttons window appears as shown in Figure 19-4;** then click Add New in the Material tab.

   • **If Add New is not available;** then click the X in the first line of the Material tab, which has the Deletes Link to This Datablock tooltip. The Add New button appears, as shown in Figure 19-4, and you can now click it.

   The Buttons window changes to contain four sections, as shown in Figure 19-5:

   • **Preview:** This is where you preview the color and texture.

   • **Material:** This is where you can set the color and give your material a unique name so that you can choose it again for future work.

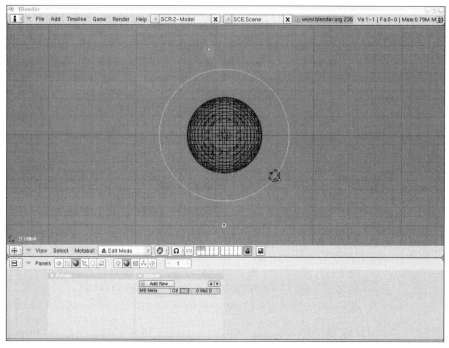

Figure 19-4:
Adding
a new
material.

- **Shaders:** You can adjust the lighting of the object. (Blender also allows you to add external light sources to the object, but the controls here adjust the light source that you already have and the ambient light.)

- **Texture:** This allows you to clear a texture if you applied one or to choose one, but to do that you first need to assign a new texture using the instructions in the section "Adding textures" that follows.

4. **To change the material name to something other than the default name, you can click in the topmost text box in the Material pane on the word MA:Material. A cursor appears, allowing you to rename the word Material. Don't change MA:.** (You don't have to give your material a different name. Blender appends the next consecutive number to each new material, making each material name unique anyway.)

5. **Choose either RGB (Red, Green, Blue) or HSV (Hue, Saturation, Value) and adjust the sliders to achieve the color you want, as shown in Figure 19-5. The bottom slider is for transparency, which you can adjust as well.**

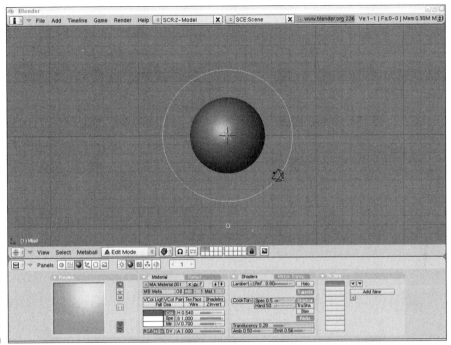

The colors appear in the Preview window, and the 3D image in the 3D window should appear somewhat rendered with those colors as well. You can choose Textured, Shaded, or Solid from the Viewport Shading list in the header of the 3D window to choose the rendering that you like the most.

6. **Choose the lighting effects from the sliders and buttons in the Shaders tab, shown in Figure 19-5.**

7. **When you finish adjusting the material, click the X in the first line of the Material tab, which has the Deletes Link to This Datablock tooltip.**

   The Add New button appears, as shown earlier in Figure 19-4.

Applying an existing material to a model

After you create a material, as described in the preceding section, you may want to apply that material to many of the new objects that you create. To apply an existing material, you can do the following:

1. **Be sure you're in Object mode. If you're not, position the cursor in the 3D window and press Tab.**

2. **Select the object that you want to apply the material to. (If anything is already selected, deselect it by having the cursor in the 3D window and pressing A. Then press B and click and drag over part of the object to select it.)**

3. **Click the Shading button on the Buttons window header (or press F5) and then click the Materials button on the Buttons window header**, as shown in Figure 19-4.

4. **If the Add New button appears in the Material tab, click it.**

   Four panes appear in the Buttons window.

5. **Click the box to the left of the material name, which has the Browses Existing Choices Or Adds NEW tooltip.**

   A pop-up menu appears with all the names of the materials that you created, as shown in Figure 19-6.

6. **Select the material from the pop-up menu.**

   The material is applied to the object.

7. **Click the X beside the material name with the Deletes Link To This Datablock tooltip.**

If you make any changes to a material that already exists, every object that has that material applied will reflect those changes.

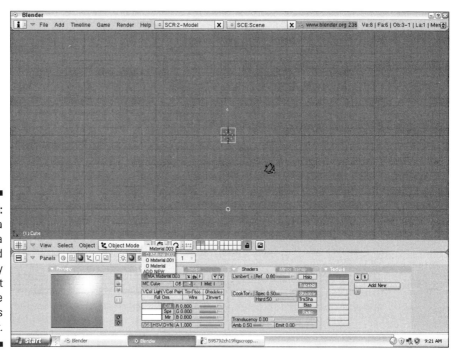

Figure 19-6:
Apply a material to a selected object by choosing it from the Materials list.

Adding textures

You may want to add a ready-made texture to an object, or you may want to import a texture. To add textures to an object, you can do the following:

1. **Select the object that you want to add a texture to in the 3D window.**

2. **Press F5 (or click the Shading button on the Buttons window header) and then click the Texture button on the Buttons window header.**

   The Texture buttons appear in the Buttons window.

3. **Click Add New in the Texture tab.**

   More buttons appear.

4. **From the Texture Type drop-down list, choose one of the following:**

   - **A texture,** such as Marble, Wood, Clouds, Magic, and so on.

   - **None,** if you don't want a texture, or to remove a texture.

   - **Image,** if you want to import an image as a texture.

5. **If you chose a texture or None, go to step 6; otherwise, if you chose Image, click the Load Image button in the Image pane of the Buttons window, navigate to and select the graphic file containing the image that you want to load, and click Select Image.**

   You can use the buttons in the Image pane to adjust the loaded image, which you will find especially easy if you're the world's smartest person.

6. **To view the image with the texture applied, you can render it, as described earlier in this chapter.**

7. **Click the X in the first line in the Texture tab with the Deletes Link To This Datablock tooltip.**

   The Add New button appears in the Texture tab.

Editing the geometry of an object

You can put 3D objects together to make new 3D shapes, and you can also edit the geometry of mesh 3D objects or curves or surfaces by dragging points on them and stretching or collapsing their shapes. To edit the points on a 3D mesh object or curve or surface, you can do the following:

1. **If anything is selected, then position the cursor in the 3D window and press A (to deselect all the objects).**

2. **If you're in Object mode, then position the cursor in the 3D window and press Tab to change to Edit mode. Also, in the Viewport Shading list in the 3D window header, choose Wireframe.**

   Points appear on the objects in the 3D window. If you don't see any points, zoom in.

3. **Position the cursor in the 3D window and press B (which stands for Border Select) and drag over a point or points on an object to select them.**

   The selected points turn white.

4. **Now you can move the point by positioning the cursor in the 3D window and pressing G (which stands for Grab) and moving the cursor. Click to end the move.**

   The shape changes.

 To undo, you can press Control+Z, but you need to be in the same mode as the step that you want to undo. For example, if you're in Edit mode, then Control+Z undoes the previous step that you did in Edit mode. If you're in Object mode, Control+Z undoes the previous step you did in Object mode.

Extruding a Logo

One handy use of a good 3D modeling program, besides creating the next *Incredibles* movie, is to create a 3D logo. To do that, you insert text; extrude it; add some color, texture, lighting, animation, a few trips to Starbucks; and you have a masterpiece. . .or something.

To extrude a logo, first you add text. To add text, you can do the following:

1. **If anything is selected in the 3D window, with the cursor in the 3D window, press A to deselect all objects.**

2. **Click where you want the text to appear.**

   The 3D cursor appears at the spot you clicked.

3. **Choose Add➪Text.**

   The word *Text* may appear with a cursor.

4. **Backspace to delete the word *Text* and type in the text that you want to appear.**

5. **Press Tab to switch from Edit mode to Object mode.**

   The 2D text appears.

6. **Click the Editing button in the Buttons header or press F9.**

   Three panes appear in the Buttons window, as shown in Figure 19-7.

7. **In the middle pane of the Buttons window, entitled Curve and Surface, click on the right arrow on the right side in the Ext1 box to increase the Ext1 value from 0.000 to 0.100.**

   The text extrudes.

8. **If you want a larger extrusion, then in Step 7, click on the right arrow in the Ext1 box until your extrusion is the size you want.** (The left arrow decreases the value).

   You can middle-click and drag in the 3D window to more closely inspect the extrusion. (Mac users with a one-button mouse can Alt+Ctrl+Shift+click and drag.)

9. **To create a nice beveled effect, rather than a sharply defined extrusion, you can input values into the two boxes below the Ext1 box, which are the Ext2 and BevResol** (which stands for Bevel Resolution).

   You may want to enter, for example, 0.02 in Ext2 and maybe 10 in BevResol. Your extruded text changes as you change the parameters.

Figure 19-7:
Extruding text with Blender.

Rendering and Animating a Model

You may need to add many objects and adjust them to get your 3D model the way you want it. After you have done so, or at any time while you're creating your model, you can take a look at it at a higher resolution than the resolution of the 3D window. Blender can render the model as it appears in the Camera view.

Also, you may want to add animation. Doing so isn't as hard and complicated as it sounds; although, like almost everything in Blender, it can drive you crazy if you're just starting out. Stay positive; think fun.

To animate, you set keyframes, and Blender automatically interpolates the position, scale, or rotation of the object in between the keyframes. You set a few a keyframes and then let Blender figure out what happens in between.

When you render the animation, Blender generates a rendered image for each frame and numbers them sequentially and stores them in a folder of your choosing.

Rendering an image

You may want to look at an image at a higher resolution to see whether you like the colors, lighting, and transparency that you selected. To render an image at a higher resolution, you can do the following:

1. **Check to see what your model looks like in Camera view.**

   If you don't already have a Camera view, choose View⇨Camera from the 3D window header. You may need to move the model around or move the camera around to get the model to be seen by the camera. (Think of it as a game and have fun!)

2. **To render the model, click the Scene button from the Buttons window header.**

   The Buttons window changes to four panes: Output, Render, Anim, and Format.

3. **Click the big Render button in the Render section.**

   A window appears with the rendered image, as shown in Figure 19-8.

Figure 19-8:
Render a
single frame
or an
animation
using the
Scene
panel.

Animating a 3D model

Animating your 3D model is not a complicated task, although getting it to
look just right may take some tweaking. To animate the 3D model, you can do
the following:

1. **Be sure that you're in Object mode. If you're not, position the cursor
   in the 3D window and press Tab to switch from Edit mode to Object
   mode.**

2. **Select the object that you want to move, rotate, or change the size of
   in the animation.**

3. **Set the Frame number in the Buttons window header to the frame
   number that you want to keyframe.** (When you start an animation, this
   is probably Frame 1.)

   To change the frame number, click the arrow keys beside the number;
   press the arrow keys on your keyboard; or click the frame number, type
   a new frame number, and press Return.

 4. **Position the model where you want it.**

 Make sure you watch the model in Camera view, because this view shows how it will render. You can rotate, resize, or just move the model to where you want it to start (or end, depending on which keyframe it is).

 5. **With the cursor in the 3D window, press I (which stands for Interpolate).**

 The Insert Key menu appears.

 6. **Choose one of the following:**

 • If you want to move the object and you want to keyframe its location, choose Loc.

 • If you want to rotate the object and you want to keyframe the start or end of its rotation, choose Rot.

 • If you want to change the size of the selected object or objects, choose Size.

 • If you want a combination, choose either LocRot or LocRotSize.

 7. **Repeat steps 3–7 for each keyframe that you want to set.**

 You can test the animation at any time by changing the Frame number to 1 and pressing the right arrow on your keyboard. Or watch it in reverse by pressing the left arrow.

 8. **To render your animation, first select the Scene button from the Buttons window header.**

 The Buttons window changes to four panes: Output, Render, Anim, and Format, as shown in Figure 19-8.

 9. **Click the Anim button.**

 This renders all frames from the frame number in the bottom-right button of the Anim section to the frame number in the bottom-left button of the Anim section, by default this may be 250 frames. If you want other frame numbers rendered, click the right or left arrows on either box to increase or decrease the numbers, or click in the box and type in the frame number and press Return.

 10. **To play the animation, click the Play button in the Anim section.**

Loading and Saving Files

The process of saving and opening Blender files is similar to saving and opening files from any other application, only the Save As and Open dialog boxes look a bit unusual to Windows XP and Mac OS X users.

To save a file, do the following:

1. **Choose File⇨Save.**

   The Save As dialog box appears, as shown in Figure 19-9.

2. **Open the file folder that you want to contain your file. You can navigate through your file folders by clicking on a folder name or clicking the P button in the upper left-hand corner of the dialog box to move up one level.**

3. **Type the name of your file in the second line of the Save As dialog box and type .blend after it.**

4. **Click the Save As button.**

   The file is saved in the folder that you specified.

To open a file, choose File⇨Open, select the file that you want to open, and click Open.

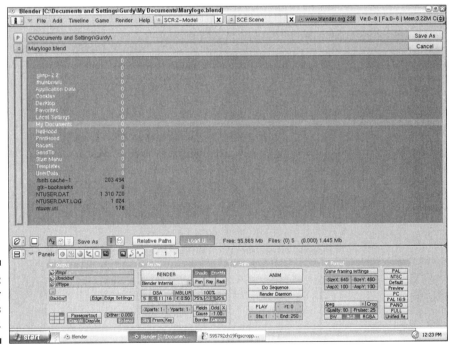

Figure 19-9:
The Blender
Save As
dialog box.

Chapter 20

Recording Sound with Audacity

*A*udacity is a free software program for recording and editing sound that is easy to use and records at amazingly good quality. You audio fanatics out there will be pleased to know that it can record and edit 16-bit, 24-bit, and 32-bit (floating point) samples and can record at up to 96 KHz. Granted, the Philadelphia Symphony Orchestra would not use Audacity to record their albums, but for a hobbyist, Web designer, businessman, and others it can give you good sound — good enough for using on Web sites, presentations, and a million other places. And it's not hard to learn. In fact, my seven-year-old was recording songs on her own after only a two-minute demonstration. This chapter introduces you to the basics of using Audacity.

Importing Sound

Audacity imports MP3, WAV, AIFF, AU, and Ogg Vorbis files, in addition to its own .aup format. You can import a sound file in two ways:

- ✔ **Open the sound file into a new project,** which means it opens into a new window of its own. To open the file as a new project, choose File ⇨ Open, navigate through your files and select your sound file, and click Open.

- ✔ **Import a sound file into an existing project** by choosing Project ⇨ Import Audio. The sound file appears on a new track or tracks below your existing track or tracks.

Recording Sound

To record, hook up a microphone to the microphone input on the sound card of your PC or to the Microphone In jack on your Mac. You can also hook up a USB microphone to your USB port, if you want.

If you have more than one choice in the Line In drop-down list on the Mixer toolbar, then choose the appropriate setting for your microphone. Be sure that your microphone is turned on and click the Record button, shown in Figure 20-1, to record. You may want to watch your sound levels on the Input level meter, also shown in Figure 20-1. Your goal is to record at the highest volume level without clipping it. The Clipping indicators to the right of each meter light up red and stay lit if any sound in the recording or playback gets distorted because it is too loud.

If the Clipping Indicator lights up, you probably want to decrease the volume of your microphone.

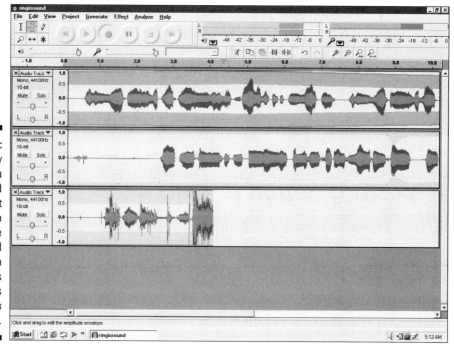

Figure 20-1:
Audacity
allows you
to record
or import
sound on
multiple
tracks and
edit it in
various
ways, as
well as
add effects.

Layering Sound

Audacity automatically layers your sound on tracks, so that the sound already imported or recorded in Audacity plays while you record the next track. Using headphones for this is a good idea; otherwise, you may be re-recording the sound coming over your speakers. You may also want to expand your Audacity window so that you see more tracks at once.

New tracks appear automatically every time you start a new recording. (You can pause your recording and then continue it on the same track; however, once you click Stop, the next time you click record, a new track appears.) You can start recording at the beginning of the track, or you can click anywhere in any track (be sure that the Selection tool is selected before you click) and start the recording from that point (on a new track, of course).

You can use the Mute buttons on any track to temporarily mute that track. Or if you just want one track to play while you record, you can click the Solo button on that track. To delete a track, click the close button on the upper-left corner of the track.

Adjusting Track Volumes Using the Envelope Tool

Some tracks may be recorded softly and some loudly. Usually, you want to adjust your sound levels so that all tracks have about the same levels of volume. Surprisingly, you probably don't need to actually listen to your clip to adjust the volumes of your tracks. You can do it visually by adjusting the size of the waveforms, so that they all appear roughly the same size. And you can do that by using the Envelope tool.

To use the Envelope tool, click the Envelope Tool button. The tracks appear with shaded areas, white areas, and blue inner borders. Click and drag up or down in a track to increase or decrease the volume. The first time you click and drag, the entire track changes volume. Each time you click and drag, an edit point appears, so that the volume changes only from one edit point to the edit points surrounding it. This feature allows you flexibility to make adjustments for louder or softer sections of your clip, or to fade in or fade out a track.

You may want to use the Normalize effect on your tracks before adjusting their volumes with the Envelope tool. For details, see "Normalize, Noise Removal, Echo, Tremolo, and Other Effects" later in this chapter.

Selecting, Cutting, Pasting, Silencing, and Trimming Sound

You can select any part of your clip on any track and manipulate it by cutting it, pasting it, silencing it, or silencing everything else (which is called trimming). To copy and paste or silence sections of your clip, select the desired part of the clip by clicking the Selection button and clicking and dragging the appropriate section in the track. Or click in a track and then Shift+click to select everything between the two clicks. To silence your selection, click the Silence Selection button. To get rid of everything but what you selected, click the Trim button. To cut, click the Cut button, or press Control+X (Windows or GNU/Linux) or Command+X (Macintosh) . You can paste your selection by clicking anywhere in a track and choosing Edit ➪ Paste, or pressing Control+V (Windows or GNU/Linux) or Command+V (Macintosh). The part of the track that you cut appears where you pasted it.

Normalize, Noise Removal, Echo, Tremolo, and Other Effects

If you are not used to editing sound, the Noise Removal filter may seem nothing short of miraculous. It takes an ordinary recording and makes it sound 100 percent more professional by getting rid of popping p's, hissing s's, and other annoying noise. It's not perfect, but it still works wonders. To remove noise, select the track or tracks from which you want to remove the noise. (To select a single track, click anywhere below the name of the top track you want to select. To select multiple tracks, select one track, then Shift+click anywhere below the name of the last track you want to select.) Click Effect ➪ Noise Removal, and click Remove Noise. (I just leave the slider halfway between Less and More.)

Audacity can create other effects, such as Normalize, Echo, Tremolo, Wahwah, Amplify, Equalization, and more. All the effects work roughly in the same way. Select the track, tracks, or part of a track to which you want to add an effect, then choose Effect ➪ *the name of the filter*. Start with the default settings, and click OK. Listen to your effect. Does it need more? Is it too much? If so, then choose Edit ➪ Undo and try the effect again, this time adjusting the settings differently.

You can use Normalize to make soft clips louder and loud clips softer. However, if your clips change in volume and you want to adjust for it, you'll probably want to use the Envelope tool, as well.

Exporting Files to MP3 or WAV

You can save your project in Audacity's .aup file, but they are not readable by any program except Audacity. To export to MP3 or WAV, choose File ➪ Save As MP3 or File ➪ Save As WAV. Give your file a name and click Save. (The first time you choose File ➪ Save As MP3, a dialog box appears informing you that "Audacity does not export MP3 files directly. Would you like to locate lame_enc_dll now?" Click Yes. The "Where is lame_end.dll" dialog box appears. Open the lame-3.96.1 folder that you downloaded and put somewhere, select lame_enc.dll, and click Open.) When you save as MP3 a dialog box appears where you can fill in the Title, Artist, Album, Track Number, Year, Genre, and comments as you like and click OK. Your files are now exported to WAV or MP3.

Part V
More Powerful, Free Software

The 5th Wave   By Rich Tennant

"Do you remember which military web site you downloaded your Bot software from?"

In this part . . .

We cover some of the best educational software, including Tux Paint, Tux Typing, Celestia, Solfege, Flight Gear, and Gcompris. And I describe ten of the most popular free software games: GNU Chess, Super-Tux, Freeciv, Trackballs, Enigma, Circus Linux!, GLtron, BilliardGL, LBreakout2, and Crack-Attack! Of course, many more great games exist—this is just a sampling.

Even though you don't need to run the GNU/Linux desktop to use the best of the free software, you may want to try out SimplyMEPIS, which is the topic of Chapter 21. SimplyMEPIS is probably the most user-friendly GNU/Linux desktop and is the easiest to install, since it automatically detects your hardware and installs the necessary drivers for you.

Chapter 21

Learning with Free Educational Software

*T*he free software world offers hundreds of educational games and programs for children and adults. This chapter covers a few programs, but many others exist as well. If you're looking for a particular area of educational interest, you may want to check out the sites listed in Chapter 2, "The Best Places to Get Free Software."

Training Your Ears with Solfege

Solfege is a serious program for music students but can be used for fun, too. It offers drills in identifying pitches, rhythms, chords, and scales. Each exercise can be configured to the student's level — from a novice to a level that probably only a professional orchestra composer can ace. It also has singing exercises to train the voice to the correct pitch. This program is great for any serious student of music, and even kids might find some of it fun, such as the rhythm exercise.

Solfege provides the following exercises and more:

✔ **Identify Chords:** Click the Chords button and then click New Chord for Solfege to play, as shown in Figure 21-1. Then identify the type of chord from the buttons on the left.

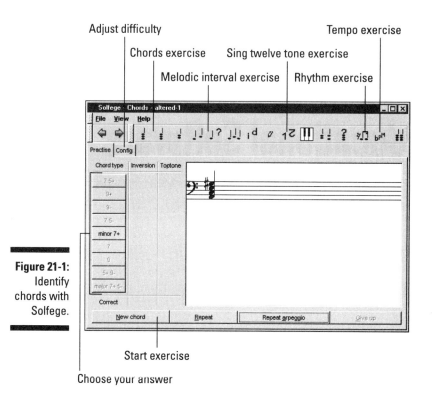

Figure 21-1:
Identify chords with Solfege.

✔ **Identify Melodic Intervals:** Click the Melodic Interval button, shown in Figure 21-1, and click the New Interval button, shown in Figure 21-2. Solfege plays two notes and you need to identify what interval they are by clicking the buttons.

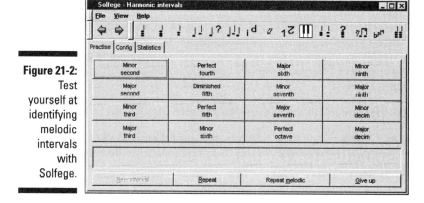

Figure 21-2:
Test yourself at identifying melodic intervals with Solfege.

✔ **Sing Twelvetone:** Click the Sing Twelvetone button, shown in Figure 21-1, and then click the New button, shown in Figure 21-3. The singer sings the notes, then listens to Solfege or sings with Solfege.

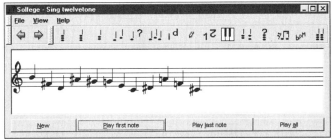

Figure 21-3:
Sing the twelve tones of the scale with Solfege.

✔ **Identify Rhythm:** Click the Rhythm Exercise button, shown in Figure 21-1, then click the New button, shown in Figure 21-4. Solfege plays a rhythm and you get to reproduce that rhythm in musical notes. This exercise is probably the easiest for a novice. And fun, too!

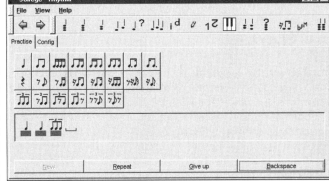

Figure 21-4:
Reproduce Solfege's rhythms in musical notation.

Most of these exercises can be configured to be easy enough for a novice. Click the Config tab on each lesson to configure them.

To download Solfege for Windows, go to www.solfege.org/Main/Download and under the Official Releases heading, click MS Windows Installer (For Windows). To install Solfege, close any programs that are running in Windows. Double-click on the solfege-win32 file and follow the instructions of the Installation Wizard. (For more information about using the Installation Wizard, see the Appendix.)

No official packages are available for the Mac OS X yet, although users are working on it. Check back at the aforementioned link for news about when it will be available. Many GNU/Linux users can install Solfege using KPackage. For more information on installing programs with KPackage, see the Appendix.

Tux Paint for Kids

Tux Paint is a fun painting program for kids. It's designed for kids from square one, with large buttons, meaningful icons for non-readers, a huge supply of cute stamps, and fun tools such as rainbow paint and sparkles. The sound effects are delightful. Each time your child clicks on a tool, a fun sound accompanies it. Tux Paint even allows the child to save his work, or you can exit the program and the artwork comes up on the screen when you start again. (No more tears!)

Tux Paint is also customizable. Moms may want to add stamps of gemstones so their daughters can design their own necklaces. Or make stamps of clothes and a doll's body to play virtual paper dolls. A teacher may use stamps to teach rocks and minerals or a thousand other things.

Getting started

Tux Paint opens with an empty drawing area. Click a tool on the right — either Paint, Stamp, Lines, Shapes, Text, Magic, and so on — and the Tools on the left of the screen change accordingly. You can choose the size of the paint brush, or choose the stamp and choose an arrow to increase or decrease the size of the stamp, as shown in Figure 21-5.

Customizing stamps

If you want to add your own customized stamps to Tux Paint, you can do so using the GIMP. Be sure the image is no bigger than 100x100 pixels. The edges of the picture should be transparent, not white. Then save the image as a PNG file in the following directory:

- ✔ **Windows:** C:\Program Files\TuxPaint\data\stamps
- ✔ **Mac:** /Users/youraccountname/Library/Preferences/stamps
- ✔ **GNU/Linux:** /usr/local/share/tuxpaint/stamps or /usr/share/tuxpaint/stamps

Figure 21-5:
A Tux Paint masterpiece by my seven-year-old daughter.

You can draw in rainbow colors!

Where to get Tux Paint

You can find Tux Paint at www.newbreedsoftware.com/tuxpaint/download. To download and install it, do the following for your operating system:

✔ **Windows:**

- **To download Tux Paint,** click on the Windows (Installer Version) link. Then click the tuxpaint-windows-installer download link under the Programs header. (This Web site uses mirrors. For more information on mirrors, see the Appendix.) After the download completes, go back to the download page and click on the tuxpaint-stamps-windows-installer to download the stamp images used by the stamp tool within Tux Paint.

- **To install Tux Paint,** double-click on tuxpaint-0.9.14-win32-installer-1.exe and follow the instructions of the Installation Wizard. Double-click on tuxpaint-stamps-2004.10.03-win32-installer.exe and follow the instructions of the Installation Wizard.

- **To run Tux Paint,** choose Start⇨Programs⇨Tux Paint.

✔ **Mac OS X:**

- **To download Tux Paint,** click on the Mac OS X link, click the download link under the Tux Paint heading, and then click the download link under the Rubber Stamps Collection heading. (This Web site uses mirrors. For more information on mirrors, see the Appendix.)

- **To install Tux Paint,** double-click on each of the two downloaded files. A folder called Tux Paint with a Tux Paint file in it appears, and a folder called Tux Paint Stamps with a file called Tux Paint Stamps Installer appears. Click on the Tux Paint Stamps Installer icon. If you have multiple users on your Mac, then a dialog box appears. Install Tux Paint Stamps for Current User, All Users, or Tux Paint Application. If you're not sure, then choose Current User and click Install Stamps.

- **To run Tux Paint**, double-click on the Tux Paint icon in the Tux Paint folder.

✔ **GNU/Linux:** See the Appendix for instructions on installing applications using KPackage.

Exploring the Cosmos with Celestia

Celestia is a software application that allows you to explore the universe. You can see planets, asteroids, stars, the moon, and spacecraft up close. For example, I took a close look at Jupiter, as shown in Figure 21-6. You can even orbit the moon and planets. But Celestia is more than just seeing planets, asteroids, and more up close in 3D. What's truly amazing about Celestia is that you can go to any star, orbit it, see other stars and travel to any other star from there. Celestia keeps track of what star you've chosen and where you are. So, you really do explore the universe with Celestia — at least the hundreds of stars in Celestia's database — and some even have planets.

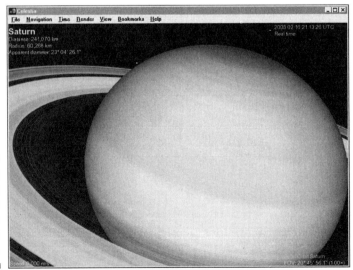

Figure 21-6:
Take a trip around the universe with Celestia.

Moving around the universe

Check out the cool demo of Celestia by choosing Help⇨Run Demo (Windows and GNU/Linux) or Celestia⇨Run Demo (Macintosh).

Also, you may want to set the date and time before you start. To set the date and time, choose Time⇨Set Time, and fill in the information in the dialog box.

Celestia allows you to move around the universe in the following ways:

- ✔ **To move closer to an object,** click on the object, such as a star, to select it; then press G.
- ✔ **To return to our sun,** press H to select the sun, then press G to return to it.
- ✔ **To go to any planet (in our solar system) or other objects, such as a spacecraft,** right-click on the sun (or control-click if you have a Macintosh) and choose the planet or object, then press G to go to it.
- ✔ **To orbit a planet,** right-click (or control-click if you have a Macintosh) and drag around the planet.

Further controls can be found by choosing Help⇨Controls.

Information about the star or planet is listed in the upper right-hand corner of the window.

Where to get Celestia

Mac OS X and Windows users can go to http://sourceforge.net/projects/celestia. Scroll down and under Latest File Releases, click on the Download link for the Celestia-macosx or Celestia-win32-bin package. Then click on Download celestia-win32-1.3.2.exe or Download Celestia-macosx. Then click in the download column of any location near you. To install the downloaded file double-click on it, and then (for Macintosh) simply double-click on the Celestia icon in the celestia-osx folder or (for Windows) follow the instructions of the Installation Wizard. (For more information about the Installation Wizard, see the Appendix.)

Many GNU/Linux users can use KPackage to download and install Celestia, as described in the Appendix.

Learning to Type with Tux Typing

Tux Typing is a delightful learning-to-type program for youngsters. My 7-year-old daughter and 10-year-old son spent hours playing this game and still didn't tire of it. It's arcade-like action with the purpose of learning to type, as shown in Figure 21-7. And the antics of the penguin are charming.

Figure 21-7:
The Fish Drop game kept my seven-year-old daughter enthralled for hours.

The only instruction you need to know in Tux Typing is to use the Esc key to end the games and return to the menu. (My kids figured that out on their own!)

Tux Typing offers two arcade-like games, Fish Cascade and Comet Zap. They both have the same rules but with different graphics. You get three or four levels of play: Easy, Medium, and Hard, or Space Cadet, Pilot, Ace, and Commander. You also get six types of exercises: Alphabet, Finger Exercises, Plants (yes, Begonia, Daffodil, and so on), Short Words, Medium Words, and Long Words.

The goal is to type the letters or words dropping from the top of the screen before they hit the bottom of the screen. Visually, they either get zapped by laser beams or eaten by the penguin. The game keeps score, of course.

Tux Typing also offers a practice mode, shown in Figure 21-8. For the serious student of typing, this looks like a great start.

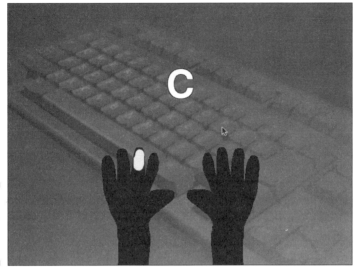

Figure 21-8:
Tux Typing's
practice
mode.

To download and install Tux Typing for Windows and Mac OS X, go to `http://tuxtype.sourceforge.net/download/` and do the following for your operating system:

✓ **Windows:**

- **To download Tux Typing,** scroll down and in the TuxType 1 (Stable Branch) Binary section, click on the Windows link. Then click in the download column for the location near to you. (For more information on mirrors, see the Appendix.)

- **To install Tux Typing,** double-click on the downloaded file, and follow the instructions of the Installation Wizard. (For more information about the Installation Wizard, see the Appendix.)

✓ **Mac OS X:** The stable version is not available yet, although a newer development version is available. Check back periodically for the development version to become the stable version.

✓ **GNU/Linux:** Many GNU/Linux users can use KPackage to download and install Celestia, as described in the Appendix.

Learning Fun with Gcompris

Gcompris is an educational software package with 45 different activities for kids 2–10. It has colorful and inviting screens, and the activities range from learning to play chess to learning to control the mouse. It's easy to navigate within the program, and every activity is geared toward learning. Gcompris is available in many languages. And it has verbal tool tips — when you move the mouse over a button, the function of the button is spoken.

The full-blown version of Gcompris works on the Mac (using X11) and GNU/ Linux. The Windows version, however, has only ten activities available on it. But these ten are nice activities. The developer of Gcompris is currently working on porting the rest of the activities to Windows, and would like Windows users to contribute about $26 if they want more than the ten activities on what he considers the Windows demo version.

The ten activities included with the Windows Gcompris version are

- **Math activities:** Addition, Subtraction, and Multiplication exercises, as shown in Figure 21-9.
- **Addition:** Add scores of a target game, as shown in Figure 21-10.
- **Counting:** For kindergarten and preschool.
- **Games:** Tower of Hanoi, Super-Brain (which was too hard for me!)
- **Mouse skills:** Click on moving fish to erase hidden pictures.
- **Typing letters**
- **Piloting a submarine:** Not as easy as it looks!
- **Drawing and identifying colors**
- **Identifying letters:** Shown in Figure 21-11.

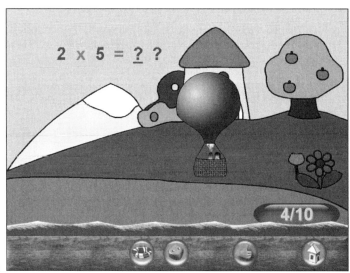

Figure 21-9:
Keep the balloon up in the air by answering the equations as they appear.

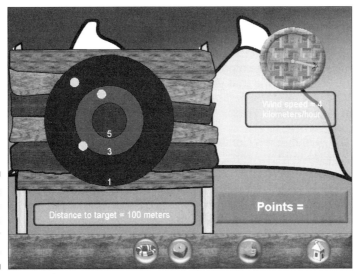

Figure 21-10:
Shoot the arrows, then add up your score.

Within each game, click on the life preserver symbol at the bottom of the screen and choose Manual to find out the instructions for each game.

Clicking on the House at the bottom of the screen brings you back to the last menu.

Figure 21-11:
Click on the spoken letter.

To download and install Gcompris for Windows, go to `http://source forge.net/project/showfiles.php?group_id=6865` and click on the next to last link in the Gcompris downloads: gcompris-6.1-setup.exe for Windows. Then click in the download column for the location near to you. (For more information on mirrors, see the Appendix.) To install the program, double-click on the file that you downloaded and follow the instructions in the Installation Wizard. (For more information on the Installation Wizard, see the Appendix).

Many GNU/Linux users can download and install this program using KPackage. For instructions on installing programs using KPackage, see the Appendix.

Flying with Flight Gear

Flight Gear is a flying simulation program that can let you pilot any one of dozens of aircraft, large and small, including a balloon and a helicopter. You can visit any one of 20,000 airports worldwide! Flight Gear offers a three-DVD set of the world terrain, which you can buy, or you can install a program that downloads the terrain as you need it — on the fly? Flight Gear allows you to fly in different weather conditions or different times of the day and has an extensive 109-page manual that you can download, as well as tutorials. Serious pilots probably want to invest in a joystick and rudder pedals.

Levels of difficulty

Flight Gear comes with a couple levels of difficulty, to help you get started. You may want to start out flying a smaller plane, such as a Piper Cub, and then move up until you're flying the big jets. Figure 21-12, and than in a couple of pages 21-13 show Flight Gear in action.

Where to get Flight Gear

You can download and install Flight Gear in the following ways for the following platforms:

- ✔ To download Flight Gear, for Windows go to `www.flightgear.org/ downloads`. Under the heading Download Flight Gear, click Windows. Under the Windows heading, click either the Mirror-1, Mirror-2, or Mirror-3 link. Then to install Flight Gear, double-click on the downloaded file and follow the instructions of the Installation Wizard.

Figure 21-12:
Expert pilots can take a jumbo jet around the world with Flight Gear.

✔ Mac users need to go to macflightgear.sourceforge.net and click Download. Then click on the icon under the Download heading for a location near you. After the file downloads, a folder appears containing a folder named FlightGear and a file named OpenAL.pkg. (If you haven't already installed OpenAL and you're using Mac OS X 10.3, then double-click on OpenAL.pkg and follow the instructions in the installer that appears.) Drag the FlightGear folder to the Applications folder or any-where you want to keep it. Double-click the FlightGear folder to open it, and inside that folder, double-click the FlightGear icon to start the appli-cation. FlightGear for the Mac requires OS X 10.3 or later.

✔ Many GNU/Linux users can download and install Flight Gear using KPackage. For instructions on installing programs using KPackage, see the Appendix.

For the manuals or tutorials, go to www.flightgear.org/docs.html.

Flight Gear has five active mailing lists, plus an IRC Channel for live discus-sions. You can find all these at www.flightgear.org/mail.html.

Chapter 22

Fun with Arcade, Simulation, Puzzle, Strategy, and 3D Games

. . . .

In This Chapter

▸ SuperTux and Circus Linux! for kids

▸ Freeciv and Gnu Chess for teens and adults

▸ Enigma, Crack Attack!, Lbreakout2, Trackballs, BilliardGL, and GLtron for everyone

. . . .

A huge pile of games have been written and made available as free software. Many have been ported from GNU/Linux to Windows or to the Mac. In this chapter, I present ten of the most popular games, but keep in mind that there are many more. Refer to Chapter 2 for likely places to find them. Free software games usually have large and active gaming communities, which often add to the fun.

GNU Chess

GNU Chess is a chess game that you can play with XBoard for Mac OS X or GNU/Linux, or with WinBoard for Windows. XBoard and WinBoard are graphical interfaces for Gnu Chess, as shown in Figure 22-1. In other words, they let you see the chessboard instead of a screen with the words telling you what the move is. But WinBoard and XBoard are not only the front end for GNU Chess; they also let you do the following:

> ✔ **Play chess with other people over the Internet, or watch the moves of someone else playing chess.**

> ✔ **Show the moves of any of sixty games of Bobby Fischer.**

> ✔ **Use other chess engines besides GNU Chess.** GNU Chess was developed with standard file formats, so you can try out a whole slew of chess programs that are compatible with XBoard and WinBoard. See which ones you can beat!

✔ **Play correspondence chess.** For XBoard only, you can make a move and automatically generate an e-mail using the CMail program to send the move to your opponent, who can then view it using XBoard.

Active moderated forums for WinBoard and XBoard are found at `http://wbforum.volker-pittlik.name/`. You can enter tournaments; discuss WinBoard, XBoard, or the chess engines; or just discuss chess.

You can download WinBoard from `www.tim-mann.org/xboard.html`. Scroll down the page and click on the link Download Stable WinBoard. To install WinBoard, double-click on the downloaded file and follow the instructions of the Installation Wizard.

To download and install XBoard for GNU/Linux, use KPackage. For instructions on using KPackage, see the Appendix.

GNU Chess is installed by default with Mac OS X along with a proprietary graphical interface by Apple named Chess. You can find Chess in the Applications folder on your Mac.

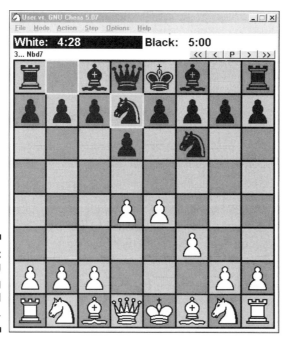

Figure 22-1:
Play GNU
Chess using
WinBoard
or XBoard.

Freeciv

Freeciv is inspired by the popular game Civilization, which *Time* magazine dubbed the greatest computer strategy game of all time. However, because Civilization is not open source and free, the free software community created its own game with similar game play and strategies and the same empire-building goal. Freeciv, shown in Figure 22-2, is very popular and considered by some to be the best open source strategy game for both single and multiple players. It has eleven active forums on different topics, including a Multi-player Online Gaming forum.

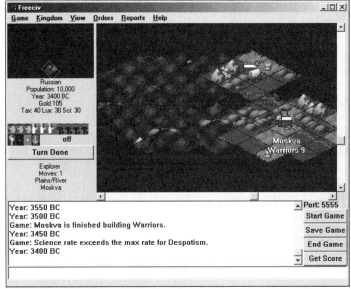

Figure 22-2: Freeciv is an empire-building multiplayer strategy game.

Freeciv has been translated into many languages, so you can play with people all over the world.

Freeciv can be downloaded for Windows by going to www.freeciv.org. Under the Get Started header, click on Download. Then scroll down the page and choose the download for your respective operating system. Windows XP, 20000, NT users can click on the Freeciv-2.0.0-win32-gtk2-setup.exe link. Double-click on the downloaded file to install it.

You can download and install Freeciv for GNU/Linux using KPackage. For details of how to use KPackage, see the Appendix. For the rules of the game and FAQs, go to www.freeciv.org.

To download FreeCiv for Mac, go to `www.freeciv.org` and click on Download under the Get Started header. On the new Web page that appears, choose the download for Mac OS X. Double-click on the downloaded file to unpack it, and then click on the FreeCiv folder that appears and drag it to your Applications folder or wherever you want to keep it. This will copy the FreeCiv folder from its current temporary location to a permanent location on your hard drive. To run FreeCiv on the Mac, you need Mac OS X version 3 or later and X11. For information on how to install X11 on your Mac if you don't have it already, see "Downloading and installing the GIMP for Mac OS X or GNU/Linux" in Chapter 1.

SuperTux

SuperTux is a 2D, side-scrolling, Super Mario-type game with 26 levels and a story to go with it. It can be played with a joystick or with just the keyboard arrows. There are lots of enemies to jump over and lots of boxes with prizes in them. The graphics are appealing, as shown in Figure 22-3, and the music and sound effects are very similar to Super Mario.

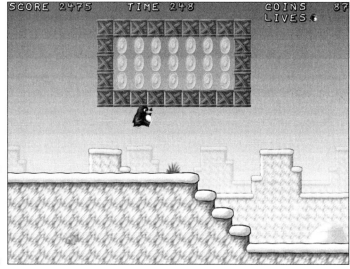

Figure 22-3:
Help
SuperTux
rescue
Penny.

SuperTux starts with a story line. His penguin friend, Penny, is kidnapped by the big boss penguin, Nolok, and SuperTux needs to rescue her. A map appears, showing the route he must take. Press the arrow keys to start him on his journey and when he reaches an obstacle, press Return or Enter (depending on your keyboard) to start a level. If you want to quit a level, press the Esc key.

To jump really high or run really fast, press Control + Arrow key. (On some keyboards, only the right control key will produce the effect.)

To download and install SuperTux, Windows and Mac OS X users can go to `http://super-tux.sourceforge.net/download.html` and click on the link next to your operating system. Then click in the downloads column for a location near you. (For more about mirrors, see the Appendix.)

To install SuperTux in Windows, double-click on the downloaded file and follow the instructions of the Installation Wizard.

To install SuperTux on the Mac, create a new folder in your Applications folder or anywhere you want to keep SuperTux. Then double-click on the file you downloaded to unpack it. A folder appears containing the SuperTux applications and assorted documentation. Drag the contents of this folder to the new folder you created in Applications or wherever.

GNU/Linux users can download and install SuperTux using KPackage. For details of how to use KPackage, see the Appendix.

To run SuperTux, double-click on the SuperTux icon.

Trackballs

Trackballs is inspired by the game Marble Madness on the Amiga. It's a ball rolling and bouncing game with steep and skinny 3D paths and lots of obstacles, as shown in Figure 22-4. It has seven courses and three levels of difficulty for each course. You move the ball with the mouse — and, of course, the ball moves faster on steeper slopes. Press the spacebar to jump.

You can download and install Trackballs for GNU/Linux using KPackage. Windows users can download Trackballs at `http://trackballs.source forge.net/`. To install, double-click on the downloaded file, and the program extracts into a folder named Trackballs v1.0.1. Open the folder and double-click the trackballs icon.

Figure 22-4:
Roll the ball past obstacles while keeping it from falling off the cliff in Trackballs.

Circus Linux!

Circus Linux! is inspired by the Atari game Circus Atari. It's a fun game where you click the mouse, then try to position the seesaw at the bottom of the screen to catch the clown flying through the air, as shown in Figure 22-5. If you catch the clown, the other clown launches into the air. Don't miss! The goal is to get as many points as possible. The game keeps track of high scores. The sound effects are fun, too.

Circus Linux! offers several variations of the game as well, and it can be played in one-player or two-player mode or a two-player cooperative mode.

Windows and Mac OS X users can download Circus Linux! by surfing to `http://www.newbreedsoftware.com/circus-linux/download/` and clicking the download link for your operating system.

The Windows link is zipped, so to install it, first right-click on it and choose Extract Files. Click OK in the dialog box that appears. Open the extracted folder and double-click on the circuslinux application file. The game starts immediately.

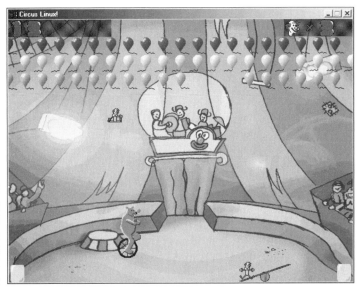

Figure 22-5:
Catch that clown in Circus Linux!

Macintosh users should double-click on the downloaded file to unpack it and open the CircusLinux folder if this doesn't happen automatically. Create a new folder in your Applications folder or anywhere you want to keep CircusLinux. Then drag the contents of the CircusLinux folder into the new folder you created in Applications or wherever. Double-click on the CircusLinux icon in the new folder to start the game.

GNU/Linux users can download and install Circus Linux! using KPackage. For details of how to use KPackage, see the Appendix.

Crack Attack!

This game is inspired by the Nintendo game Tetris Attack. It is also similar to a game mode called Marathon in the Nintendo 64 Pokemon Puzzle game. The object is to put the brackets around two cubes and switch them so that you get three colors in a row or three in a column, as shown in Figure 22-6. When you do so, the cubes disappear. The goal is to get as many cubes to disappear as possible and not let the pile grow too high. This game gets quite strategic when it is played by two players at the same time. An advanced player can cause his blocks to fall on the other player's stacks.

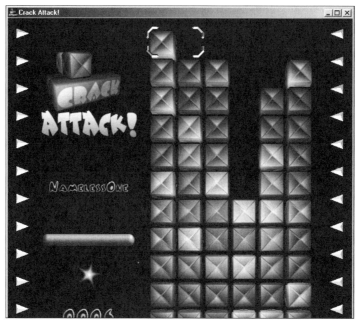

Figure 22-6:
Crack
Attack! is
similar to
Tetris Attack
and can be
played
alone or
with two
players at
the same
time.

Windows or Mac OS X users can go to http://aluminumangel.org/attack/ to download the game.

To install it in Windows, double-click on the downloaded file and follow the instructions of the Installation Wizard. To run it choose Start➪Programs➪ Crack Attack➪Crack Attack.

To install it in Mac OS X, double-click on the downloaded file to unpack it if this doesn't happen automatically. Double-click on the Crack Attack folder to open it and then double-click on the Crack Attack application icon to start the game.

GNU/Linux users can download and install Crack Attack! using KPackage. For details of how to use KPackage, see the Appendix.

Enigma

Enigma is a popular ball-rolling puzzle game that has 141 levels. Each game is different and after you win one game, you move on to the next. It is timed, and the highest score is noted. In the Welcome Game, for example, the boxes in the middle and on the borders open to reveal a color when hit by the marble that you roll, but close when the marble hits the next box unless it is the same color. The object is to open the central boxes and have them remain open. With 141 levels, Enigma can keep you busy for hours!

If you want to quit a level, press the Esc key.

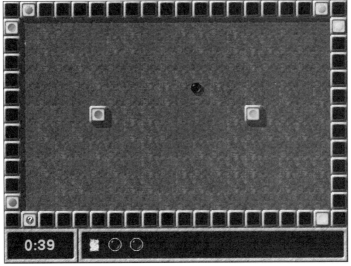

Figure 22-7:
Enigma has many levels to choose from for ball-rolling, puzzle fun.

Windows users can go to http://www.nongnu.org/enigma/ for downloads. GNU/Linux users can download and install Enigma using KPackage. For details of how to use KPackage, see the Appendix.

BilliardGL

BilliardGL is a game of 3D pool. It has remarkable 3D graphics that are intuitively easy to maneuver and use. This is fun for anyone, whether you have a real pool table or not. It has two modes: View and Aim. In View mode, you can use the arrow keys to move closer to the action, and click and drag the mouse to change the angle of the view. Pressing the spacebar changes to Aim mode, as shown in Figure 22-8, and then the arrow keys just move you around the cue ball, or closer or farther from the cue ball. This time when you press the spacebar, the cue ball moves directly upward, colliding with any ball in its way. Pressing the spacebar longer gives it more momentum. Hopefully you aimed well!

Figure 22-8:
BilliardGL is
a 3D pool
game
experience.

To download and install BilliardGL for Windows, go to `www.tobias-nopper.de/BillardGL/download-en.html` and click on a link for your operating system; then click in the Downloads column for a location near you. (For more information about mirrors, see the Appendix.) BilliardGL is 792 kB. Install the program by double-clicking on the file that you downloaded and following the instructions in the Installation Wizard.

GLtron

GLtron is inspired by the movie *TRON*. You control a car, called a lightcycle, which creates a wall behind it as it travels, as shown in Figure 22-9. The object is to be the last lightcycle that has not crashed. You can do this by causing the three other lightcycles to crash into the wall created by your car or others, or they can crash into the boundary of the game board. These other three light-cycles can be other players or computer-driven.

Four players can steer four lightcycles from a single keyboard. Player 1 uses A for left turn and S for right turn. Player 2 uses K for right and L for left. Player 3 uses 5 and 6. Player 4 uses left arrow and right arrow. For Single- player view press F1. For Two-player view press F2. For Four-player view, press F3. Or you can press F10 to toggle between three camera modes. You can pause the game any time by pressing the spacebar. (This game goes so fast, you'll probably want to press the spacebar a lot of times.)

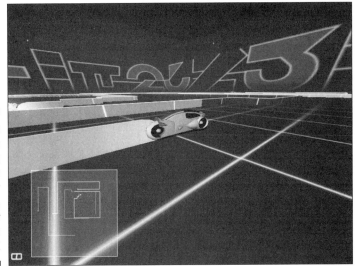

Figure 22-9:
GLtron is a
fast-moving
game with
up to four
players,
inspired by
the movie
TRON.

Windows and Mac users can go to http://www.gltron.org/ for downloads.

For Windows, double-click the downloaded file and follow the instructions of the Installation Wizard.

For Macintosh OS X, double-click the downloaded file to unpack if your computer doesn't unpack it automatically. Then double-click the GLtron icon to start the game.

GNU/Linux users can download and install GLtron using KPackage. For details of how to use KPackage, see the Appendix.

LBreakout2

LBreakout2 is a multiplayer or single-player game with over 50 levels of play. Basically, you press the spacebar to start the game, then use the arrow keys or mouse to move the paddle at the bottom of the screen from side to side to keep the ball or balls from falling. When a ball hits the paddle it bounces up to hit the boxes above, as shown in Figure 22-10. LBreakout2 offers features such as goldshower, joker, explosive balls, bonus magnets, chaos maluses, darkness maluses, weak balls, growing bricks, explosive bricks, regenerative bricks, and more. You can set the game for three skill levels: Kids, Medium, and Hard.

TIP

If you want to quit a level, press the Esc key.

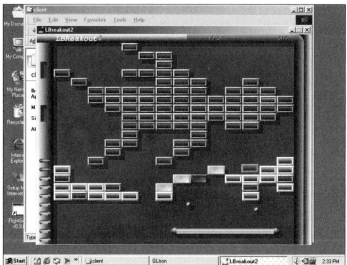

Figure 22-10:
Bounce the
balls to
uncover the
hidden
contents
of the
boxes.
Use
single-
player
mode or
multiplayer
mode.

To download LBreakout2 for Windows go to `http://lgames.sourceforge.net/index.php?project=LBreakout2` and click on the download ending with .zip for Windows, or .dmg for the Mac. Then click in the Download column for a location near you.

To install LBreakout2 for Windows, right-click the downloaded file and choose Extract files, and click OK in the Extract dialog box. Then open the extracted folder and double-click the lbreakout2 icon in the Client folder.

To install LBreakout2 for Macintosh, unpack the .dmg file you downloaded by double-clicking it. The lbreakout2 window appears. Drag the lbreakout2 icon from that window to your Applications folder or anywhere else you want to keep it. This will copy the application to your hard drive. Double-click on the lbreakout2 icon to start the game. LBreakout2 requires Mac OS X 10.3 or later.

GNU/Linux users can download and install LBreakout2 using KPackage. For details of how to use KPackage, see the Appendix.

Chapter 23

A Friendly, Free, and Powerful Alternative to Windows XP

*G*NU/Linux is a free open source alternative to Windows. Hundreds of versions of GNU/Linux exist. The reason is that it is free, people download it and tinker with it, and then distribute it. SimplyMEPIS Linux is a popular version of GNU/Linux and ranks in the top ten for the following reasons:

- ✔ **Powerful and polished:** SimplyMEPIS is designed to be user-friendly while not losing any of the power of the GNU/Linux operating system.

- ✔ **Runs from CD-ROM or hard drive:** It can run from the CD-ROM, giving you a chance to try it out and see whether you like it before you install it on your hard drive. It takes only about three minutes to boot it.

- ✔ **Ease of installing:** SimplyMEPIS is probably the easiest GNU/Linux distribution to install. It automatically detects your hardware and installs drivers automatically without your needing to do anything.

- ✔ **Tons of applications:** SimplyMEPIS installs with tons of useful free software applications, all in one stroke, such as Mozilla Firefox, OpenOffice. org, the GIMP, Audacity, and many more.

- ✔ **No worries about viruses, worms, Trojan Horses, or anything else that may infest a Windows computer:** You don't need anti-virus software when using GNU/Linux. One reason is that the design of GNU/Linux was inspired by the design of the Unix operating system, which is used for large mainframe computers for which security was important.

  ✔ **Contains a firewall to restrict anyone from using your computer remotely:** Except you, of course, if you need to.

  ✔ **Includes KPackage:** Use this to download and automatically install free software from the Internet.

For someone who wants a reliable desktop, packed with applications for almost every conceivable purpose — especially when you consider the KPackage program that can download and install thousands of free programs from the Internet — SimplyMEPIS may be right for you. It takes about three minutes to run from the CD-ROM, and it seems to run flawlessly.

Downloading SimplyMEPIS

To install SimplyMEPIS, you can surf the Web to www.mepis.org and click on the Download MEPIS Linux link (under Discover MEPIS) to download. Click on one of the Mirror links and click the link titled Released. Then click on the topmost link, which in this case is SimplyMEPIS–3.3.iso.

Downloading SimplyMEPIS takes quite a while because it is 693 Mb. (You probably don't want to try this if you're using a modem connection.) If you don't have a fast Internet connection, you can buy the CD-ROM for $9.95 by clicking on the link in the Buy From MEPIS section on the www.mepis.org home page.

When it is finished downloading, burn it to a CD with a CD burner. If you don't have a CD burner or don't want to use it, again you could just buy the CD-ROM.

Installing SimplyMEPIS

You can install SimplyMEPIS in two ways:

  ✔ **To run from your CD-ROM:** Boot your computer from the SimplyMEPIS CD-ROM as described in the next section, and you'll have a full-blown GNU/Linux environment with lots of applications installed and working in seconds. When you run it from the CD-ROM, however, applications load a little slowly because CD-ROM drives are slow compared to hard drives. But you can still try it out and use the applications and see how you like it.

✔ **To run from your hard drive:** After you install SimplyMEPIS from the CD-ROM, you can use it or further install it by clicking on the INSTALL ME icon on the SimplyMEPIS desktop. (See the later section "Installing SimplyMEPIS onto Your Hard Drive" for more details.)

Booting SimplyMEPIS from a CD-ROM

To boot SimplyMEPIS from a CD-ROM, follow these steps:

1. **Place the SimplyMEPIS CD-ROM in the CD-ROM drive of any Windows computer and reboot the computer.**

   A window appears, as shown in Figure 23-1. SimplyMEPIS boots automatically in 30 seconds, which means you have 30 seconds to interrupt the booting, if you want to do the following:

   • **If your computer is older,** you can use the arrow key to choose Boot 2.4 (older hardware).

   • **To explore the Help,** click F1.

   • **If you want a language other than English, press F2** and choose German, Spanish, French, Italian, Dutch, or Swedish. Use the arrow keys to navigate the list and press Return after making your selection. To start booting, press Return.

   • **To choose a different screen resolution,** other than the default, press F3 and navigate through the choices with the arrow keys and press Return to make your selection. Press Return again to start booting.

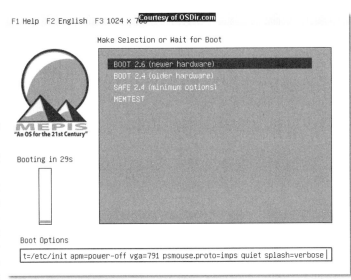

Figure 23-1: The first installation screen that appears when booting Simply-MEPIS.

After about two minutes, a new screen appears, requesting your Username and Password.

2. Click demo.

SimplyMEPIS fills in the words, using demo as your Username.

(You probably don't want to choose Root, because if you're just trying out or even installing the program permanently, you probably don't need the power of being the system administrator that Root gives you. You can save your work in demo mode, just like you can save it as Root.)

3. Type demo in the Password input box.

The SimplyMEPIS desktop appears after about a minute, with the KMix application running.

4. You can use the sliders of KMix to adjust the volume of your computer, if you want.

5. Go ahead and explore the SimplyMEPIS menus by clicking the K in the lower left-hand corner,

A menu appears, as shown in Figure 23-2.

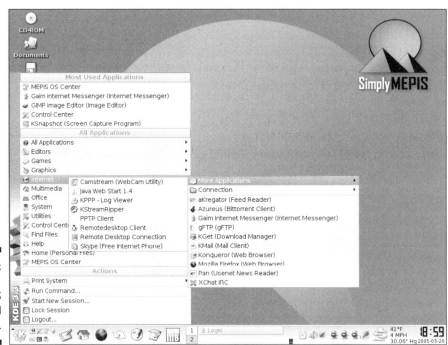

Figure 23-2:
The Simply
MEPIS
desktop and
menus.

Configuring your Internet connection

You can start Mozilla Firefox by choosing K⇨Internet⇨Mozilla Firefox and see whether you can surf the Web. If not, here's how to adjust your Internet settings:

1. **Choose K⇨SimplyMEPIS OS Settings.**

   A dialog box appears requesting the root password.

2. **Type in the root password, which by default is "root" (without the quotation marks).**

   The MEPIS OS Control Center dialog box appears, as shown in Figure 23-3.

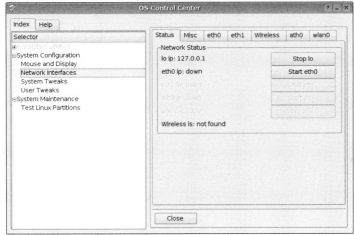

Figure 23-3:
The Simply-
MEPIS OS
Control
Center.

3. **Choose Network Interfaces.**

   If you have an Ethernet card, click the tab labeled eth0 and choose Use DHCP if you automatically get an Internet address from your Internet provider. Or choose Use Static IP Settings if you need to type the numbers.

4. **Click Apply.**

   A dialog box appears, saying that the eth0 config has been updated. The new config will take effect when you restart the network.

5. **Click OK.**

6. **To make your changes take effect by restarting the network connection, click the Status tab and click the Start eth0 button.**

Applications That Install with SimplyMEPIS

SimplyMEPIS comes with lots of free software installed. It also comes with KPackage, which enables you to download and easily install any free software from the Internet. On the K menu of the SimplyMEPIS desktop, you'll find the following applications and more. Table 23-1 includes the highlights.

Table 23-1	SimplyMEPIS Applications	
Menu Category	*Subcategory*	*Application*
Games	Arcade	Frozen Bubble
		KSirtet
		TuxRacer
	Board Games	KBackgammon
		KMahjongg (Tile Game)
		Penguin Taipei
	Card Games	Penguin Canfield
		Penguin Freecell
		Penguin Golf
		Penguin Solitaire
		Pengiun Thornq
	Tactics and Strategy	KBattleship
		KMines
		Penguin Mastermind
		Penguin Merlin
		Penguin Minesweeper
		Penguin Pegged
Graphics		Acrobat Reader
		Digikam (Photo management)

Menu Category	Subcategory	Application
		The GIMP
		KdeprintFax
		KFax
		Kooka (Scan & OCR program)
		KPaint
Internet		aKregator (Newsfeed reader)
		Azureus (Bittorrent client)
		Gaim Internet Messenger
		gFTP
		KGet (Download Manager)
		Mozilla Firefox
		Pan (Usenet news reader)
		XChat IRC
		Camstream (WebCam utility)
		Skype (Free Internet phone)
Multimedia		Gtkpod (iPod manager)
		K3b (CD & DVD burning)
		KMix (Sound mixer)
		KsCD (CD player)
		RealPlayer 10
		Xine (Video player)
		XMMS (Multimedia player)
		Audacity
		KAudioCreator (CD ripper)
		Kino (Video editor)
		Xawtv (TV viewer and capture)

(continued)

Table 23-1 *(continued)*

Menu Category	Subcategory	Application
Office		Checkbook tracker
		KNotes (Pop-up notes)
		Kontact (Personal information manager)
		OpenOffice.org
		Scribus (Page layout software)
System	Security	Guarddog (Firewall)
		KPackage Package Manager
Utilities		Kdict (Online dictionary)
		KPilot (PalmPilot tool)
		KAlarm
		KPalmDOC (PalmDOC converter)
Editors		Kate, KEdit, KWrite

Anti-virus software is not necessary with SimplyMEPIS, because GNU/Linux operating systems do not currently suffer from viruses, worms, and other malicious programs that can attack Windows computers.

When you first choose an application on the K menu, such as the GIMP, you may need to install it. Doing so is simple. Just let the Installation Wizard do the work for you and accept any of the default settings, unless you're experienced with the application and want to do otherwise.

Installing SimplyMEPIS onto Your Hard Drive

After you've booted SimplyMEPIS onto your computer, you may want to install it on your hard drive so that it will run faster. To install SimplyMEPIS on your hard drive, perform the following steps:

1. **Click the INSTALL ME icon on the SimplyMEPIS desktop.**

   A dialog box may appear, asking you to enter the Root password.

2. **Type the word *root* in the Password input box and click OK.**

   After a few seconds, the SimplyMEPIS OS Control Center dialog box appears.

3. **Click Install MEPIS on Hard Drive.**

   The SimplyMEPIS Linux Copyright information appears in the pane on the right. It is both copyrighted and released under the GNU Public License. That's okay. It's still released under the GNU Public License, which means it's free software.

4. **Click Next.**

5. **Choose the disk for installation.**

   (This is a no-brainer for me. I have only one disk.)

6. **Select Auto-install Using Entire Disk and click Next.**

   You could arrange for disk partitions and run Windows and SimplyMEPIS on the same computer — but why not just dedicate an entire computer to it? This makes installation easy, although it also erases everything on your hard drive.

   A dialog box appears with the message, "OK to format and use the entire disk for SimplyMEPIS?"

7. **Click Yes (assuming you don't mind deleting everything on your hard drive).**

   A progress bar appears in the pane on the right with the title Installation in Progress, Formatting Home Partition. After about ten minutes, a new pane appears, entitled Select Boot Method, with some default settings.

   Anything you saved on the computer while you were running SimplyMEPIS from the CD-ROM gets erased when you format the disk.

8. **Click Next.**

   The "OK to install GRUB bootloader at hda?" dialog box appears.

9. **Click Next.**

   The "Grub installed ok" dialog box appears.

10. **Click OK.**

    The pane on the right changes to User Account and Root (Administrator Account).

11. **Type whatever you want your user account name to be in the User login name box. (You may want to use all lowercase letters.) Then type what you want to use for your User password and the same password in the Confirm User Password input box. Type what you want to use for your Root password for the Administrator account and type it again in the Confirm Root Password input box. Click Next.**

    The pane on the right changes to Computer Network Names.

12. **Type in the name of your computer, computer domain, and workgroup. You can type in what you want here, or accept the default. Click Next.**

    The pane on the right changes to Services to Start and Select Display Driver.

    Guarddog firewall service and PPP service for dialup, adsi, and pptp networking are selected by default.

13. **Click Next.**

    The pane changes to Localization Defaults.

14. **If you're in the U.S., choose US. Also choose the Locale as en_US. If you're not from the U.S., choose your locale from the list. Click Next.**

    The pane changes to include information where you can get support.

15. **Click Finish.**

    A dialog box appears asking whether you want to reboot the computer without the CD-ROM. It informs you that you need to take the CD-ROM out of the computer. (But if you try to do so, the CD-ROM will not open at this time, so you need to click OK first.)

16. **Click OK.**

    Your computer starts to shut down.

17. **Before the computer reboots, get the CD-ROM out of the computer.** (This is not the time to take a break. You have only a few seconds to get the CD-ROM out between the time the computer stops using the CD-ROM and the time it tries to boot with the CD-ROM again.)

    Then the computer reboots, and after about a minute a screen appears, requesting your username and password.

18. **Type in your username and password.**

    You're now running SimplyMEPIS from your hard drive!

Downloading and Installing More Free Software Applications

SimplyMEPIS comes with two software packages that can download and install free software applications from the Internet with ease. They are Synaptic and KPackage. Appendix A provides instructions for using KPackage.

Getting Support

If you run into any problems and need help, you can go to www.mepis.org and www.mepislovers.com for support. Both have active forums with knowledgeable people who are happy to give you good advice.

Part VI
The Part of Tens

The 5th Wave   By Rich Tennant

HOW TO CREATE XML SCHEMAS

"Can't I just give you riches or something?"

In this part . . .

1 include a chapter with ten great reasons to switch to free software and a directory with ten categories of more free software for you. Why switch to free software?

- ✔ **It's free in terms of cost.** You don't need to buy it, and you don't need to buy upgrades.

- ✔ **It's free in terms of freedom.** You can give it away, sell it, study it, modify it. Whatever you want to do, you can do — except restrict someone else's freedom to do the same.

- ✔ **It's worry-free.** No more concerns about accidentally violating restrictive end-user agreements.

- ✔ **It's powerful.** And getting more powerful all the time.

- ✔ **It's virus-free and free of other malicious software.** Plus it's spyware-free. Because the source code is freely available, there's no place for viruses, spyware, and other undesirable programs to hide undetected.

- ✔ **You can get support easily** via enthusiastic communities of well-wishers eager to give something in return for getting this powerful software.

Considering these compelling reasons and the great software available, why not give it a try?

Chapter 24

Ten Lists of More Great Free Software and Stuff: A Directory

*F*ree Software For Dummies goes into depth about lots of the best free open source software packages. But many more exist that aren't covered. This chapter lists some more of the top free software, as well as places to get free photos, graphics, fonts, sound effects, music, and movies. But I can only skim the surface here. For more free software programs, you may want to check out the Web sites mentioned in Chapter 2.

Podcasting

Podcasting is an exciting new technology that can let anyone become their own radio station. The free software application iPodder, discussed in Chapter 12, lets you subscribe to audio programs or music, developed to be listened to on iPods or other portable media players. But what if you want to create and distribute podcasts, not just listen to them? It's easy with Easypodcast.

> **Easypodcast:** You can create your own podcasts by using Audacity, described in Chapter 23, to create and save your audio file. Then you can use Easypodcast to tag your file, create an RSS feed for it, and upload it for podcasting. Easypodcast is available for Windows and GNU/GNU/Linux, at www.easypodcast.com.

Internet

You can video conference over the Internet using Gnomemeeting, add a shopping cart to your Web site using osCommerce, turn your computer into a Web server with the Apache Web server, remotely control your computer using TightVNC, and more:

- ✔ **Apache Web server:** Turn your computer into a Web server. This is by far the most popular Internet server software in use, as evidenced by the 68 percent of the Web sites on the Internet that use Apache. For information and downloads, go to httpd.apache.org.

- ✔ **Bit Torrent:** Peer-to-peer file sharing for Windows, Mac OS X, and GNU/Linux. It's a way of cooperatively distributing files, so that a huge demand for downloads does not crash your Web site. For information and downloads, go to www.bittorrent.com. For examples of files that are legal to share with Bit Torrent, visit www.legaltorrents.com.

- ✔ **FileZilla:** This is an FTP client for Windows. FTP stands for File Transfer Protocol; it's a fast way to transfer files from one computer to another. You can FTP files over the Internet or over your local network. FileZilla has an intuitive interface and is easy to use. For more information and downloads, go to http://filezilla.sourceforge.net.

- ✔ **Gaim:** Instant messaging software that supports multiple protocols, so that from one window on your computer, you can be logged into, send, and receive instant messages on multiple networks simultaneously. (including AIM, ICQ, Yahoo!, MSN Messenger, IRC, Jabber and more). GAIM supports many of the features of the various networks, such as away messages, file transfer, typing notification, MSN window closing notification, and it also supports features unique to GAIM such as Buddy Pouncing. Information and downloads at http://gaim.sourceforge.net.

- ✔ **Gnomemeeting.org:** This is an Internet phone/video conferencing tool for Windows and GNU/Linux. It's like Microsoft's NetMeeting. The voice and video quality are good. You can go to www.gnomemeeting.org to download it.

- ✔ **Mozilla Composer:** You can download this Web authoring system for Windows, GNU/Linux, Mac OS X, and Windows from www.mozilla.org. It's part of the Mozilla Suite.

- ✔ **Nvu:** This complete Web authoring system for Windows, GNU/Linux, and Mac users is a powerful, free alternative to FrontPage and Dreamweaver. For more information and downloads, go to www.nvu.com.

- ✔ **osCommerce:** This is an online shopping cart. For more information and to download, go to www.oscommerce.com.

- ✔ **Pears:** This easy-to-use newsfeed aggregator (RSS reader) works on Windows, GNU/Linux, and Mac OS X. For more information and downloads, go to http://project5.freezope.org/pears.

- ✔ **Perl:** To download this programming language for many Web functions, go to www.cpan.org.

- ✔ **PHP:** This is another programming language for many Web functions. Download at PHP.net.

- ✔ **TightVNC:** From another computer, you can see your own desktop and use your computer, as if you were right there in front of it. TightVNC works on Windows and GNU/Linux. For downloads go to www.tightvnc.com.

Graphics

More great free graphics programs are as follows:

- ✔ **Inkscape:** This vector graphics program is similar to Adobe Illustrator, Macromedia FreeHand, and Corel Draw. It runs in Windows and GNU/Linux. For more information and downloads, go to www.inkscape.org/.

- ✔ **QCad:** This is a computer-aided drafting program. Using QCad, you can create architectural plans, mechanical plans, and other technical drawings. You can get more information and download QCad at www.ribbon soft.com/qcad.html.

- ✔ **Wings 3D:** This 3D modeling tool is simple and powerful, and is for Mac OS X, Windows, and GNU/Linux. For more information and to download Wings 3D, go to www.wings3d.com.

Utilities

Here are some free utilities. Some are free as in gratis, and some are "free as in freedom."

First, here are the gratis ones. Their source code isn't available, and they can't be freely modified, so they're not "free as in freedom" and thus don't have all the advantages of free software described in Chapter 25. Ad-Aware and Zone Alarm also offer fuller-featured versions that are not gratis.

- ✔ **Ad-Aware by Lavasoft:** This program protects your Windows computer from data-mining, aggressive advertising, parasites, scumware, some Trojan horses, dialers, malware, Browser hijackers, and tracking components. For more information and to download, go to www.lavasoftusa.com/software/adaware/.

✔ **Spybot — Search & Destroy:** Spybot detects and removes spyware for Windows. For more information and to download, go to `www.safer-net working.org/en/`.

✔ **ZoneAlarm:** This is a free firewall for Windows. For more information and to download, go to `www.zonelabs.com/store/content/home.jsp`. The gratis version is for non-business use only.

And these (like all the other software packages described in this book, except for Ad-Aware, Spybot, Zone Alarm, Skype, and a few multimedia components of SimplyMEPIS) are "free as in freedom."

✔ **7-Zip:** This file archiver compresses and decompresses lots of different formats and has a high compression rate. It's for Windows only. For more information and to download, go to `www.7-zip.org`.

✔ **ClamWin:** Free anti-virus program for Windows. (You don't need anti-virus software for GNU/Linux and Mac OS X.) For more information and to download, go to `www.clamwin.com`.

Learning

An exciting new online learning opportunity may be the Dokeos campus, where teachers can create online courses and make them available to students. Also, Childsplay is a delightful collection of fun and educational games for small children. The following describes these and other educational programs:

✔ **Childsplay:** This suite of educational games for children runs on Windows, Mac, and GNU/Linux. For more information and to download, go to `childsplay.sourceforge.net`.

✔ **Claroline:** This software is for creating and administering courses through the Web. It provides forums, document repositories, a calendar, chat, assignment areas, links, and more. It works with Windows, Mac OS X, and GNU/Linux. For more information and downloads, go to `www.Claroline.net`.

✔ **Dokeos:** For online multimedia authoring for courses and online learning, go to `www.dokeos.com/campus/dokeos`. Teachers use Dokeos to create courses using up to 50 Mb or more and can make them available, either for pay or for free, at the Dokeos online campus. Learners can then take courses either for free or for a charge, depending on the course.

✔ **jDictionary:** This program contains over 1.4 million words and 250,000 links. It can run on Windows, Mac OS X, and GNU/Linux. For more information and to download, go to `www.jdictionary.sourceforge.net`.

✔ **Stellarium:** This program renders realistic skies in real time for Windows, GNU/Linux, and Mac OS X. You can see whatever you could really see with a small telescope or just your eyes. For more information and to download, go to `www.stellarium.free.fr`.

If you're interested in a particular academic subject, and you're using Windows, you'll probably want to check out `http://osswin.sourceforge.net` as described in Chapter 2, for more free educational software.

Multimedia

Windows XP and Mac OS X both come with free video editing software, but if you use Linux, you'll probably want the free open source video editing program, Kino. Also, if you need a free CD player, there are plenty of them:

✔ **JazzPlusPlus:** This full-featured MIDI sequencer is for GNU/Linux and Windows. For more information and to download, go to `www.jazzware.com`.

✔ **Kino:** This is video editing software for GNU/Linux. It is included in SimplyMEPIS. For more information, see `http://kino.schirmacher.de`.

✔ **Zinf:** This audio player is for GNU/Linux and Windows. It plays MP3, Ogg/Vorbix, and WAV, and offers audio CD playback, SHOUTcast/Icecast HTTP streaming, RTP streaming, and music browsing with theme support, and a download manager. For more information or to download, go to `www.zinf.org`.

Office

Powerful, free accounting software, databases, project management software, customer relations software, and more are available:

AbiWord: This word processing program is like Microsoft Word. It is slimmer, trimmer software than OpenOffice.org Writer, and works with Windows, GNU/Linux, and Mac OS X. For more information and to download, go to `www.abisource.com`.

✔ **Firebird:** This free database is based on source code from Borland and runs on Windows, GNU/Linux, and Mac OS X. It's been used since 1981. For more information and to download, go to `http://firebird.sourceforge.net`.

✔ **Gantt Project:** This project management tool is for Windows, GNU/Linux, and Mac OS X. For more information and to download, go to `http://ganttproject.sourceforge.net`.

- **GnuCash:** This is a personal or business accounting package for Mac OS X and GNU/Linux. It lets you track bank accounts, stocks, income, and expenses. For more information and to download, go to `www.gnucash.org`.

- **MySQL:** This popular free database has over six million installations, including Yahoo!, NASA, Suzuki, Associated Press, and more. It runs on Windows, Mac OS X, and GNU/Linux. For more information and to download, go to `www.mysql.com`.

- **Open For Business:** This program offers nearly everything you would want for a retail business as well as for other types of businesses. It offers e-commerce, catalog management, promotion and pricing, order management, customer management, warehouse management, shipping, accounting, manufacturing management, content management, and more. For more information and to download, go to `www.ofbiz.org`.

- **Open Workbench:** This program is touted as The Open Source Alternative to Microsoft Project, for serious project scheduling. For information and downloads, go to `www.openworkbench.org`.

- **osCommerce:** For more information and to download this online shopping cart, go to `www.oscommerce.com`.

- **Quasar Accounting:** Business accounting software for Windows and GNU/Linux. For more information and to download, go to `www.linuxcanada.com`.

- **SugarCRM:** This is Customer Relationship Management software. For more information and to download, go to `www.sugarcrm.com`.

- **TurboCASH:** This accounting software is for Windows only. It can be configured for any country and has plug-ins that link TurboCASH to osCommerce. For more information and to download, go to `www.turbocashuk.com`.

- **WebCalendar:** Web calendar and scheduler version 2.9 for Windows, GNU/Linux, and Mac OS X. It can be used by a single individual or by groups, or as an event calendar for Web sites. For more information and to download, you can go to `www.k5n.us/webcalendar.php`.

Photos and Graphics

It used to be that in order to find a single nice-looking public domain image, you needed to wade through hundreds of uninteresting photos taken by government officials who are not photographers. But those days are over. New Web sites have emerged, such as PDPhoto, which offers many beautiful public domain photos. Even the government sites such as NOAA and NASA are featuring very nice photos.

Even if a photo is public domain, you don't want to use anything with a logo on it or any picture with someone's face without his or her permission.

- **Gimp-Savvy:** This is a community-created index with links to more than 27,000 government photos that you can easily browse and download. Check out gimp-savvy.com/PHOTO-ARCHIVE.

- **GNUart:** Free photos, music, paintings and more at www.gnuart.net

- **NASA:** Check out the Image of the Day gallery and archives. You can find some cosmic stuff at www.nasa.gov/multimedia/imagegallery.

- **NOAA:** This is the National Oceanic and Atmospheric Administration photo library. It contains more than 30,000 public domain images in several categories. Go to www.photolib.noaa.gov.

- **Open Clip Art Library:** Over 3000 vector graphic images in the public domain at www.openclipart.org

- **PDPhoto:** This site has more than 2,000 good photos taken by a fellow named Jon Sullivan. They are mostly public domain, but you need to check in the text below the image before you use it to be sure. Surf to www.pdphoto.org.

- **Wikipedia's List:** A huge list of links to public domain images on the Web, at Wikipedia, the fabulous free encyclopedia on the Web. Visit en.wikipedia.org/wiki/Public_domain_image_resources.

Movies and Sound

The future will probably bring lots more free movies and sound, but even now there's plenty out there.

Check out these sites for your movie and sound needs:

- **Free Music! – MIT:** Links to high-quality, free classical music recordings and more, at hebb.mit.edu/FreeMusic/.

- **Free Music at cyper-media.com:** A few more links to free music at orcyber-media.com/freemusic/.

- **Internet Archive:** This site has more than 3,000 open source movies and thousands of free books and songs, too. Check out their audio collection at www.archive.org/audio/ (and books at www.archive.org/details/texts) To check out their movies, go to www.archive.org, choose Open Source Movies from the search list, and type a topic of interest. Remember, you can't publish any faces or logos without the actor's or company's approval.

- ✔ **Links to Tens of Thousands of Legal Music Downloads:** The title says it all, at `www.goingware.com/tips/legal-downloads.html`.

- ✔ **List of Free Music Advocates:** Links to bands and others that support free music at `www.ram.org/ramblings/philosophy/fmp/fma.html`.

- ✔ **Mutopia:** Free sheet music for hundreds of compositions at `www.ibiblio.org/mutopia/`.

- ✔ **Opsound:** Free music is available at `opsound.org/opsound/pool guide.html`.

Fonts

You can easily find thousands of great free fonts on the Web. Use them in your logo or elsewhere for a unique look:

- ✔ **Free Fonts archives!:** This site, at `Jeff.cs.mcgill.ca/~luc/free fonts.html`, has links to tons of sites with free fonts.

- ✔ **Fonts.goldenweb.it:** This is just one of the sites listed at the Free Fonts Archives site above. GoldenWeb, at `Fonts.goldenweb.it`, offers more than 12,000 free TrueType fonts.

Chapter 25

Ten Unreasonable Advantages of Free Software

In This Chapter

▶ Ending virus and spyware worries

▶ Saving money on software and upgrades

▶ The power of free software and why it's going to get even more powerful

▶ Why support is readily available

Some software is free as in free lunch — it's freeware available at no charge. And some software is free as in freedom; it's free in the sense that it's published with a license specifying that its source code — all the underlying logic and instructions that cause the program to function — is freely available and free for anyone to study, modify, and redistribute.

This book explores software that is free in both senses — it's free as in gratis and free as in freedom (with the exception of ZoneAlarm, Spybot, Ad-Aware, and a few multimedia extensions to Mepis, which are gratis but not open source). Getting powerful software for free can be an extremely attractive economic proposition, but it turns out that, in the opinion of many, software that is free in the sense of freedom provides you with many more far-reaching benefits. This chapter takes a look at what these benefits are.

It's Free

One great thing about free software is indeed that it doesn't cost you anything, except for the time needed to download and install it. So your initial acquisition of it is free. Then the upgrades are free. And if you want to migrate from one free software package to another, or have all your employees use the software, that's free, too. What if you want to give it to your friends or family? That's free. When you think of all the money that you could spend on buying software that isn't free, it adds up to a lot of money that you don't have to spend. And because the software is free, and the cost of trying it is, therefore, extremely low, you're more likely to try out new software that can increase your productivity.

It's Powerful

Virtually all the software packages described in this book are as powerful as their proprietary counterparts. In some cases, the free software is even more powerful than the proprietary alternatives. For example, Mozilla Firefox has many features not available in the current version of Internet Explorer.

Free software can become powerful because it's easy for smart people all over the world to work on it, because the source code is available and the Internet makes intellectual collaboration easy. When one person or company makes an improvement to the source code of a free software program for their own benefit, they can share it with others effortlessly, and everybody benefits. Because the source code isn't shrouded in secrecy, software developers can easily build on the work of their predecessors without having to constantly re-invent the wheel. This means that it's easy for free software to continuously gain more and more powerful features at the same time that it's being made easier to use.

It's Virus-Free

Because free software is developed out in the open where anyone can examine the source code, the possibility for malicious programmers to secretly attach code for software viruses, worms, or Trojan horses to it is quite small. The source code of a free software package may be scrutinized by hundreds or thousands of developers who are under no pressure to meet artificially scheduled release deadlines. This generally results in software that is robust and well-designed without the dramatic vulnerabilities of, for example, Windows software. Microsoft has been aware of the need to make their software more secure and more resistant to viruses in the last few years but are still way behind compared to the virtually virus-free environment of the free software world. Many people feel that proprietary software can never be as virus-free as free software, because the source code of proprietary software can't be improved by the large communities of developers that are available in the free software world.

If your computer has ever been attacked by a software virus, worm, or Trojan horse (which is fairly likely, if you've been running Windows), you know what an inconvenience or even a disaster it can be.

So, why pay for software that's unsafe when you can have virus-free software for free?

It's Worry-Free

As shown in this book, free software doesn't cost you anything, and it's virus-free, so already you're heading for no worries.

But there's more. The licenses accompanying free software (if it is really free, in the sense of freedom) permit you to improve, redistribute, and even sell the software's source code, all of which is typically illegal with proprietary software. Some people ignore the end-user license agreements of proprietary software and give copies of it to their friends or family or "borrow it" for use on their machine, but that's not legal and could cause you problems, particularly if the software is being used in a business. With free software, you don't have to worry about that. You can burn copies of free software on a huge stack of CD-ROMs and sell them or give them away on a street corner, if you want, and it's all completely legal and even encouraged.

It's Supported by Enthusiastic Communities

Because free software is based on the idea of sharing, a tremendous amount of goodwill is generated around popular free software projects. Almost any free software package that you're likely to use probably has an enthusiastic group of supporters who will answer technical questions for free on a community Web site. These online forums are usually easy to search, which means that if you need help with your software, the answer is usually just a few keystrokes away. And if it isn't, you can post a question on the forum and often get good answers back within a few hours. The cost to you per support incident is precisely zero dollars, and the monthly unlimited support plan also costs you precisely zero dollars.

It's Not Locked into a Single Platform

The free software packages discussed in this book run on Windows, Macintosh, and Linux, which covers just about any desktop computer you might use. The free availability of the underlying source code of the software makes it easy in many cases for free software to be translated to work on just about any kind of computer. That means that if you have a Windows computer at work, for example, and a Macintosh or Linux computer at home, you don't have to learn another program when you change platforms. This flexibility also gives you the freedom to migrate away from the costly upgrade cycles and vulnerabilities of, for example, Windows, if you want to. You can choose whatever computer and operating system you want.

Choice Is Good

Free software is currently one of the only viable competitive alternatives to the world of Microsoft software. Do you really want to live in a world where one software maker controls the way everyone interacts with computers, especially when computers are playing an increasingly central role in so many different areas of life from business and education to health, government, and even entertainment?

And because of the negligible cost of downloading and trying out new free software and because of the tens of thousands of free software packages available, you're likely to have a choice of free software available for almost any use. Isn't that better than being locked into the proprietary file formats of a single powerful software manufacturer?

Nobody Is Spying on You

Spyware is a relatively recent arrival on the software scene, but unfortunately it is now fairly rampant in the Windows world. Spyware is software that may be secretly embedded in other useful software; it may secretly monitor your activities on your computer and pass on the information elsewhere on the Internet without your knowledge. A recent study by the National Cyber-Security Alliance showed that spyware has infected 80 percent of home computers. Interestingly, in the world of Mac OS X and GNU/Linux, spyware is for all practical purposes non-existent. It's no coincidence that this is true, because Mac OS X and GNU/Linux are built on free software. (Not everyone is aware of this, but Mac OS X is a proprietary layer of Apple software built on top of Apple's modifications of FreeBSD, a UNIX-like system that is very similar to GNU/Linux and for which the source code is freely available.)

Again, because free software is developed out in the open, it is virtually impossible for secret code for spying on you to be attached to it.

Upgrades Are Easy

Upgrades are easy with free software. Even if it's two o'clock in the morning, you can download your free upgrade from the Internet in a matter of minutes and have it up and running quickly. No more phone calls to venders and waiting for FedEx. No agonizing about the benefits of an upgrade versus its cost. No more long activation codes that you need to redo three times to get right and that you need to file somewhere off your computer where you will never lose them (gulp).

Basically, you can always have the latest upgrades with the latest new features, improvements, and bug fixes, and you can have them with no cost and virtually no effort.

No Worries About Data Lockout

The history of the computer industry is littered with proprietary software packages that are no longer sold. WordStar, Lotus 1-2-3, DEC, Wang, and many others used to be gigantic industry leaders, and where are they now? They've merged into oblivion or something close to it.

So, in a few years from now, what's going to happen to all of your archives of some old software program that saves files into a proprietary format that is not supported anymore by the original program vendor? You may only be able to access those files with the original program, but if it doesn't work on any current computer, or if you can't find the original program, your files may be as good as lost because they're indecipherable. With free software, however, your files are probably never going to be irretrievable, no matter how old, because the formats in which they are saved are not proprietary. The source code will always be available and, perhaps with some programming help, you will be able to find someone who can modify or has modified that code to open those files on your new computer.

Appendix

Installing Programs Using KPackage and Installation Wizards

*I*n this Appendix we cover the easy ins and outs of installing programs, either using the easy Installation wizards of the Mac OS X and Windows desktops or using the comprehensive KPackage program used by many versions of GNU/Linux, including SimplyMEPIS.

Using KPackage, you can access about 10,000 free software programs available to download and install in SimplyMEPIS, and other versions of the GNU/Linux operating system often offer a similar selection of programs via KPackage. KPackage automatically downloads and installs the programs that you specify in its list, plus it figures out what other programs may be required by the program you specified. And then it downloads and installs them as well. You can also use KPackage to update all your programs to the latest versions.

KPackage is divided into 30 or so major categories, including: Admin, Games, Graphics, Math, Science, Sound and more. The games category alone contains over 500 games, including FlightGear, Freeciv, Gcompris, Xboard and lots more. (Who has time to play all those games?)

Installing Free Software Using KPackage

For anyone running a GNU/Linux desktop, such as SimplyMEPIS, you will love KPackage. This program comes already installed in many GNU/Linux desktops, including SimplyMEPIS. You can use it to find and install a huge variety of free software on the Internet.

In GNU/Linux, you can install programs while other programs are running. Unlike in Windows, you do not have to exit your programs before installing others.

To use Kpackage, you can do the following:

1. **In SimplyMEPIS or other GNU/Linux KDE desktops, choose K⇨System⇨KPackage.**

   KPackage opens with a list of 10,000 free software programs that you can download and install.

2. **Unless you want to explore the programs in the Admin folder, click the minus sign beside the Admin folder to collapse it.**

   The next folder appears with a minus sign next to it.

3. **Continue to collapse folders until you see the folder that you want to explore, such as Games, for instance.**

4. **Click to select the name of a program that you are interested in.**

   The pane on the right reveals a description of the program.

5. **If you want to download and install the package, click in the Mark column beside the name of the program.**

   A check mark appears, as shown in Figure A-1.

6. **To download and install the software that you selected, choose Packages⇨Install Marked.**

   A dialog box appears, requesting the password for the root account.

7. **Type the password of the Root account, which you created when you installed your GNU/Linux desktop and press Return.**

   The Install KPackage dialog box appears, showing you what programs it plans to install.

8. **Click Install.**

   A log of the download and installation appears in the large pane on the right, as shown in Figure A-2. When the installation is finished, a button labeled "Done" appears next to the Install button.

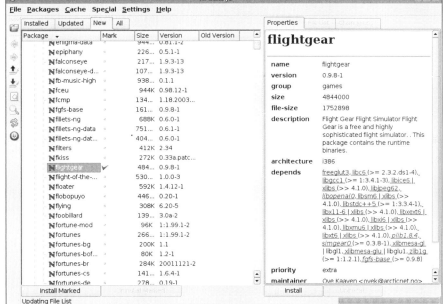

Figure A-1:
Use
KPackage
to download
and install
free
software
programs
for
GNU/Linux.

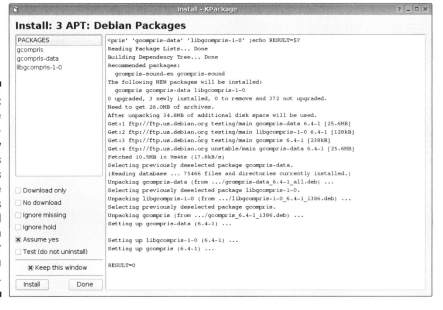

Figure A-2:
KPackage
auto-
matically
downloads
and installs
the
programs
needed
to run
whatever
you
selected.

9. **Click Done.**

The Install KPackage dialog box disappears. Now you can run your program from the K menu.

Installing Using an Installation Wizard

I had a friend who used a computer daily but would never install any program herself. When I asked her why, she replied, "It's too confusing. There's too much to read." I was so surprised to hear that anyone actually tried to read everything presented by the Installation wizard. Imagine reading every word of a license agreement before installing a program! Or even worse, imagine reading that Important Information dialog box that some programs come with! Yes, the one that's usually filled such technical stuff that no ordinary user could ever fathom. Okay. Nuff said.

Here's a summary of what some typical dialog boxes of the Installation wizard may contain:

Authentication: You may need to enter the name and password for the system administrator account.

License Agreement: For programs in this book, this is often the GNU license, which is very favorable. It allows you to use the program for free, give it away for free, sell it for money, change it and improve however you like. The only prohibition is basically that you are not allowed to keep anyone else from having the same rights to the program.

Select a Destination: You may be asked to provide a location for the installation. Fortunately, a default location is generally chosen for you and you can just click Continue.

Important Information: This is very important information, at least, to someone. But whether or not you really want to read this information is your choice. I know what I always do.

Localization: This is to select the language that you want to appear in the program. Sometimes, even if you speak English, you need to choose what kind of English, such as En – USA, for example.

Downloading with Mirrors

Many free software programs are so popular that the demand to download them could crash a site, if that site is the only place they are available for download. To solve this problem, some free software is available for download using mirrors, which are multiple sites that take on the downloading job.

If a page appears with lots of places that you can choose from to download your software, that's a sure sign that you are downloading via a mirror. To use a mirror, just click on the Download link of a site near to you. It's always good to choose a link near you, but don't worry if you can't. I used a mirror from Australia once, even though I was in Iowa, and it downloaded just as quick as if I chose Phoenix.

One thing to keep in mind when using mirrors is that sometimes a mirror site may get overloaded with downloads, or for other reasons the mirror that you choose may be slow. If you are downloading a big program, such as OpenOffice.org, you may want to check how fast your download is taking place. No sense in spending two hours waiting for a download that would take ten minutes downloaded from another mirror. You can always cancel your download and try it again from another mirror.

To cancel a download, using Firefox, choose Tools ⇨ Downloads to view the Downloads window, if it is not already visible, and click Cancel beside the name of the program you are downloading. (For more about Mozilla Firefox, check out Chapter 9.)

Index

• E •

(continued)